# The MACHINERY of WAR

# An illustrated history of weapons

Peter Young

# The MACHINERY of WAR

Crescent Books · New York

Granada Publishing Limited
First published in Great Britain 1973
by Hart-Davis, MacGibbon Limited
Park Street St Albans Hertfordshire
and 3 Upper James Street London W1R 4BP

517120798


Made by Roxby Press Productions
55 Conduit Street London W1R 0NY
Editor Michael Leitch
Picture Research Penny Brown
Design and art direction Ivan and Robin Dodd
Printed in Great Britain by Oxley Press Limited

This edition is distributed by Crescent Books
a division of Crown Publishers, Inc.
by arrangement with Roxby Press Limited

**right** By the close of the Churchillian era, in 1945, the pattern of warfare had already changed radically from that to which he referred in 1941; and twenty-five years later not all the tools in the USA could finish the Vietnam job – barring, that is, the ultimate deterrent. In the photo a South Vietnamese helicopter searches rice fields in Cambodia for traces of the enemy.

## INTRODUCTION

# GIVE US THE TOOLS AND WE SHALL FINISH THE JOB

*WINSTON S CHURCHILL*
*February 1941*

This book is a general survey of the weapons which men have used in war – the tools of the soldier's trade – told largely in the terms of land warfare.

The art or science of war has a long history going back to ancient times. No military historian would deny that Alexander the Great, Hannibal and Julius Caesar, to name but three of the great commanders who lived before the Christian era, contributed to its development in much the same way as later commanders such as Gustavus Adolphus, Frederick the Great and Napoleon. The strategical principles upon which they acted remained very much the same down the ages, as did the political and diplomatic reasons which made one group, tribe or nation attempt to secure its ends by the application of violence. Similarly the procedures, by which such group violence was organized, have changed but little. The chief levels of planning and execution may be summarized under the following headings:

**Grand Strategy**

The planning of a war; usually formulated by *civilians*, i.e. politicians, the head of state.

**Strategy**

The planning of a campaign within a war; carried out by a nation's *military* leaders.

**Grand or Battle Tactics**

The business of trying to defeat the enemy's forces in the field. Battle tactics are the responsibility of the commanders-in-chief of the armies involved.

**Tactics or Minor Tactics**

The execution of some part of the grand tactical plan for winning a battle; in general the term covers the ways in which officers interpret the orders of their superior commanders.

## The Elements of Strategy

The distinguished military historian the late Basil Liddell Hart defined strategy as 'the art of distributing and applying military means to fulfil the ends of policy'. It is a definition which serves very well – at least for wars of the pre-nuclear age, as we shall shortly see.

In the past, as we have said, the strategical principles that helped to guide the great commanders remained much the same. Although the priorities of one commander may not have been shared even by his immediate contemporaries, and while no single analysis of strategical theory could be called universal, certain basic elements do recur. These, under the heading of 'The Principles of War', were first codified for use by the British Army during the First World War by Colonel (later Major-General) J. F. C. Fuller. With certain modifications, as described in the table below, Fuller's Principles remain valid today.

**The Principles of War**[1]

1 Maintenance of the Aim (this category was formerly called the Objective).
2 Maintenance of Morale (added after the Second World War).
3 Offensive Action.
4 Surprise
5 Security
6 Concentration of Effort
7 Economy of Force
(4–5 and 6–7: These pairs are complementary.)
8 Flexibility (formerly called Mobility).
9 Co-operation (between Allies, Services and Arms).

[1] Although it is not conventionally included in this list, Efficient Administration is a further, no less vital factor which may best be considered as forming part of the Principles of War.

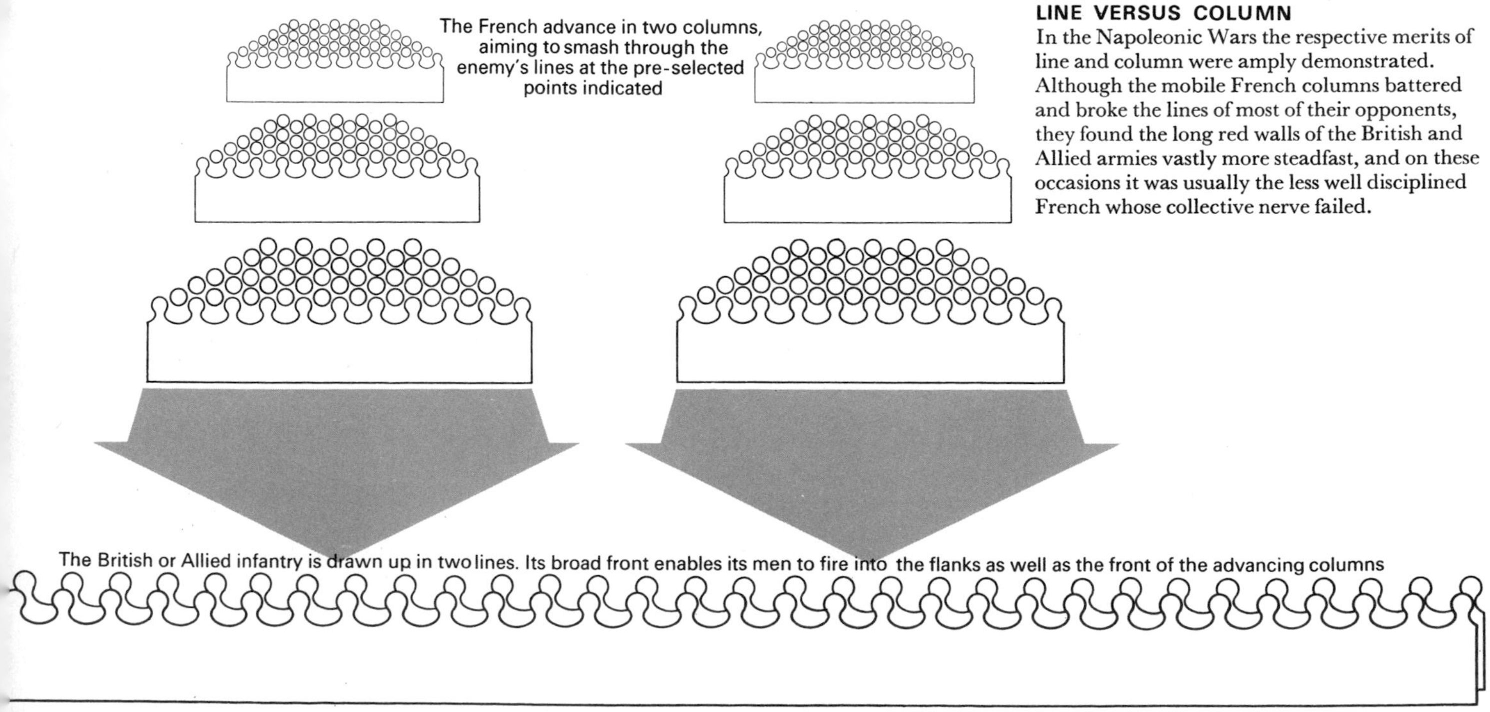
The French advance in two columns, aiming to smash through the enemy's lines at the pre-selected points indicated
The British or Allied infantry is drawn up in two lines. Its broad front enables its men to fire into the flanks as well as the front of the advancing columns

**LINE VERSUS COLUMN**
In the Napoleonic Wars the respective merits of line and column were amply demonstrated. Although the mobile French columns battered and broke the lines of most of their opponents, they found the long red walls of the British and Allied armies vastly more steadfast, and on these occasions it was usually the less well disciplined French whose collective nerve failed.

If the Principles of War, as they are listed above, appear to be fairly simple, even self-evident, the art of strategy is in reality very complex. Its complexity is due to the fact that the resources available are seldom equal to all the demands made upon them. To take a straightforward example from naval warfare, in 1812 Britain, which had enjoyed 'command of the sea' since 1805, found herself at war with the United States of America, whose naval force consisted of a mere handful of frigates. But the American vessels somewhat outclassed the average British frigate of the day, and their intervention at the height of Britain's continuing struggle – on the opposite side of the Atlantic – with Revolutionary France posed for her Admiralty a problem of strategic distribution of the utmost complexity. To take another, more recent situation, in the Second World War the Allies gradually won 'command of the air', but nevertheless their long-range aircraft were limited in number. The first problem was the allotment of resources to both Pacific and European theatres. In Europe the planners had then to satisfy – if they could – the conflicting demands of sailors who wanted to put an end to the submarine menace; of airmen who wanted to press the strategic bomber offensive against Germany to the exclusion of all else; and those of soldiers who wanted the maximum air support for the invasion of Europe. Faced with problems of this sort the theoretical notions of strategists – and more particularly of *academic* strategists – often seem to be no more than impracticable platitudes.

As we can see, the art of strategy is in part a question of deploying one's resources to the best advantage. This is a question of time as well as place. It is as dangerous to have an outdated weapons system as it is to be the prisoner of an obsolete tactical doctrine. Mussolini's Italy, the first country to re-arm after the First World War, found herself at a serious disadvantage in the Second against the forces of nations which had re-armed later.

**Weapons and Tactics**

The history of weapons cannot be divorced from the history of tactical development and training. An army must be taught formations and tactics suitable for the weapons it possesses. For example, certain formations – variations on the *line* – are generally best for *fire*, whilst some form of *column* is often handiest for *movement*. This was still so in the Second World War, although it could not be demonstrated with the beautiful clarity of the old close-order battles of the days of Wellington and Napoleon (see diagram).

**THE BEATEN ZONE**

The beaten zone represents the area within which one side's missiles can be expected to fall. At the Battle of Marathon (490 BC) the problem for Miltiades, the Greek commander, whose army was stretched across a one-mile front, was to cross the beaten zone of the Persian archers as speedily as possible and yet to avoid arriving in disorder amongst the enemy.

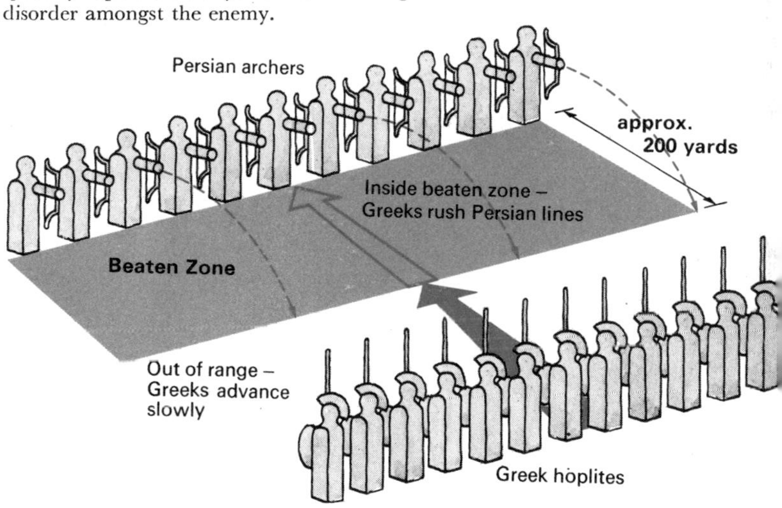

Persian archers
approx. 200 yards
Inside beaten zone – Greeks rush Persian lines
Beaten Zone
Out of range – Greeks advance slowly
Greek hoplites


**TAKING COVER**

If the blue lines indicate possible arcs of fire from the enemy's guns then A is in a very exposed position and B is exposed to air bursts or shells from howitzer or mortar, whereas C has dug himself beyond immediate danger; even if a shell exploded in the entrance to his dug-out he would still be protected in the end section, which lies at an angle to the entrance.

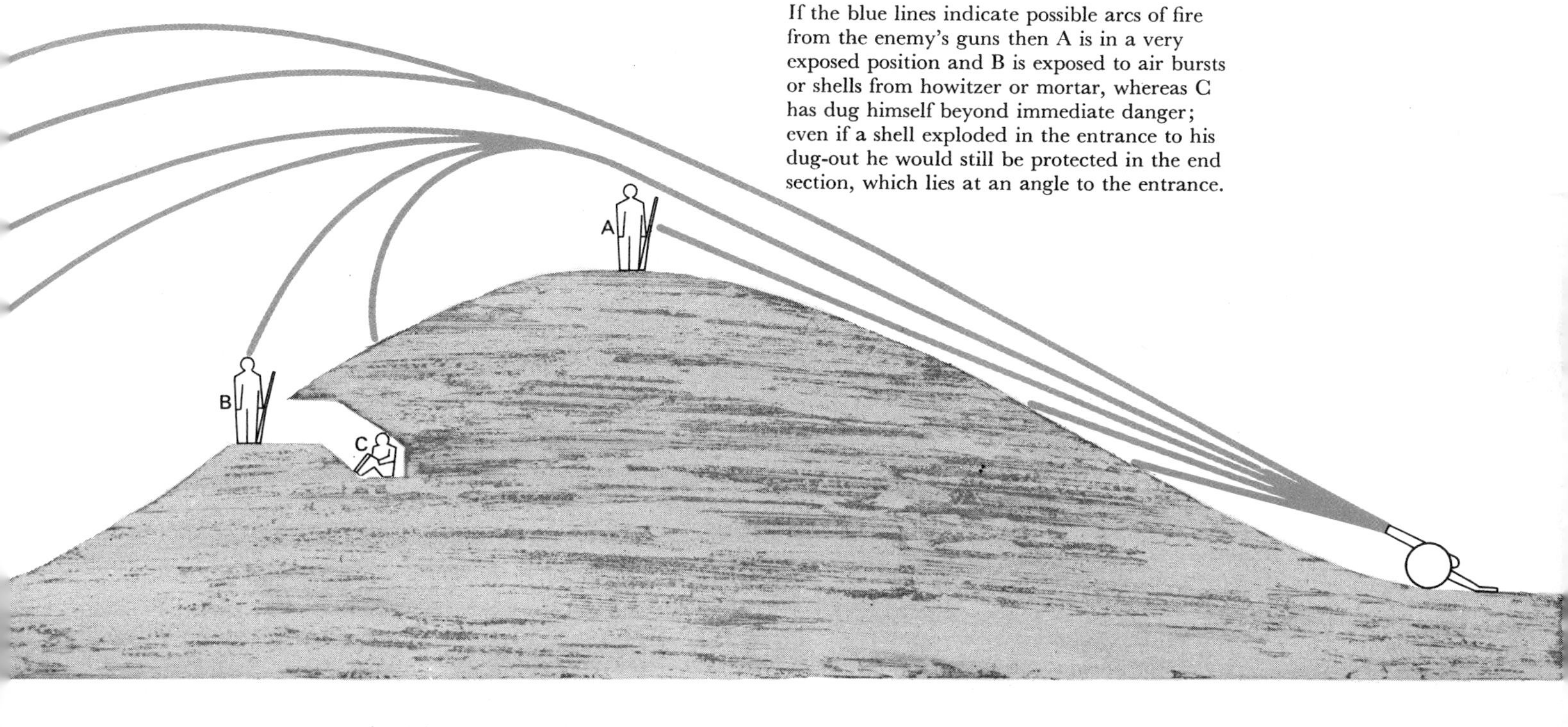

A
B
C

**above** Unorthodox fighting methods. The American destroyer *Campbeltown* is seen shortly before she blew up in the dock at St Nazaire, France, in 1942 – the climax of a brilliant raid designed to prevent the German battleship *Tirpitz* from using the dock. **below** Undercover warfare. Angolan guerrillas camouflage themselves before a combat mission.

The choice of suitable formations depends not only upon the weapons of one side but upon those of its enemy as well. It is obvious to the meanest intelligence that one must position one's own weapons in order to make the best use of their characteristics – range, beaten zone (see diagram), rate of fire, and so on. What is not quite so obvious is the extent to which a commander can cut down casualties by studying the characteristics of enemy weapons. In attack one's formations should never flatter the characteristics of the weapons the enemy is using in defence. In the First World War infantry was sent into the attack in waves deployed in more or less extended order, a formation which might have been specially devised to ensure that medium machine-guns, placed to give an enfilading or raking fire, were presented with the best possible targets. Again, there are those who not unreasonably dislike being shelled by enemy field guns. It is possible, however, to study the habits of enemy artillerymen and to discover where they can put their shells and where they cannot (see diagram).

Sound commanders well-versed in the tactics and training techniques of their day will always be in demand in any army. But the truly great tactician is he who is ready to throw the textbook aside and has the flair to improvise his tactics, if need be on the spur of the moment. This has often been achieved by those who were not afraid to use some weapon for a purpose for which it

The urban bombthrower at work, from *Chicago 1886*, a modern painting by Flavio Costantini. The bombthrowing revolutionary first rose to prominence in the second half of the nineteenth century: at that time General Cluseret, one of the commanders-in-chief of the Paris Commune of 1871, described the future role of the bomb as the 'speciality of the popular uprising'.

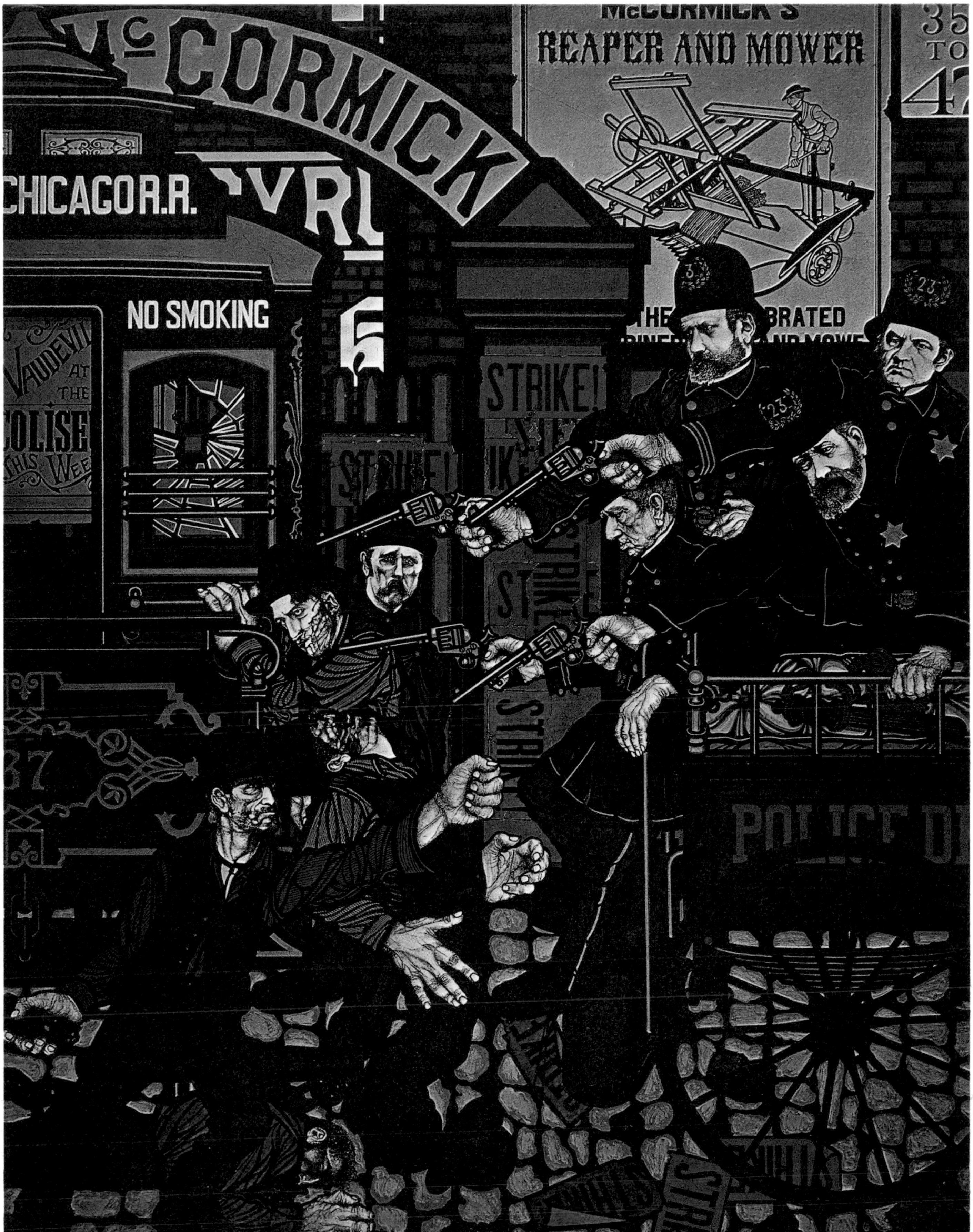
McCORMICK
REAPER AND MOWER
CHICAGO R.R.
NO SMOKING
STRIKE!

was never intended. In 1940 when the German armour was scything through France there were instances of Allied 25-pounder field-guns, which were normally expected to engage their targets at a range of some seven miles, being used not in batteries but individually – to engage German tanks at point-blank range. A rather more extreme example of the tactical value of unorthodox improvisation may be drawn from the St Nazaire raid of 1942, when the Allied destroyer *Campbeltown* was filled with explosives and driven, a mighty self-propelled missile, into the Forme Ecluse, the only dry-dock on the German-held Atlantic coast which could take the great battleship *Tirpitz*.

### New Forms of War

'Give us the tools,' said Mr Churchill, 'and we shall finish the job.' That was all very well in 1941, before Hiroshima and Nagasaki. Now one might say 'What job?' War has become so dangerous that since 1945 strategists have concerned themselves more and more with peace-keeping and with disarmament, or at least with arms control. But although there has been no Third World War the years since 1945 have been far from peaceful. All sorts and sizes of groups from urban guerrillas upwards have found it possible to advance their interests simply because the weapons of total war are too devastating to be used against them.

It is true that the Israeli campaigns of 1956 and 1967 were examples of the Second World War *blitzkrieg*, or lightning war, brought up to date; in this they followed, however brilliantly, a well-established pattern. Nevertheless much of the fighting that has gone on in the world since the Second World War has been of the pattern foreseen by General Cluseret, one of the commanders-in-chief of the Paris Commune of 1871. He regarded the bomb as the 'speciality of the popular uprising' – but, of course, he was thinking of a very different sort of bomb to the thermo-nuclear weapons of today. It seems unlikely that the major powers will indulge in a nuclear war – even by accident. At the same time there is no prospect of an end to the violence of the sort that has been going on in Vietnam or Ulster.

In the past the patterns of violence have changed and they will no doubt continue to change. In the past, however, the lessons of experience have been slowly digested. It was, for example, evident as long ago as the Korean War that air power alone was insufficient to stop determined ground forces; but the lesson has gone largely unheeded in Vietnam. Similarly the British have not been quick to see that the IRA cannot be defeated by half-measures; while the Egyptians now at last seem to recognize that to cross the Suez Canal in the way the Allies crossed the Rhine in 1945 is not likely to produce a successful tank campaign in the Sinai Desert. What conclusions these powers will draw from their recent combat experience is a matter for speculation. It is not impossible, for example, that the Egyptians may decide that push-button warfare against Israeli centres of population is more attractive than conventional desert warfare in the old El Alamein style. Equally it is possible that, appreciating the vulnerability of targets such as Cairo, Alexandria and the Aswan Dam, they will content themselves with threats of violence.

In effect the advent of nuclear weapons seems to have driven nations back to older forms of warfare which stop short of total war. Disarmament and even arms control, however desirable, are as yet the dreams of men who believe that the element of force is not a necessary part of international intercourse. In fact the element of force does come into international relations, and though it can be intelligently controlled – and indeed must be – there is no question of its being eliminated. What is, however, being eliminated is the old clear-cut distinction between peace and war. It is beginning to be appreciated nowadays that strategy is really rather more comprehensive than Liddell Hart told us, when he described it as 'the art of distributing and applying military means to fulfil the ends of policy'. It comprises in addition an understanding of international affairs, of the social and economic aspects of politics, and above all of weapons technology. Indeed it is time that we added to the so-called Principles of War the maxim: 'Thou shalt keep abreast of the technological developments of thy day.'

The ends which may be attained by war, and the machinery of war, have changed. The deterrent policies of modern times may keep a potential aggressor from the paths trod by the Hapsburgs in 1914 and by Hitler in 1939. But while total warfare has receded into the background, other forms of violence still attract elements that seek to press their advantages.

Speaking for myself I find no reason to depart from a passage which I wrote in 1965 – the concluding paragraph of *World War 1939–1945*:

> 'We live in a technological age. But it is an age in which people whose interests are opposed still strive to solve their problems by force, though their methods may be those of the economist, the politician and the diplomat. Perhaps two World Wars have bred a brand of statesman capable of keeping the lid on Hell. It does not seem likely, for we are not specially skilful in selecting our masters. Let us therefore remember the words of Santayana: "He who forgets his History is condemned to relive it".'

On his long march Everyman, with an ingenuity worthy of a better cause, has succeeded, century by century and generation by generation, in producing weapons ever more deadly and destructive. It seems a pity that this history does not have a happy ending with some supernational power exercising arms control, and with the machinery of war being confined to an international police force. Unhappily the United Nations, like its predecessor the League of Nations, is still very far from fulfilling that dream.

Egyptian charioteer, from a wall painting in the rock temple of Rameses II (1292–1225 BC) at Beit El-Wali, Nubia.

CHAPTER I

# The Ancient World

SOME PUT THEIR TRUST
IN CHARIOTS,
AND SOME IN HORSES....

*PSALMS XX 7*

Man's first weapon was himself, a complex and adaptable shock weapon, with teeth to bite, feet to kick, hands to hold, fingers and nails to scratch and gouge. Why and when he first resorted to war are questions that may well defy solution for all time, but the means that he employed present a less formidable problem. Undoubtedly the earliest weapons were not invented for use exclusively in war: the first man lived by hunting and gathering the edible parts of plants, and for the former weapons were needed.

**Stone Age Weapons for Hunting**

The stone was perhaps man's first weapon. In the beginning he used it in the way that some animals use them today, to break open shells or bones to reach the food inside. From this it is not a far step to wielding the stone in the hand as a primitive club, and then to the discovery that the stone can be thrown, giving the thrower a wider range of offensive possibilities and an improved defensive position. Now he could keep his adversary – at this time almost invariably an animal – at a distance where the creature's own shock weapons, horns, teeth and claws, could not be used. Thus was born the missile weapon. It is likely, too, that at much the same time man found that tree branches of varying sizes could be used as clubs and also thrown with considerable accuracy; thus the two basic elements for making a stone-headed spear were now available to him – once he could find out how to give the spear a sharp point.

This last discovery had to wait for the next step in the evolution of man the tool-maker, when he developed the process of shaping or knapping pieces of flint. Presumably he first noticed that flints which had been broken naturally sometimes had a sharp edge; he must then have realized that in these he had the makings of a tool with which to cut or chop rather than to pound. The first steps in flint-knapping were directed towards flaking off the outer parts of a large flint to make the inner portion into an axe. This was originally held in the hand (the so-called hand-axe) and later was fitted with a helve or handle. This produced a more efficient weapon because the person using it could impart far greater momentum, and therefore striking power, to the weapon by swinging it through a greater arc. Men also in time discovered that the flakes chipped from the core of the flint were as useful, if not more useful, than the core itself. These flakes could be turned into arrowheads, spearheads, knives and, finally, primitive swords. Before then, spears had merely been sharpened staffs, usually charred around the tip in a fire to harden the point. The use of flint greatly improved the spear: the point was harder and sharper, therefore more efficient and durable. In some areas it was also fitted with barbs.

**First Steps in Mechanical Power**

Man could never hope to match the strength of the larger animals, or the speed of many of the smaller species. He needed some other agency than his own relatively puny muscles to deliver missile weapons. The answer was mechanical power – as great a revolution in weapons as the discovery of the stone. The first of these mechanical aids was the spear-thrower, still to be seen among the Australian aborigines. This consists of a grooved piece of wood, in which the spear lies with its butt against a solid block at the rear of the groove; the front end of the thrower is held by the man, and as he hurls the weapon, the thrower acts as an extension of his arm and thereby imparts a greatly increased momentum to the spear.

Then there was the bow. This was at first merely a length of springy wood bent into a curve by means of a length of rawhide tied between the ends – a simple weapon, but one that could shoot what was in effect a miniature spear many times the distance that a man could hurl its larger brother, even with the aid of a spear-thrower. Another weapon introduced during this phase was the sling. This worked on the same principle as the spear-thrower, but discharged its smaller missile, a stone or pebble, with a much higher velocity, which gave the missile much the same striking power as the larger and slower weapons. It also served the shepherd in his work: using it he could direct his flock by dropping stones on or around the leading sheep or goat.

The succeeding millenia of the Stone Age, until the advent of the Bronze Age in the Mediterranean area *c.* 3500 BC, produced no important new weapons, but witnessed a gradual improvement in the existing ones. New weapons, such as the blow dart, appeared locally where materials suggested a special use, but the mainstream of development in the rest of the world lay in the sophistication of the art of flint-knapping. The introduction of polishing and grinding made it possible to remove, on the rough sides and edges of flints, the jagged surfaces that so often resulted in breakages; holes drilled in the flint heads of axes enabled the warrior to socket the helve into the head of the axe rather than tie it on. The primitive sword made its appearance in the form of a flat piece of wood with a row of small, sharp flints along the edges, but this was an unsatisfactory weapon that was to be completely revitalized by the introduction of bronze. In the Stone Age defensive equipment amounted to nothing more than fur or hide clothing, replaced and supplemented later by thick cloth and quilted garments, and primitive shields of wicker or hide, the latter stretched on wooden frames.

**Copper – Its Uses and Limitations**

In about 3500 BC came the most important step so far in man's development of tools and weapons: when he discovered how to smelt copper. Metals, notably gold and silver, were known before this time, but these were so soft that they could serve no warlike purpose. By approximately 4000 BC the first copper implements had appeared, but these too were often merely decorative and confined to small objects because man had only found small quantities of the metal in a usable form, and had no method of working it except by heating it and then beating it into shape. Although this had the very important effect of doubling the strength of the metal, the result was still weak and could serve no practical purpose apart from the manufacture of small implements such as fish hooks, needles and brooches.

A more important development was the invention of smelting, by which the metal is separated in molten form from its ore. By this process a far greater quantity of copper became available. Now the process of smelting produced useful quantities of sufficiently pure copper to enable the peoples of the Nile, and later the Tigris-Euphrates valleys, to evolve the first civilizations based on the use of significant quantities of metal. But copper is still a very malleable metal even after it has been hardened by hammering, so the only copper weapons produced were daggers, which had wide, triangular blades to overcome the weakness of the metal. Larger weapons of copper were out of the question as they would hardly have been able to support their own weight without buckling.

As skill in the working of copper increased, the use of the metal for weapons became more widespread. Daggers

**STONE AGE WEAPONS**
The diagram shows the evolution in three principal phases of weapons in Stone Age times, before man had learned the secrets of metal working. The weapons are also divided vertically into two classes, those of the shock type (usually held in the hand and used for chopping, cutting, etc.) and the missile type (thrown or mechanically propelled).

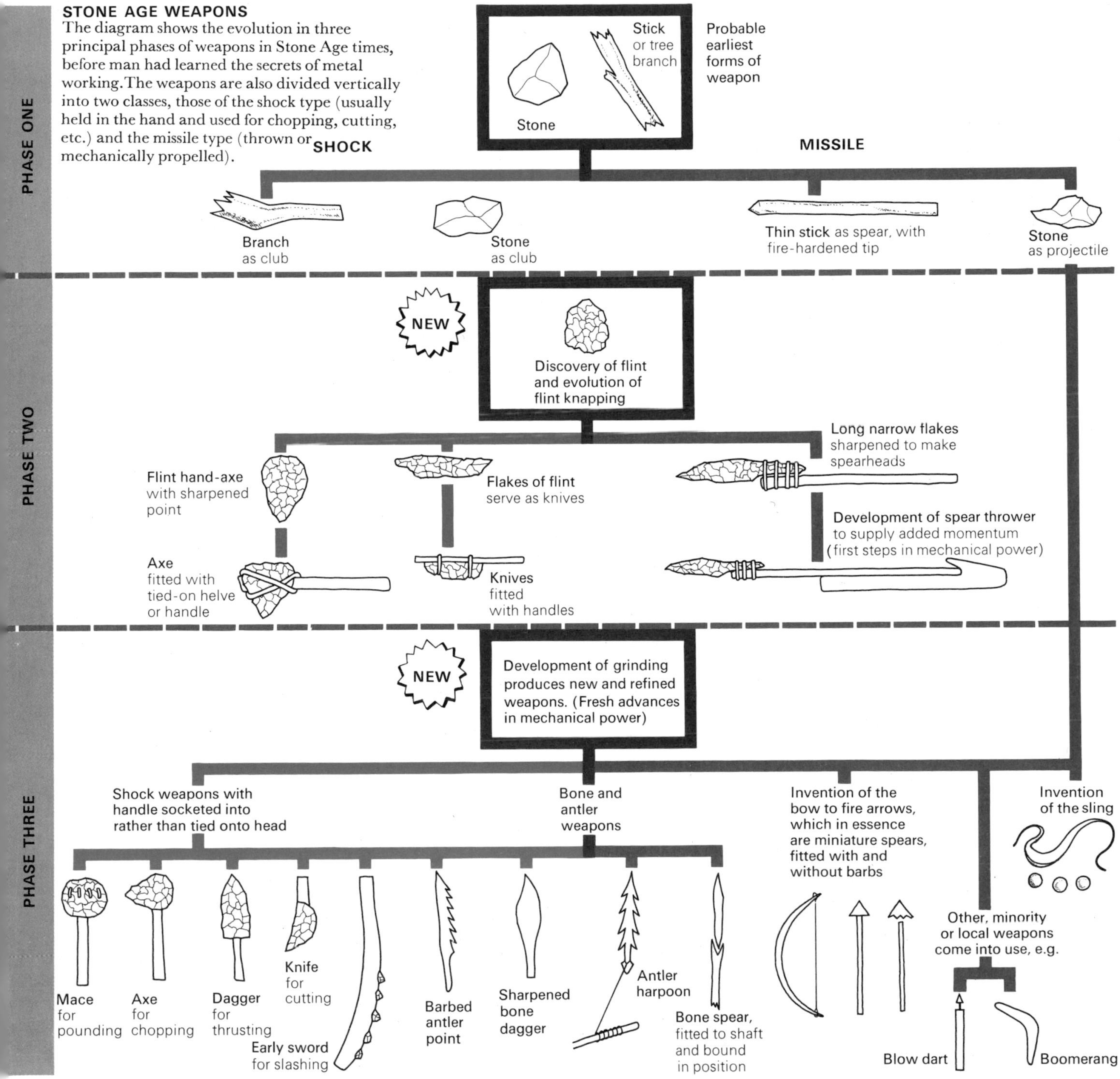
PHASE ONE
Stone
Stick or tree branch
Probable earliest forms of weapon
SHOCK
MISSILE
Branch as club
Stone as club
Thin stick as spear, with fire-hardened tip
Stone as projectile
PHASE TWO
NEW
Discovery of flint and evolution of flint knapping
Flint hand-axe with sharpened point
Flakes of flint serve as knives
Long narrow flakes sharpened to make spearheads
Development of spear thrower to supply added momentum (first steps in mechanical power)
Axe fitted with tied-on helve or handle
Knives fitted with handles
PHASE THREE
NEW
Development of grinding produces new and refined weapons. (Fresh advances in mechanical power)
Shock weapons with handle socketed into rather than tied onto head
Bone and antler weapons
Invention of the bow to fire arrows, which in essence are miniature spears, fitted with and without barbs
Invention of the sling
Other, minority or local weapons come into use, e.g.
Mace for pounding
Axe for chopping
Dagger for thrusting
Knife for cutting
Early sword for slashing
Barbed antler point
Sharpened bone dagger
Antler harpoon
Bone spear, fitted to shaft and bound in position
Blow dart
Boomerang

were improved by narrowing the blade, the necessary stiffening being provided by spines down the centre of each side of the blade, and axeheads and arrowheads were cast roughly and then finished by hammering.

Hand in hand with the improvements in weapons went a gradual sophistication in the organization of armies. Early warfare had taken the form of combat between individuals or groups who were personally involved in a dispute, but the civilizations of the Nile and Mesopotamian valleys went one better. They were able to provide sufficient food in their fertile lands to support, when the need arose, an additional and expressly warrior class. These men were equipped homogeneously as groups of spearmen, bowmen and slingers, and they fought for the community.

Tactics were still simple, if not crude, and consisted of the two armies forming up in two facing lines, bombarding each other with a shower of arrows or stones and then closing to fight it out hand to hand. Any tactics more advanced than this were accidental. Furthermore, the development of weapons had reached an *impasse*. Copper was in a way an advance over stone, but it was soft and incapable of taking an edge that could match a flint in sharpness. What was needed was a stronger metal.

## The Hyksos – Warriors of the Bronze Age

The first people to find the new metal were the Sumerians of Mesopotamia, and the substance they found was bronze, an alloy of tin and copper, which if worked properly has a strength far exceeding that of either of its constituent metals. How the Sumerians discovered bronze is a mystery, but it very likely came about when copper and tin ores became mixed accidentally before smelting. With the use of bronze, existing weapons could be improved, and at last it became possible to make an effective sword.

The use of bronze was confined to Mesopotamia until the Hyksos invasion of Egypt in about 1700 BC. The Hyksos people were a mixed though predominantly Semitic race; they overran Egypt with the aid of their bronze weapons, horse-drawn chariots and composite bows, all of which were unknown to the Egyptians before that time. Their chariots were two-wheeled and drawn by pairs of horses, and apart from the tactical surprise they inflicted on the Egyptians, they had a very considerable shock value; in effect they increased battlefield mobility by a previously unheard-of degree. The composite bow, in which the original wooden stave was replaced by a sandwich of wood, horn and sinew, was more reliable, had a longer range and was capable of dispatching its arrow with a greater velocity than its wooden counterpart.

At about this time, too, the composition of armies began to alter as urban civilizations became more numerous: a form of militia – in the sense of a 'citizen army' – now provided the basis of armed forces. Whereas earlier

Stone Age warfare: spear-armed Dani warriors of New Guinea prepare for battle. Inter-village encounters still occur in some areas of the island, and usually take either of two forms. One is a stylized, ritual clash but in the other, more deadly type lives are fiercely sought to avenge the ghosts of men slain in earlier fights.

armies had been composed of smaller numbers of professional warriors, the new ones were larger and had a considerable force of lightly-armoured militia equipped with pikes (thrusting spears) and shields. These men formed a solid base around which the more highly-trained archers, slingers and horse-drawn nobility could operate. Another advantage enjoyed by the Hyksos lay in their superior defensive armour, which included plates of bronze sewn to leather or quilted material to protect the most critical parts of the body. These plates were small and looked like scales and spread in rows across the helmet and over the chest, shoulders and arms.

**Egyptian Swords**

The most important weapon brought to Egypt by the Hyksos was the sword, the development of which, as we have seen, was dependent entirely on bronze. It seems likely that the Hyksos took the idea of the sword (as well as that of the chariot) from the Sumerians and improved on it to produce a fairly long and straight-bladed weapon. As an offensive weapon the sword fulfils two roles, those of cutting and thrusting. The perpetual problem in the design of swords is to make the two apparently conflicting requirements compatible. The root of the problem is that, generally speaking, the thrusting sword should be straight and the cutting sword – the modern sabre – curved. The Egyptians, in developing their own bronze swords after the example of the Hyksos, opted for the curved cutting sword, and this example was followed by most of the Middle Eastern and Oriental nations. But when the sword appeared in Europe it took the form of a straight thrusting sword, made with edges so that it could slash as well as thrust. The culminating products of the two designs were the curved Arabian scimitar on the one hand and on the other the long, straight rapier, which had no cutting edge.

The Egyptians learned the lessons of the Hyksos invasions well, and in about 1600 BC drove the invaders from their land, in turn pressing forward their own conquests into Palestine and Mesopotamia. For the most part Egypt held sway over the Middle East until she met the Hittites in Eastern Anatolia. The latter had one of the answers to Egypt's military might – they had discovered how to make weapons of iron. Iron had been known for some 1,500 years before this date, but the metal had not been used for any practical purpose because no one knew how to work it. But in about 1400 BC it was found that if iron and carbon were heated together, hammered into shape and then cooled quickly, the result was a weapon or tool far surpassing bronze in strength and sharpness. The process was expensive and difficult, however, and the success of the Hittites over the Egyptians appears to have been due as much to their superior discipline and training as to their possession of iron weapons. Nevertheless, the knowledge of how to work iron was a secret that the Hittites jealously guarded, and it was not until their Empire was broken up by the arrival of the Thracians and Phrygians in Asia Minor that the use of iron spread elsewhere. In the consequent dispersal of the Hittite peoples, the secret of wrought iron travelled with its smiths throughout the Middle East.

**Assyria – Home of the First Professional Soldiers**

Although the Hittites had not been able to reap the full benefits of their monopoly in iron, the next major power to arrive was able, having an excellent military system, to make full use of its good iron-producing capabilities. This power was Assyria, which had shaken off the domination of Babylon, with which it was culturally allied, in about 1900 BC. By 1100 BC or thereabouts Assyria had become the most powerful nation in the Middle East, reaching the peak of her power during the reign of Tiglath-pileser III (745–727 BC).

The Assyrians, whose militia army had freed them from Babylon, soon realized that the militia system was impractical for any kind of prolonged campaign because it meant that their generals had to make do with improperly trained troops, while the food and manufacturing industries at home were deprived of a large part of their manpower for considerable periods. At the height of her power, therefore, Assyria relied on a large standing army, the first in history, and by the time of Tiglath-pileser III this was largely equipped with weapons of iron.

The basic organization of Assyria's forces had been settled long before, by approximately 1250 BC, when the army was divided into chariot and infantry arms. About 950 BC the development of cavalry began, although it was as yet incapable of shock tactics since neither the saddle nor the stirrup had been invented. The cavalry of the period consisted of mounted archers who were protected while they discharged their bows by other, light cavalry equipped with spears and shields. Later the mounted archer was equipped with defensive armour and it became possible to convert the light cavalry, too, into bowmen. The infantry, which formed the solid base of any attack, was divided into two types. Firstly there were the native Assyrian heavy infantrymen, armed with bows or slings and provided with armour and helmets, and secondly there were light auxiliary forces, usually drawn from subject races and employed for screening and swift pursuit. One advantage enjoyed by Assyrian troops was the fact that they were all provided with boots, which enabled them to move faster than any of their enemies. This was, obviously, an enormous asset when long distances had to be covered.

To sum up its chief characteristics, the Assyrian military system was based on a standing army equipped uniformly with iron weapons and having a good balance of cavalry and infantry, both of which featured lightly and heavily armed units. The Assyrians were also adept at siege warfare and had special engines with which to pierce the gates and city walls of their enemies.

The downfall of Assyria finally occurred in 612 BC when Nineveh fell to the Chaldeans and the Medes. But the Babylonian resurgence, led by the Chaldeans, did not last long, and it was left to the Medes to take up the reins of empire in the Middle East. However, although they sought to emulate the military doctrines of the Assyrians they had so lately conquered, they found it impossible to train their troops to such a high pitch, and consequently they fell back on the older militia system. Advances were made, nevertheless, particularly in the way in which the infantry was turned into a more disciplined and comparatively mobile body, instead of the great solid, immobile mass that had for so long formed the main body of every army – the rock around which the cavalry or chariots could manoeuvre. This imposition of discipline on the infantry is of signal importance, as it marks the beginning of the temporary eclipse of cavalry.

**The Persians Go to War with Greece**

The Chaldean–Median empire did not last long before in 559 BC it was taken over, from within, by the Persians (a people akin to the Medes) under Cyrus II. As they consolidated their newly-won power the Persians came into conflict with the Ionian Greeks, who lived on the Asiatic shore of the Aegean Sea. This set the stage for a conflict that was to bring Europe into the limelight of world affairs for the first time.

Internal dissension delayed the clash, but with the restoration of civil order under Darius I (*c.* 521–*c.* 486 BC), the Persian Army was made ready for an invasion of Europe. Oddly enough, the Persians had by that time reverted to chariots, many of which were fitted with scythes on the wheel hubs; in addition they had a large force of cavalry. As for the Persian infantry, Darius could call on contingents from every part of his empire. They, however, were most inferior militia troops who could only be used to form a solid mass as a base for the better troops – the chariots, the cavalry and the best infantry (headed by the famous Immortals, an élite body of 10,000 men). The main weapon of the infantry was the bow. Standard Persian tactics were to disorganize their enemies by showering them with enormous numbers of arrows and to exploit the ensuing confusion by sending in the ordinary infantry, hoping to prevail by sheer weight of numbers.

**Greek Armour and Discipline Win the Day**

The Persians' offensive system worked admirably in mainland Asia, and against less well-disciplined troops, but it met its match against the Greeks, who were far fewer in number but compensated for this deficiency by superb discipline and heavily-armoured infantry. As the invaded nation the Greeks were always careful to choose ground where the Persians could not use their superior numbers, or their cavalry, to advantage. The Greek warrior, the hoplite, was a militiaman – but an exceptionally well-trained one. He was substantially armoured with a breast-plate, a helmet, a large round shield and greaves to protect his shins; his weapons were a pike, or thrusting spear, and a short sword.

In battle the Greeks used a close formation known as the phalanx. They advanced in lines eight men deep: the shield on the left arm of one man covered the exposed right side of the man to his left, and a hedge of pikes sprouted from the front ranks of the formation. The Greeks did not, by the way, invent the phalanx – although it is quite commonly referred to as being of Greek origin. In fact records of similar infantry formations survive from as far back as Sumerian times. But there is little doubt that in Greece the phalanx reached new heights of mobility and effectiveness.

Darius I of Persia met the Greeks for the first time at Marathon in 490 BC and suffered a resounding tactical defeat. The clouds of Persian arrows had little effect on the heavily-armoured Greeks, and subsequent attacks by the light infantry were repulsed with very severe casualties. Darius then found that his lines of communication were threatened and he retreated back to Asia, where he died before he could invade again. Further battles between the Greeks and the Persians did take place, however, in 480–479 BC, under Darius's son, Xerxes I 'the Great' (*c.* 519–*c.* 465 BC); but the results were much the same. Such Persian successes as were gained came – as at Thermopylae – from their vast superiority in numbers. In

general the Greek hoplites and their formations were more than a measure for the Persians and their tactics. Indeed, from that point in time it was the heavily-armed and armoured infantryman who dominated battlefields for centuries to come.

**The Macedonian Phalanx**

The next stage in the developing arts of war was the bringing to perfection of the Greek hoplite. This was achieved by two Macedonian kings, Philip and his son Alexander 'the Great', between 356 and 336 BC. The Macedonian phalanx had double the depth of its predecessor, containing sixteen men who were now also equipped with a longer spear called the *sarissa*. Estimates of its length vary between twelve and twenty-four feet. If, which is not perhaps entirely likely, it was the longer of these extremes, it has been calculated that six spear-points could be offered to the enemy in front of each man. The Macedonian phalanx was superlatively drilled and extraordinarily manoeuvrable for its size and complexity, and was the supreme weapon of the world until the advent of the Roman legion. The phalanx did not operate alone, but was supported by well trained light skirmishing troops who used the traditional bow, sling and javelin (throwing spear) and by heavy cavalry equipped with spear and sword and who also carried a considerable amount of armour. With this powerful, all-arms war machine Alexander extended the Macedonian empire from Greece to the Indus Valley.

**Rise of the Roman Legion**

But already the weapon that was to beat the Alexandrine phalanx was developing: the Roman legion. The story of Rome's rise to the position of the greatest power in the ancient world begins with the expulsion of the Etruscans from Rome in 510 BC and the establishment of the Roman Republic. Her original army was made up of six classes, each reflecting the wealth of the men in it since they had to provide their own equipment, the army being a militia force. The wealthiest citizens were in the cavalry, while the poorest had merely to provide themselves with slings. The basic tactical unit was the century (of 100 men): it was organized in battle in the form of a phalanx, and this formation was retained until Rome suffered a crushing defeat by the Gauls at the Battle of the River Allia in 390 BC.

In the reformation of the Roman Army that followed, the phalanx was replaced by a legion composed of maniples, each of which in turn was made up of two centuries, now reduced in strength to sixty men each. The total strength of a legion varied between 4,000 and 6,000 men. But the biggest innovation was not in the organization of the legion so much as in its tactical disposition. The solid phalanx was now abandoned and replaced by a

Moments from the story of the world's first standing army – founded by the Assyrians. **left** Mounted archers of King Ashurbanipal (669–626 BC) charge an enemy detachment of foot soldiers; from a relief in the North West Palace, Nimrud. **above** Archers and slingers mount a combined attack; from a scene in Sennacherib's Palace, Nineveh.

The hitting power of the bow was acknowledged in ancient times throughout the Mediterranean region – and in many more primitive areas too. Archers served both on foot and in mounted units (in Assyria the latter were protected as they discharged their bows by specialist cavalrymen armed with light spears and shields). The standing bronze figure illustrated here is from Sardinia and represents a foot soldier of the sixth century BC. On the far right is an Etruscan mounted archer, also made of bronze but dating from the fifth century BC. The attitude of the figure suggests some awareness of the tactic, usually attributed to the later Parthians, in which the archer flies in real or feigned retreat before the enemy and then suddenly turns and fires at him.

heavy-infantry formation resembling either the black or the white squares on a chessboard. Between each maniple in the front rank there was an interval one maniple wide, which was covered by the maniples in the second rank, the gaps in this being in turn covered by the men of the third and rearmost rank. And no longer was wealth the qualification for equipment and position. Those in the front rank (*hastati*) were young but experienced troops, in the second rank were the veteran *principes*, while the third rank contained a mixture of veterans (*triarii*) and young, inexperienced troops (the *velites* or skirmishers who often opened a battle and then fell back). This tactical disposition enabled the front rank to retire into the second if necessary and the rear rank to move up into the second without disturbing the front line.

The standard equipment for a legionary was a metal helmet, a breastplate and a large oval metal shield, plus a javelin and a sword. Roman tactics were usually for the heavy infantry to advance on the enemy, covered by the skirmishing *velites* who then withdrew; the *hastati* then threw their spears from a distance of about twenty yards and moved in rapidly to close quarters to use their swords, which were only about two feet long, inside the reach of the opposing pikemen, whose thrusting spears were then a great hindrance to them. The great test of the system came in 197 BC, when the Romans defeated the Macedonians after a hard battle at Cynoscephalae. At a later date the basic sub-division of the legion was changed from the maniple to the cohort, which had the strength of three maniples; at the same time the oval shield was dropped in favour of a longer, semi-cylindrical

The age of the heavy infantryman. **above** An Etruscan bronze figure (*c.* 520 BC) wearing the style of armour most commonly associated with the Greek hoplite – a cuirass, a helmet, and greaves to protect the shins. The right arm is shown in the thrusting position for the heavy hoplite spear. **right** A Corinthian bronze helmet from Olympia, 460 BC.

shield. In this guise, the Roman legionary was to survive until well after the arrival of the first barbarian hordes from Germany, when the Roman Empire began to crumble. Looking back over this long period of some 600 years it was undoubtedly the Macedonian phalanx and the Roman legion that had been mostly responsible for the eclipse of the cavalry, put into the shadows by well-disciplined and well-protected infantry.

### The Genius of Hannibal

Although the Romans were undoubtedly the leading military force in the West after the death of Alexander the Great in 323 BC they did not, for all their many skills, go undefeated. And of the numerous generals who opposed them one name will always be pre-eminent – that of Hannibal.

Hannibal (247–183 BC) was a general in the army of Carthage, an ambitious civilization centred in the region of modern Tunisia. In the First Punic War (265–241 BC) Carthage had been forced to yield Sicily to the Romans. The Second Punic War (219–202 BC) was launched by Hannibal's capture of Saguntum in Spain, from which point he led an army of some 90,000 men and eighty elephants across the Pyrenees, through Gaul and over the Alps into the Po Valley. By his speed and audacity Hannibal overwhelmed Roman armies at the River Trebia, Lake Trasimene and at Cannae. The latter has been regarded by many historians as the perfect tactical victory. To achieve it Hannibal let the centre of his army be driven back by the Romans, but he kept his line intact. Then as soon as a sufficiently deep horseshoe had been formed he sent forward his infantry on each wing to envelop and crush the enemy, of whom 60,000 were slain. Indeed, until his elephants badly failed him at the Battle of Zama (202 BC) Hannibal's aggressive spirit and speed of manoeuvre made him the most dynamic leader of his age.

### Age of the Mounted Barbarian

The beginning of the collapse of Rome's military might can be traced back to the middle of the second century AD, as the empire began to lose its outer provinces to peoples moving westwards across Europe. Successive waves of ferocious mounted invaders, Goths, Visigoths, Huns and Vandals, sapped the last vestiges of Rome's former strength. By the end of the fourth century AD, Rome had ceased to exist as a mighty empire. There were several reasons for this collapse. First and foremost, the army had rotted away internally. The legionaries were no longer first-class troops from Rome itself but men from the provinces who were unwilling to train to the same extent as their Roman counterparts – or to carry the same weight of armour; their discipline was no match for the new sort of warfare with which they were faced. Moreover, the Romans in their declining years were desperately short of cavalry and often had to accept mercenary horsemen from the very peoples they were

251

fighting. On the other hand the invaders themselves had moderately well-disciplined, trained cavalry, and the falling-off of Roman discipline made it impossible for the legionaries to withstand their savage charges. The supremacy of infantry over cavalry was over. Cavalry victories such as that of Adrianople in AD 378, when the Goths smashed through the packed Roman lines, gave a clear indication that the future of warfare, for the next few centuries, lay with the horseman.

**Byzantine Cavalry**

But although Rome herself had fallen the Eastern Roman Empire, centred on Byzantium, or Constantinople as it was renamed in AD 330, was to survive for another 1,000 years. Unlike Rome, the Byzantine rulers had learned the error of their military ways, and had recognized in time that the day of the infantryman was over. What they had to do was take the military principles of the 'barbarians' they were fighting, refine them, improve on them in matters of equipment and organization, and then beat the enemy on the field of battle using the latter's own weapon. That weapon was, as we have noted, the cavalry, but it was a cavalry very different from the type encountered earlier. Two inventions brought from the East had revolutionized mounted warfare by making possible the development of a true heavy cavalry, which had a very considerable shock value, in place of earlier mounted forces that had relied on missiles. The two inventions were the saddle and the stirrup, which arrived in the Western world in about AD 350 and 500 respectively. Their introduction gave a heavily-armoured man much greater resistance to attack, enabling him to stay on his horse under quite stern battle conditions. This of course greatly enhanced his offensive power.

The mainstay of the Byzantine armies from the middle of the seventh century was the heavy cavalryman or cataphract. The evolution of this type of heavy cavalry had started about 100 years earlier with the outstanding general Belisarius (*c.* 505–65), who had reconquered large portions of Italy and North Africa for his Emperor, Justinian I (483–565). Belisarius's armies had been made up of three types of cavalry: firstly there were the heavy Byzantine troopers armed with lance, sword and bow (the latter being the primary weapon) and armoured with helmet, mail shirt (made of hundreds of interlocking iron rings) and shield; the second type consisted of more lightly armed and armoured Hunnish auxiliary horse-archers; there were also, thirdly, German or Slav heavily armoured lancers, who were employed on a mercenary

**THE RIVAL ARMIES**

| Persians<br>Darius III | Macedonians<br>Alexander the Great |
|---|---|
| 15 elephants | nil |
| 200 chariots | nil |
| 45,000 cavalry | 7,000 cavalry |
| 200,000 infantry | 40,000 infantry |

**THE BATTLE OF ARBELA (OR GAUGEMALA), 331 BC**

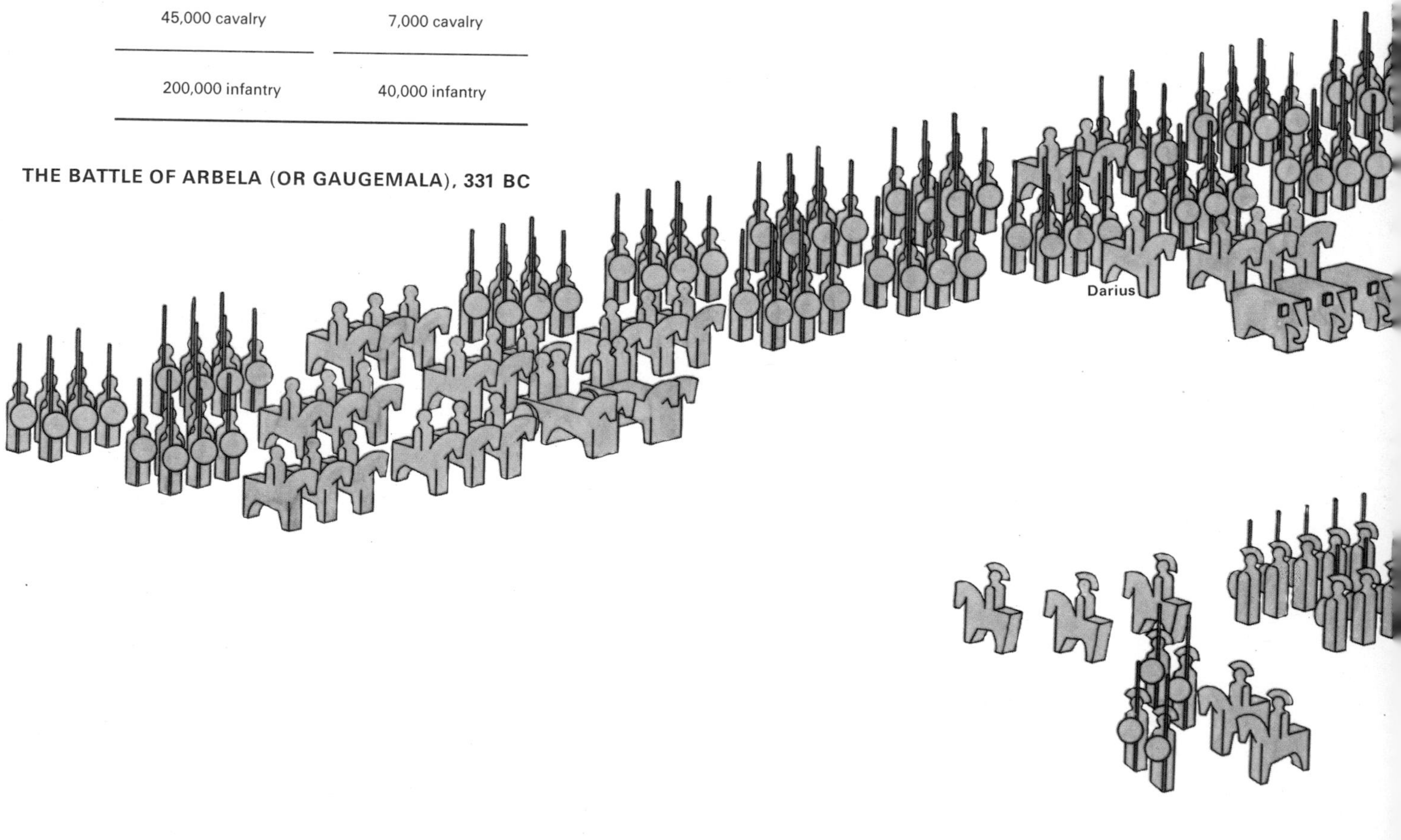
Darius

basis. Through a process of trial and error, which was speeded by initially disastrous meetings with a new enemy, the Moslems, the Byzantines had evolved their standard and successful military system by the first half of the seventh century. The key element, as we have said, was the cavalry arm, now reorganized into two types: the cataphract with his sword, lance and bow, protected by steel helmet, full mail coat, greaves and shield; and the trapezites, more lightly armoured and equipped with a bow or lance. The other major arm, the infantry, had undergone a complete transformation from the old Roman-based type, and was now made up of two varieties, corresponding to those of the cavalry: the heavy infantryman, the *scutatus*, who was clothed in a full mail coat and a steel helmet and wielded a battle axe; and the light infantryman. Some of the latter wore no armour (though others were protected by mail shirts), but all carried very powerful bows. Backed up by a good logistical organization, well trained and competently – sometimes brilliantly – led, the Byzantine army was the best of the early Middle Ages. Cavalry had come back into its own, and was to dominate the European military scene until the advent of new weapons or infantry capable of standing up to a heavy cavalry charge.

### Artillery and Siege Weapons

A subject we have not so far touched upon is that of ancient artillery and siege engines, which altered very little in their basic design during the period. There are three ways of reducing a fortified town: by starving it out, by making use of traitors within it to betray it, and by overcoming its defences by military means. The first was difficult for the ancients to achieve, as a besieging army had only a rudimentary logistical backing, and the chances were that the besieged could hold out longer than the besiegers. The second method was remarkably successful in many instances, but failing either of these recourse had to be made to siege warfare.

The first exponents of this art were the Sumerians, but their primitive and somewhat haphazard methods were greatly improved upon by the Assyrians, who had bodies of engineers to conduct the main part of the work. Mining operations were often carried out where conditions allowed it, *i.e.* where the city was not built on solid rock. The object was to undermine the foundations of the wall surrounding the city so that a section fell; this made a breach in the defences through which the attackers could then rush and try to overpower the defenders at close quarters.

Alternatively, attempts to create a breach in the wall would be made above the surface with battering rams, large logs with bronze or iron heads suspended by ropes from overhead bars so that they could be swung backwards and forwards against walls or gates. Alongside and above the ram operators, large movable towers would be

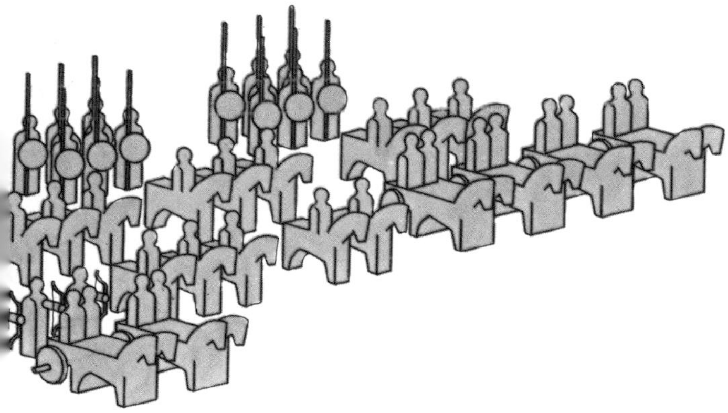

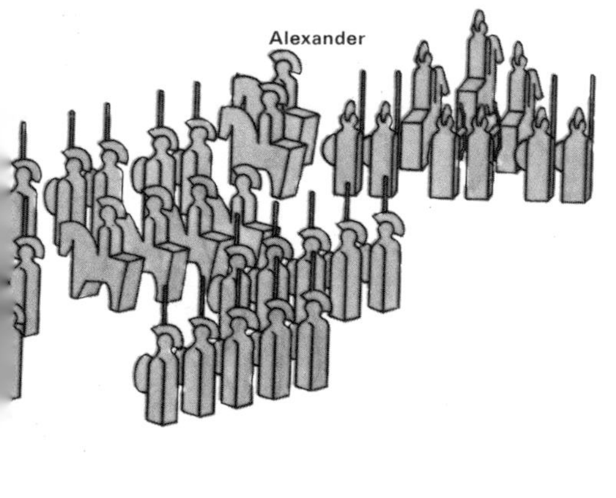
Alexander

Near Arbela, some 300 miles north of Babylon, Alexander the Great outmanoeuvred a far larger Persian force under Darius III; estimates of the numbers present vary wildly but the most conservative figures, those of Quintus Curtius, Alexander's biographer (*fl.* first century AD), give the Persians a total majority in excess of five to one (see panel for details).

As the armies faced each other Alexander decided that the Persians, who occupied a much broader front, would attempt to outflank and encircle his army. So he devised a formation with two highly mobile flying columns, one behind each wing, ready to face in any direction. The Macedonian army then began to move to its right and obliquely forward, leading the Persians away from ground which they had earlier levelled for the benefit of their scythe-bearing chariots. When the left wing of the Persian cavalry eventually charged its heavy armour brought it some initial success but the Macedonian lines held and in time drove off the attack. A follow-up charge by Persian charioteers was resisted with showers of javelins and arrows. By now gaps were opening in the strung-out Persian lines, and Alexander next led his Companion cavalry in a bold charge, heading directly for Darius. This was a decisive move; after a brief clash the Persian king panicked and fled.

In the meantime Alexander's own left-centre had been pierced by Persian cavalry and Parmenion, commander of the Macedonian left wing, was surrounded. Word was sent to Alexander, who broke off his pursuit of the routed Darius and the hordes of his terrified followers, and rode back with his Companions to free Parmenion. This was achieved after strong resistance from the right wing of the Persian cavalry, whose retreat was now effectively barred. In all Persian losses are thought to have exceeded 50,000, while Alexander lost some 500 men killed and about 5,000 wounded.

Despite its huge numerical majority the Persian army had been crushed. In fact large numbers of Persians did little but flee the field, such was the impact of Alexander's main thrust on their morale – already weakened the previous night when Darius had made his army, unnecessarily, stand-to in case of attack. Again, had Darius made use of his elephants they could have been influential in resisting the cavalry attack, since horses were known to fear them; but there is no record that the elephants were used at all.

Thus generalship and discipline brought a total victory in the field. Arbela was, too, one of the most decisive battles in history: by it Persian resistance was wrecked and Alexander then speedily overran Babylon and Persepolis, the capital of the Empire.

2740

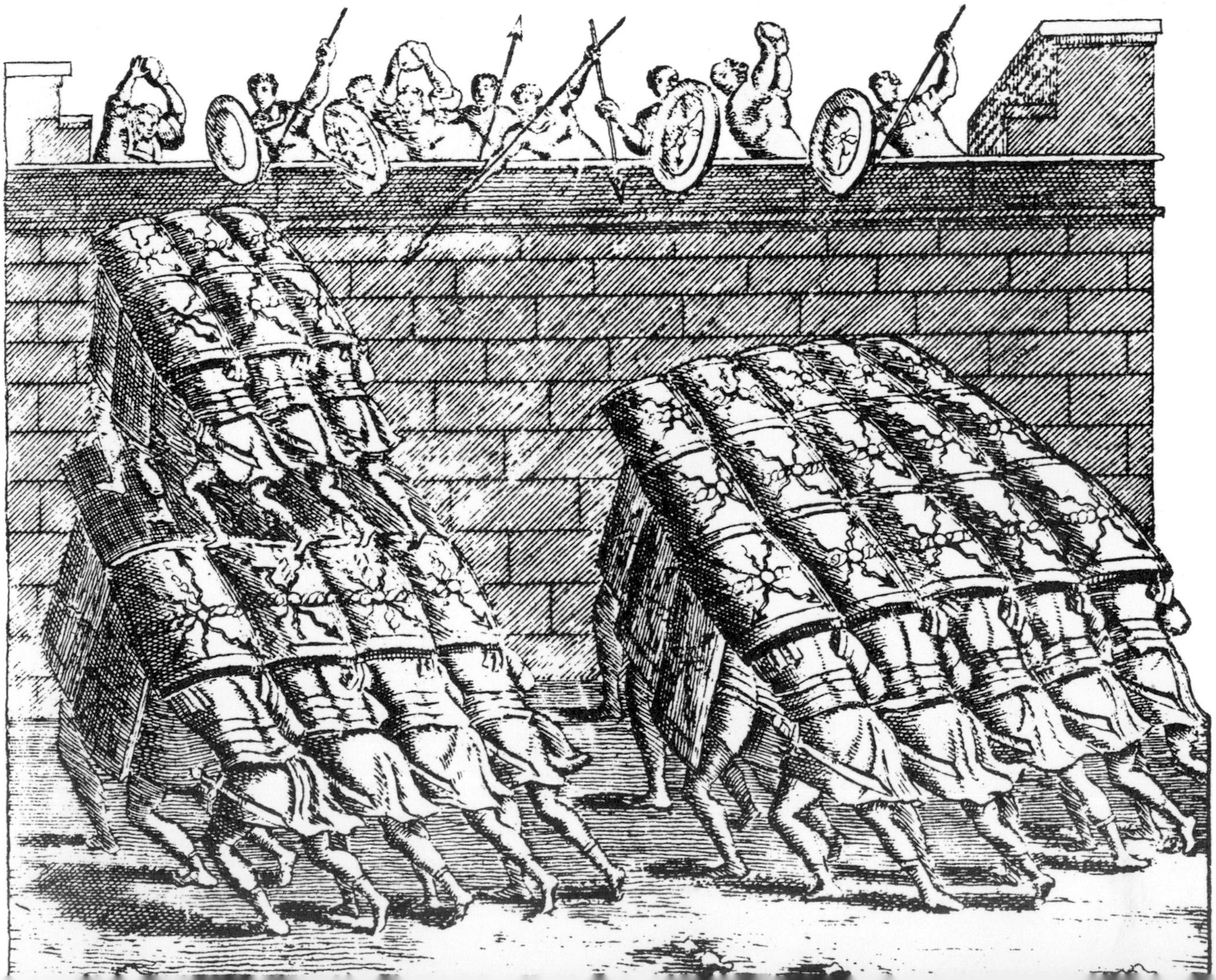

Roman arms and armour. **far left** Sword and scabbard belonging to the Emperor Tiberius (42 BC–AD 37). **left** Bronze figure of a legionary. **below left** The *testudo* or tortoise formation, used in siege warfare to protect the attacking force. **below** Battering rams. Figure A shows a straightforward ram-headed pole; in B a pointed ram is swung from a chain.

B.
A
A. Aries Simplex . B. Aries Compo

brought up to the walls, and from these superior positions archers and javelin throwers would pelt the defenders with their missiles to drive them from the walls and so prevent them from dropping stones and the like on their colleagues working the ram. These siege towers also gave the attackers a chance to go in over the wall, either directly from the towers or with the aid of scaling ladders. Sometimes ramps of packed earth were built so that the besiegers could swarm up to the level of the top of the defenders' wall with no fear that their device could be set on fire or toppled over.

The last refinement in the practice of siege warfare in the ancient world was of Byzantine origin. This was Greek fire, a powerful combustible that could not be put out by normal means. There is still doubt as to the exact chemical composition of this weapon, but it appears to have been a substance that burst into flames on coming into contact with water. Water in fact supplied the propellant for Greek fire in the form of a high-pressure jet generated by the movement of a plunger within a tube. Although the use of inflammables was by no means new in war, Greek fire surpassed by a long way any other comparable device used by the ancients.

The artillery used in the ancient world was divided into two main categories or systems, those of the *ballista* and the catapult. The former was in effect a large mechanical bow, in which the force built up in twisted ropes or some similar material was released by a trigger, hurling a large javelin or arrow up to 500 yards with considerable

THE ROMAN LEGION
The illustration shows how a Roman legion went to war in the period after 390 BC. The main body of the legion consisted of three ranks of heavy infantrymen, each armed with a metal helmet, a breast-plate and a shield and carrying a javelin and a sword. In front were the more lightly armed *velites*, many of whom wore a headdress made from a wolf's skin: they usually carried a sword and two javelins.

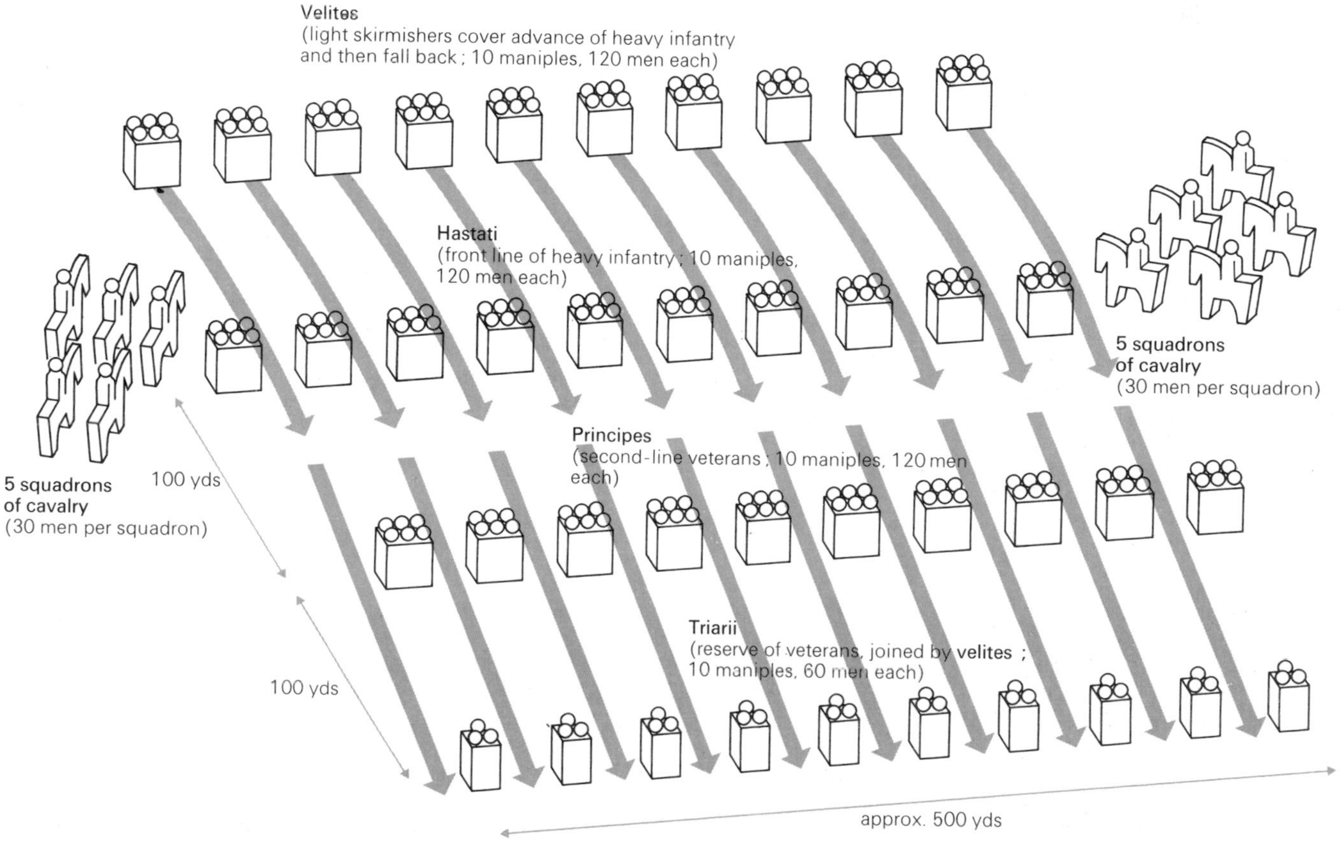
Velites
(light skirmishers cover advance of heavy infantry and then fall back ; 10 maniples, 120 men each)
Hastati
(front line of heavy infantry ; 10 maniples, 120 men each)
5 squadrons of cavalry (30 men per squadron)
Principes
(second-line veterans ; 10 maniples, 120 men each)
5 squadrons of cavalry (30 men per squadron)
100 yds
Triarii
(reserve of veterans, joined by velites ; 10 maniples, 60 men each)
100 yds
approx. 500 yds

momentum. The catapult, while deriving its motive power from the same source as the *ballista*, operated in a different way. There was a single arm, with a cup at the end of it, held down by a latch against the torsion of the ropes. Into the cup was loaded the projectile, normally a large rock, which was then hurled high into the air and down onto the enemy when the arm was released and the twisted ropes jerked the arm up to the vertical. These devices were used initially for siege operations only, since they were bulky and difficult to move, but the Macedonians improved and adapted them for use in field operations. This was done by carrying with the army only those parts which could not be rapidly improvised; the main body of the machines was constructed from local timber by engineers after the field of battle had been reached. These siege weapons were further refined by the Romans and the Byzantines, but the principle of using rope or sinew in torsion to supply the motive power remained unchanged.

While these modes of warfare flourished in the East with the Byzantines, the decline of the military arts in the West had become acute. A few able leaders still attempted to train and equip their men on the rigorous patterns of old, but skill and discipline on the field of battle had in the main given way to brute force.

**above** Greek fire – a Byzantine invention – is directed from the bow of a war galley; its composition remains unclear, but it was evidently a powerful combustible that ignited on coming into contact with water. **below** The 'barbarian' problem. Mounted Sarmatians in scale armour are driven off by the Roman cavalry; from the Trajan Column, Rome.

**CHAPTER 2**

# *The Dark and Middle Ages*

MEN OF ENGLAND
IN TIMES PAST, WHEN
THEY WOULD EXERCISE
THEMSELVES (FOR WE MUST NEEDS
HAVE SOME RECREATION, OUR
BODIES CANNOT ENDURE WITHOUT
SOME EXERCISE), THEY WERE
WONT TO GO ABROAD IN
THE FIELDS A-SHOOTING, BUT
NOW IS TURNED INTO
GLOSSING, GULLING,
AND WHORING
WITHIN THE HOUSE.

*BISHOP HUGH LATIMER*
*(c. 1485-1555) in a sermon of 1549*

Longbowmen in combat, from a fifteenth-century Flemish manuscript. The arrival of the arquebus was to save such men many hours of strenuous bow practice – as well as invoking the greater fears of Bishop Latimer (above) and fellow churchmen.

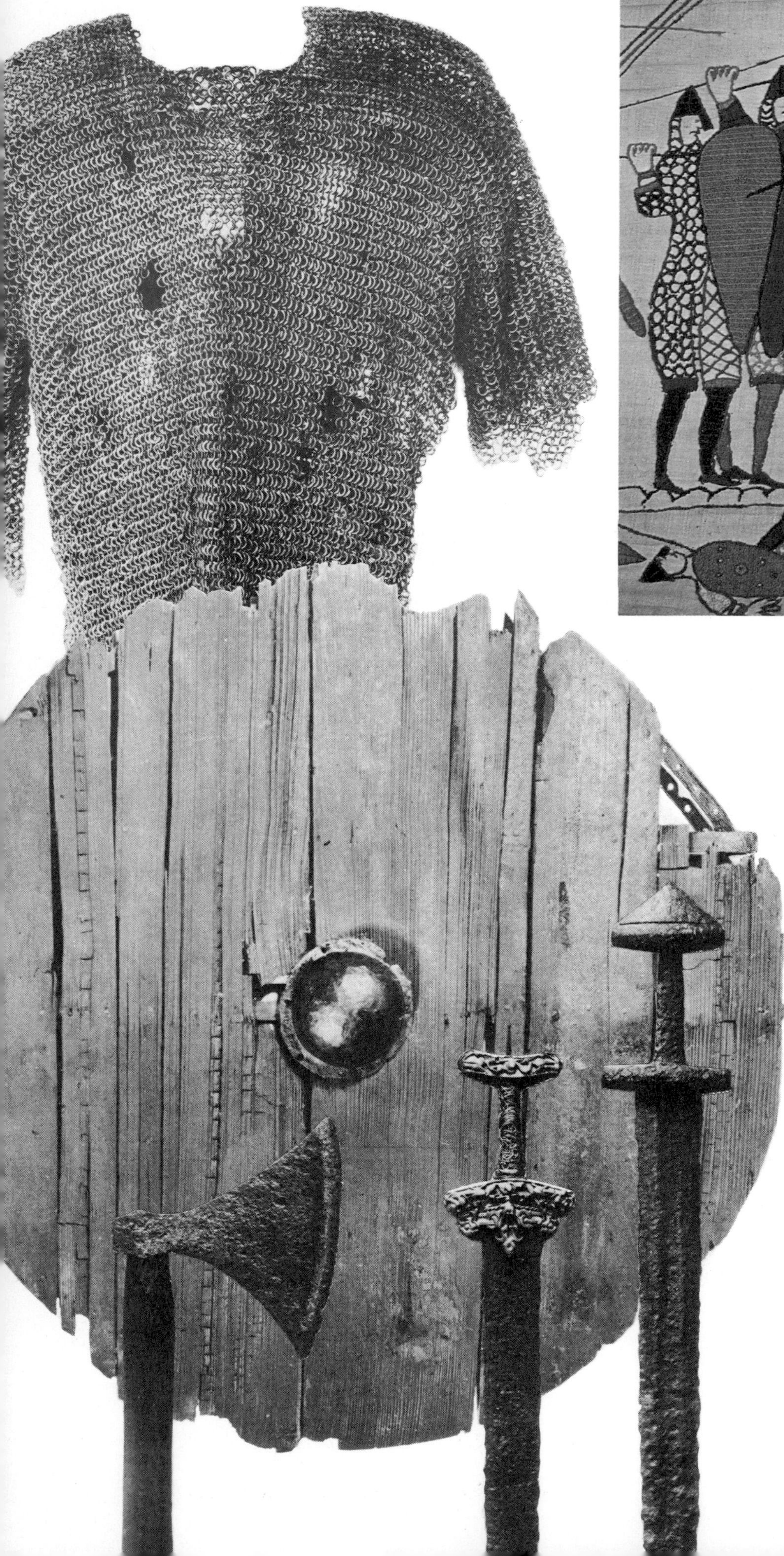

**left** Viking arms and armour. The equipment shown includes a mail shirt made of interlocking metal rings; a wooden shield fixed to a metal frame; a battle axe, and two swords. **above** English foot-soldiers at the Battle of Hastings (1066) resist a charge by the Norman cavalry; from the Bayeux Tapestry, which records the story of the Norman conquest of England.

The crossbow and its separate windlass mechanism are shown in the final phase of the weapon's development. The crossbow's effective range was about 100 yards and its rate of fire was 1–2 arrows a minute. Also shown are a Genoese bowman spanning his bow, and a machine designed *c.* 1485–8 by Leonardo da Vinci to fire four crossbows in succession.

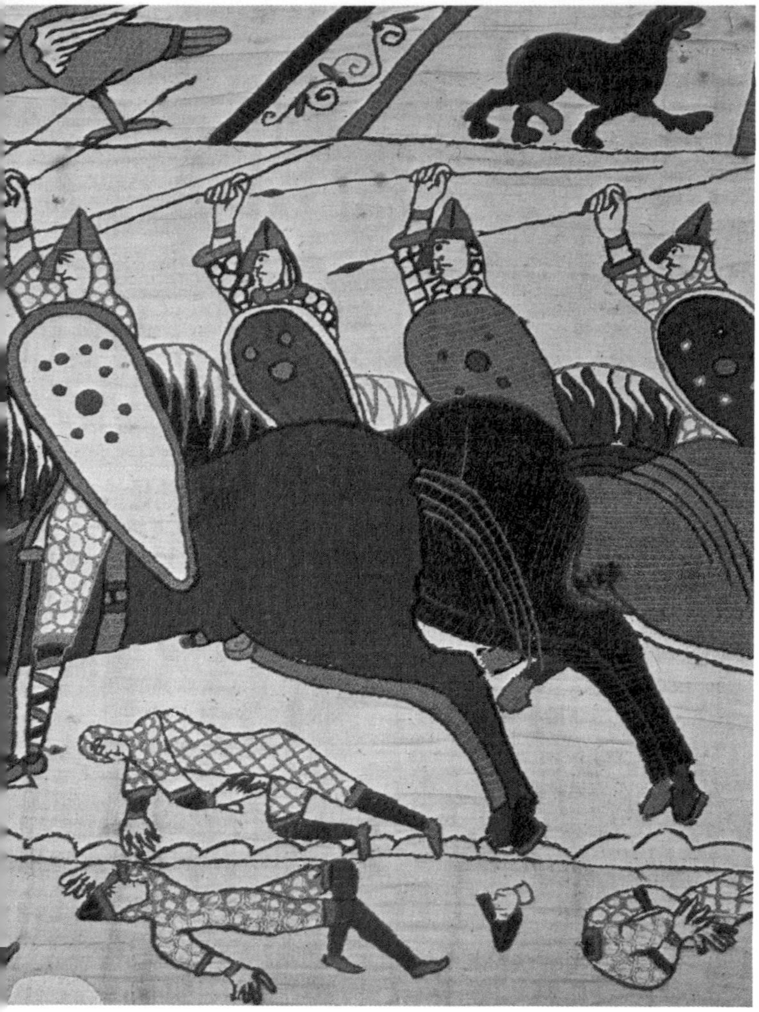

As the Roman Empire of the West crumbled and ultimately collapsed in the fifth century AD, so standards of proficiency in war also fell away. For whereas the Roman Empire had been able to support a fairly large standing army, the small states ruled by feudal kings and dukes that inherited Western Europe could seldom support more than a small corps of professional troops – effectively the ruler's personal bodyguard. In the event of war, the main body of the army had to be made up of ill trained levies drawn from an agricultural population and only available when sowing, harvesting and other bucolic pursuits permitted. Inevitably the military arts degenerated to a level comparable with the state of warfare some 3,000 years before.

The main bodies of these minor armies were incapable of manoeuvre and were poorly armed, and merely formed masses around which the nobles and the few available professionals could manoeuvre. War had returned to the stage of animal strength versus animal strength; skills were minimal. In such conditions the shock weapon was of more use than the missile, and there was a gradual return to longer swords, battle axes, maces and heavier defensive armour. Mobility decreased and battles became hand-to-hand fights between the nobles and professional soldiers or mercenaries, with the levied army of the victors rushing in at the end to finish off its defeated counterpart, the latter being now deprived of any competent or solid form of defence.

### Charlemagne's Frankish Cavalry

The first check to this decline came in about 800 and was instigated by Charlemagne (*c.* 742–814), the Frankish ruler who succeeded in uniting under his rule large portions of Western Europe, from Spain to Bavaria. Charlemagne saw that the Byzantine cataphract was the best soldier in the world, and he proceeded to model a force of Frankish cavalry on the Byzantine system. He was not entirely successful in this, as he found it impossible to enforce the adoption of the bow in the Frankish army, but he laid the foundation for the idea of heavy cavalry used in a shock rôle.

Such forces were to reign supreme in Europe for 500 years, since no feudal levy – the customary opposition – could withstand the charge of a large number of heavy cavalry moving as a concerted body. The Carolingian Empire was divided at the death of Charlemagne but his tactical theory remained in practice, albeit on a smaller scale.

### Vikings and Normans

As we have seen, the answer to heavy cavalry is well-disciplined infantry, and the first such bodies to appear were the Vikings from Scandinavia, who did so about fifty years after Charlemagne's death. Although they were originally and instinctively a marauding people, raiding their enemies from the sea, they were also highly competent at the business of set-piece battles on land. It was

THE CROSSBOW

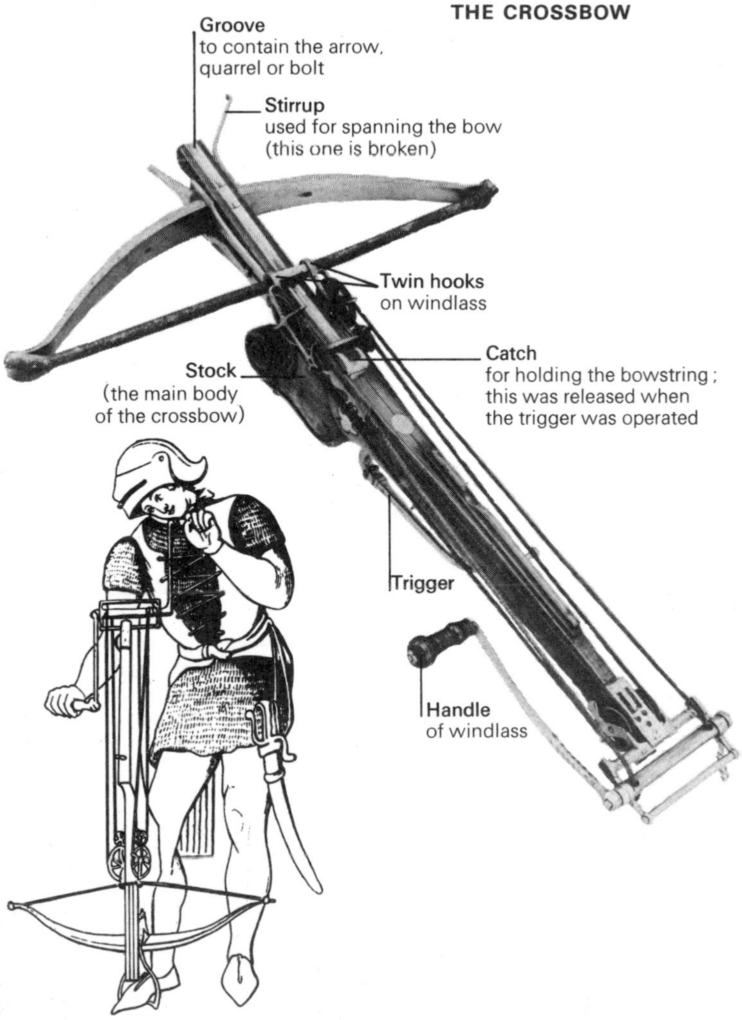
Groove
to contain the arrow, quarrel or bolt
Stirrup
used for spanning the bow (this one is broken)
Twin hooks
on windlass
Catch
for holding the bowstring; this was released when the trigger was operated
Stock
(the main body of the crossbow)
Trigger
Handle
of windlass

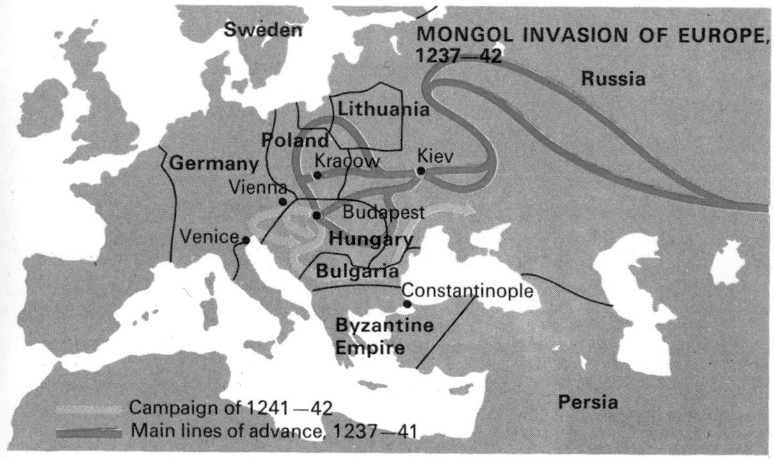
Sweden
MONGOL INVASION OF EUROPE, 1237–42
Russia
Lithuania
Poland
Germany
Krakow
Kiev
Vienna
Budapest
Venice
Hungary
Bulgaria
Constantinople
Byzantine Empire
Persia
Campaign of 1241–42
Main lines of advance, 1237–41

**top** A scene from the life of Houlun, the mother of Genghis Khan, here surrounded by mounted warriors. The Mongolian 'hordes' or field armies consisted almost entirely of light and heavy cavalry. **above** The map shows how far west the Mongolians reached in their campaigns of 1237–42; about to storm Venice, they were recalled by news of the Great Khan's death.

they who found (rather as the Greek hoplites had done before them) that the attacks of mounted opponents could be resisted by forming a shield ring or wall, with one man's shield covering half his body and half that of the man next to him, but allowing both to use their weapons – the Viking spear, sword and axe. By this time the crested Roman type of helmet had been replaced by a conical one, to which many northern Europeans fitted a nose-piece.

Once the Vikings had secured a permanent foothold in northern France at the beginning of the tenth century, they saw that there was much more to be gained by occupation than by plundering, and the resulting combination of late-Frankish and Viking military methods produced one of the best types of fighting man of the age. This was the Norman heavy cavalryman, the knight, equipped with a lance and a long sword and protected by a full-length mail coat, a conical helmet with a nose-piece and a kite-shaped shield. This last had the advantage of being long enough to cover the rider's thigh and knee without sacrificing the width needed to cover his body at the top or being too wide in the lower half for ease of movement. The proof of this type of cavalry's superiority came at the Battle of Hastings in 1066: supported by archers the cavalrymen won a hard-fought but decisive action against the ultimate form of shield-wall, the axe-equipped house-carls or bodyguard of King Harold of England.

### The Crossbow

The origins of the crossbow, or arbalest, which reappeared in Europe at about this date, are obscure, although it is known that the Romans used a version of it called a hand *ballista*. The reappearance of the crossbow in about the middle of the tenth century had far-reaching implications. Here was a cheap but powerful weapon whose arrows, also referred to as bolts or quarrels, could pierce chain-mail and so destroy the absolute superiority of the ruling and wealthier classes of warriors. It was of course in the latter's interests to suppress the widespread use of the weapon lest its possession by considerable numbers of the lower orders should make the continued dominance of the mounted knight impossible. This fear is reflected in a Papal Bull of 1139, enjoining the faithful not to use this terrible weapon against other Christians, but only against the heathen Turk. Although couched in religious terms, it is clear that the purpose of the Bull was to prevent the disordering of society as it then was.

The early form of medieval crossbow consisted of a shoulder stock, at the front end of which was mounted a strong composite bow. The bowstring was drawn by a sharp pull, but as bows became more and more powerful (being made eventually of steel) it was found necessary first to provide a metal stirrup at the front of the weapon, so that the bow could be held down by the foot as the string was drawn, and finally to provide a mechanical

The progress of the helmet, from the tubular helm (**left**), made *c.* 1300, to the more sophisticated egg-shaped bascinet with movable visor and mail aventail (**bottom**) from northern Italy, *c.* 1380–1400. Also shown is a brimmed war helmet known as a kettle hat: such helmets were widely favoured during the late Middle Ages, and this one was made in Italy *c.* 1480. **Bottom right** A domed helmet with movable nosepiece (here in raised position) *c.*1400.

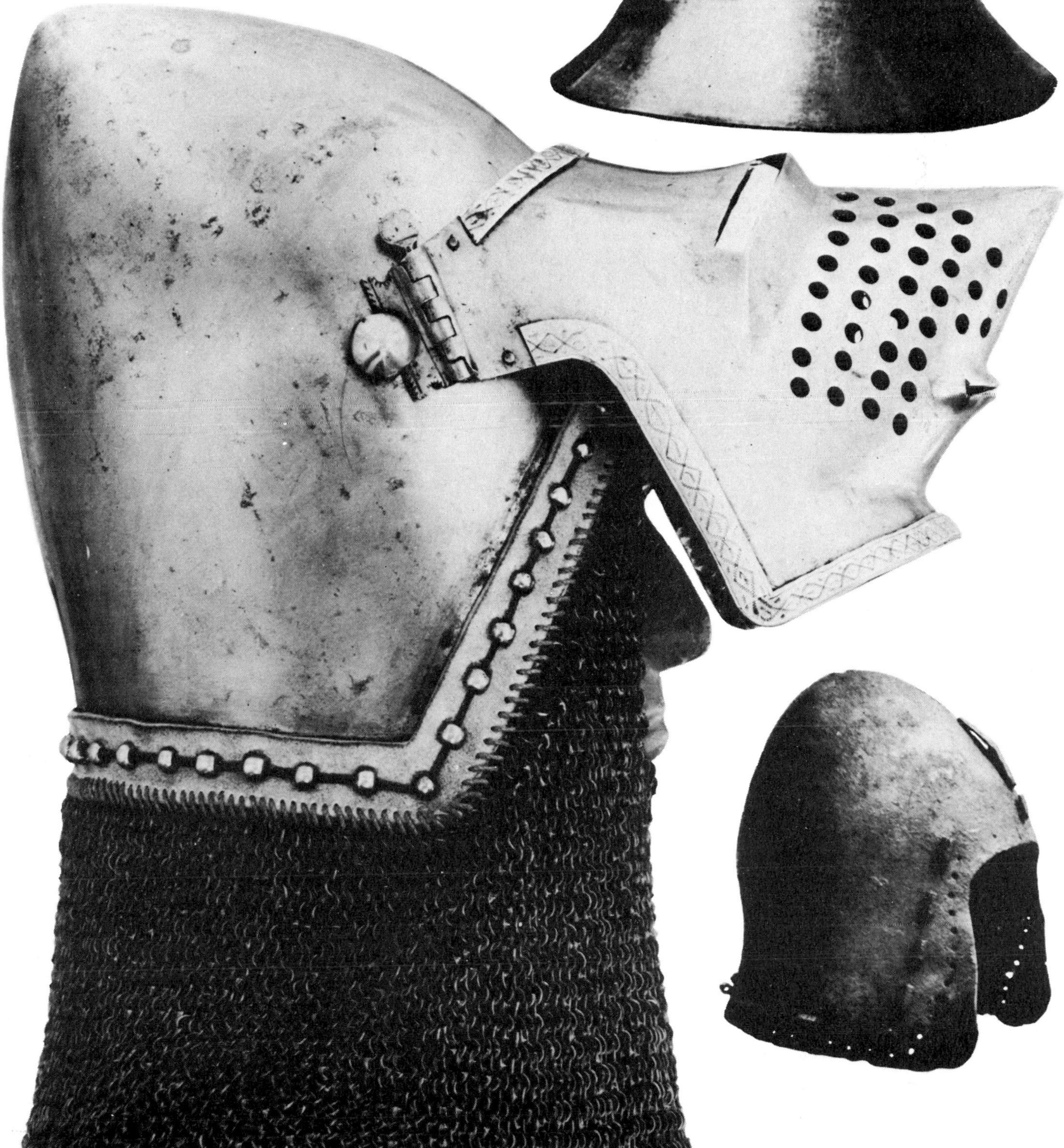

means of winding back the string. In this last form the string was pulled back via a pair of small hooks attached to lines which were wound back by a windlass fitted to the rear part of the stock. In all forms of the bow, the string was held back by a catch while the short, squat quarrel was inserted and the weapon aimed. The crossbow was shot by pulling a trigger on the underside of the weapon, which released the string with a force sufficient to pierce even the best of chain-mail armour.

The principal disadvantages of the crossbow were its slow rate of fire (not more than two arrows a minute), its fairly short range (accurate up to 100 yards) and the complete defencelessness of the arbalester (as he was known) whilst reloading. The last of these was circumvented to a certain extent by providing each arbalester, where possible, with a companion to protect him with a large two-man shield while he reloaded. This was a practical proposition during a siege, when rate of fire was not a prime consideration, but during a field action the arbalester was extremely vulnerable.

### Knights in Full Armour

Even so, the threat to the knight was a very real one, and it was the arrow as much as the increasing dangers to life and limb of hand-to-hand combat that led to the slow evolution of the fully plate-armoured knight. The problem in the early days of the transformation was the armourer's inability to produce the plates that were needed to replace chain-mail armour. The first stage was the comparatively easy one of equipping the warrior's head with a flat-topped, barrel-shaped helm, which although it provided enhanced protection against stabbing and lateral slashing cuts, was very heavy and rested directly on the head; furthermore, unlike the old conical helmet, it did not deflect a downward slash with the result that the full force of the blow was received by the wearer's head and neck, often with fatal results. Since the necessary skills to make shaped plates were still lacking, the next step was the provision of pieces of shaped leather, worn over chain-mail, to protect joints such as the shoulder and knee. These leather pieces were first

The development of armour. As the armourers of Europe grew more skilled at shaping pieces of beaten iron plate to suit the movements of the wearer, so a changeover began from mail to plate armour. At first the use of plate was confined to protecting vulnerable joints, *e.g.* at the knee and elbow, and then in time progressed to the full suit of armour. The figures shown here demonstrate various stages in the evolution of plate armour from **(far left)** the memorial brass of Sir John d'Abernon, *c.* 1277, via those of Sir John de la Pole (portrayed with his lady) and John de Erpingham (*c.* 1380 and *c.* 1415 respectively) to the Gothic-style armour worn **(right)** by the knight and his charger which dates from *c.* 1480.

boiled, then shaped and dried, and the final product made a tough substitute for plate. Meanwhile, the helmet had undergone further modifications, first by being given a rounded top to deflect downward blows, and then by being made to rest on the shoulders, thereby giving the knight better protection. The next stages in the evolution of the helmet brought the creation of a movable visor and a shaped back to protect the neck. The helmet itself was lightened. The gradual introduction of the full suit of plate armour took place as the armourers' skills found the right way to produce shaped plates and articulated joints. Thus by about 1400 fully plate-armoured knights were to be seen in Italy, France and Germany, and soon afterwards in England.

What was good for the knight was also good for his charger, which was fitted successively with plates over the front of the head, the neck, shoulders, chest, flanks, and even the tail. As can be imagined, the weight of so much armour was considerable, and horse breeding over the period 1200–1400 was devoted almost exclusively to

**top** *The Seventh Trumpet.* The seventh angel blows his trumpet above the figure of an armoured Christian engaged in battle with the heathen Saracen, *c.* 1400; from Master Bertram's workshop in Hamburg. **above** A scene from the Battle of Agincourt (1415); like Crécy before it, this battle confirmed the overwhelming superiority of the longbow over the crossbow.

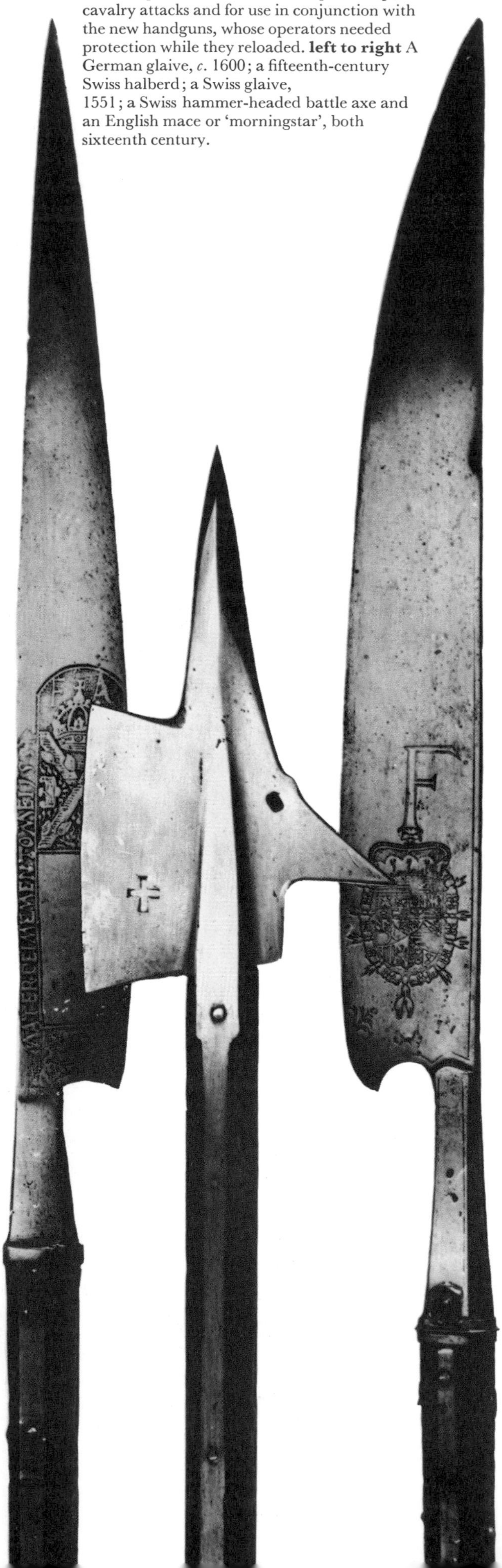

Pole weapons. These were developed to repel cavalry attacks and for use in conjunction with the new handguns, whose operators needed protection while they reloaded. **left to right** A German glaive, *c.* 1600; a fifteenth-century Swiss halberd; a Swiss glaive, 1551; a Swiss hammer-headed battle axe and an English mace or 'morningstar', both sixteenth century.

producing a mount that could carry the weight of its master, its master's armour and its own armour, and still be able to charge. 'Charge' may be a somewhat misleading word as the horses when fully loaded could do little better than a fast trot. But that was no slower than the pace at which the Duke of Marlborough instructed his cavalry to charge, 300 years later, with such devastating effect. Undoubtedly, too, the shock value of a rank of plate-armoured knights was enormous, almost regardless of the speed at which they were travelling.

Any weapons system has its drawbacks for all that, however, and medieval cavalry had two fatal ones. Firstly, when he was unhorsed a knight, who could well be wearing up to 100 pounds weight of armour, was seldom able to struggle to his feet unaided and could not therefore defend himself. Secondly, as a result of the weight carried, cavalry had lost other important characteristics of speed and mobility. But despite these shortcomings the knight remained the arbiter of the battlefield until the advent, once again, of the right weapon in the hands of skilled infantry.

### The English Longbow

The answer to the power of heavy cavalry came in the form of the English longbowman, whose fire-discipline and well practised abilities with his weapon spelt the beginning of the end for heavily armoured mounted forces. The longbow was not, perhaps surprisingly, a

The mechanics of siege warfare. **top** Pavisors (shield men) guard their archer colleagues, while a wheeled siege tower, its drawbridge lowered, is brought up to the defending wall. **centre** Machines for hurling heavy stones. **bottom** A scene from the Siege of Troyes (1429) featuring long- and crossbowmen, heavy armoured cavalry and an early cannon.

composite weapon, but was made from a single stave, generally of yew; it was six feet in length and capable of shooting its three-foot arrow twice the range of the crossbow and at up to six times the latter's rate of fire – and with the same accuracy and penetrative power. (While the rate of fire for the crossbow varied between one and two arrows per minute, a longbowman could loose off six to twelve arrows in the same period.)

The armoured knight was defeated by infantry at several battles before 1346, one such occasion being at Bannockburn in 1314, but at Crécy in that year the defeat was total. The English longbowmen, sited in good defensive positions with a stout palisade in front of them and supported by the English heavy cavalry, inflicted a crushing reverse on the best of the French heavy cavalry, killing over 1,500 of them in addition to at least 10,000 men-at-arms and levied troops. English losses did not exceed 200. The days of the heavy armoured cavalry were indeed numbered. Such, however, is the conservatism of the military mind that it was to be several hundred years before this was universally recognized.

**Pole Weapons for Cutting and Thrusting**

The next major event was the development of pole weapons as a further antidote to the massed cavalry charge. These pole weapons were of two categories, those intended for thrusting and those for cutting, with a more numerous sub-class designed to fulfil both purposes. The thrusting weapon was exemplified by the pike, a long and stout spear which was given a pointed butt so that it could be stuck firmly in the ground to withstand the shock of a cavalry charge. The cutting weapon had several forms, such as the bill and the half-moon, also mounted on stout poles so that the man on the ground could engage a man on horseback. The sub-class of dual-purpose pole weapons included the halberd.

**The Swiss Pike Phalanx**

It was with these weapons that the second great counter to heavy cavalry (the first being the longbowman) emerged in the form of the Swiss pike phalanx of the fourteenth and fifteenth centuries. This represented a reversion to the Macedonian solution to cavalry on the field of battle. Instead of passively awaiting the tremendous shock of a massed cavalry charge, the Swiss trained with great diligence to achieve the same sort of disciplined resistance that had made the Macedonians and Romans so successful. They were trained to charge cavalry with an equal shock value: to achieve this aim they used a solid phalanx of small frontage but considerable depth, the pikes of the front ranks being levelled in front of the formation. The pikes themselves were some twenty-one feet long and usually consisted of an eighteen-foot pole surmounted by three feet of steel at the tip. In action cavalry found it almost impossible to parry or hack off the steel pike-heads before the whole lethal wall of advancing pikemen crashed into them.

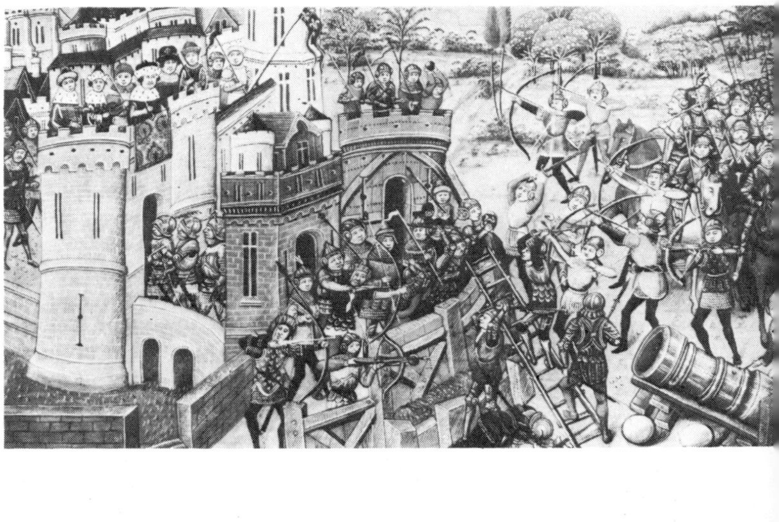

The system was evolved during the Swiss struggle for independence from Austria in the fourteenth century, and proved so successful that the Swiss phalanx was soon imitated by the German *Landsknechte*, as these foot-soldiers were known; both types then found themselves enormously in demand all over Europe as mercenaries.

**Siegecraft is Revived**

One of the effects of the Crusades, which had been going on intermittently since 1096, was a great advance in the science of fortification, for the Crusaders brought the fruits of their experience in the Middle East to the building of their own castles in Europe. Another result of the Crusades was a considerable advance in the science of steel production. This came about because the Crusaders, astounded by the superb quality of their adversaries' weapons, had taken great pains to learn the secrets of making steel comparable to that which issued from Damascus. (It was the gradual attainment of this skill that had enabled European armourers to make full suits of armour, as described earlier.)

The advances in methods of fortification also caused a resurgence of the arts of siegecraft. Old devices that had fallen into decline such as ramps, towers, sows, crows, tunnels, rams, the *ballista* and the catapult, were given new life; some of these were simply built with improved means of manufacture while others were more thoroughly brought up to date. One innovation was the fitting of a drawbridge to siege-towers so that men could rush across it high above the moat and directly invade the enemy's battlements.

The new generations of experts in medieval siegecraft also overcame the most serious limitation of ancient siege artillery, which had been based exclusively on some form of skein in torsion. The problem, more precisely, had been that the skein, whatever material it was made of, soon lost its resilience and urge to untwist rapidly, particularly in wet conditions. The chief medieval solution was a device based on a system of counterweights. In this, a heavy weight at the short end of a pivoting beam provided the counterweight to a lighter missile placed at the long end of the arm. The heavy weight was then suddenly released; the beam swung sharply through a right angle and the missile was launched towards its target. Weapons using this system were known variously as mangonels and trebuchets: these are mentioned often in contemporary accounts, sometimes synonymously, but nowhere is there an exact description of either. However, it is likely that one main type had a cup on the end of the throwing arm, into which missiles were placed, while another commonly used version was armed with stones carried in a sling. But although the mechanics of these weapons are imprecisely documented, it is certain that by such means a variety of missiles, including dead animals (to spread disease), captured spies (to spread a sense of

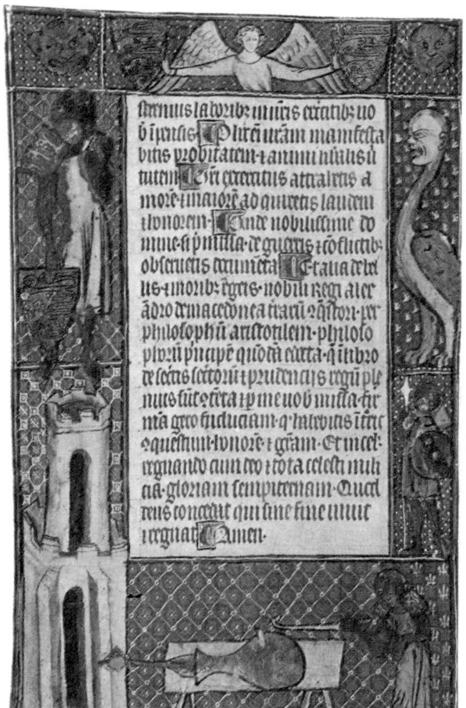

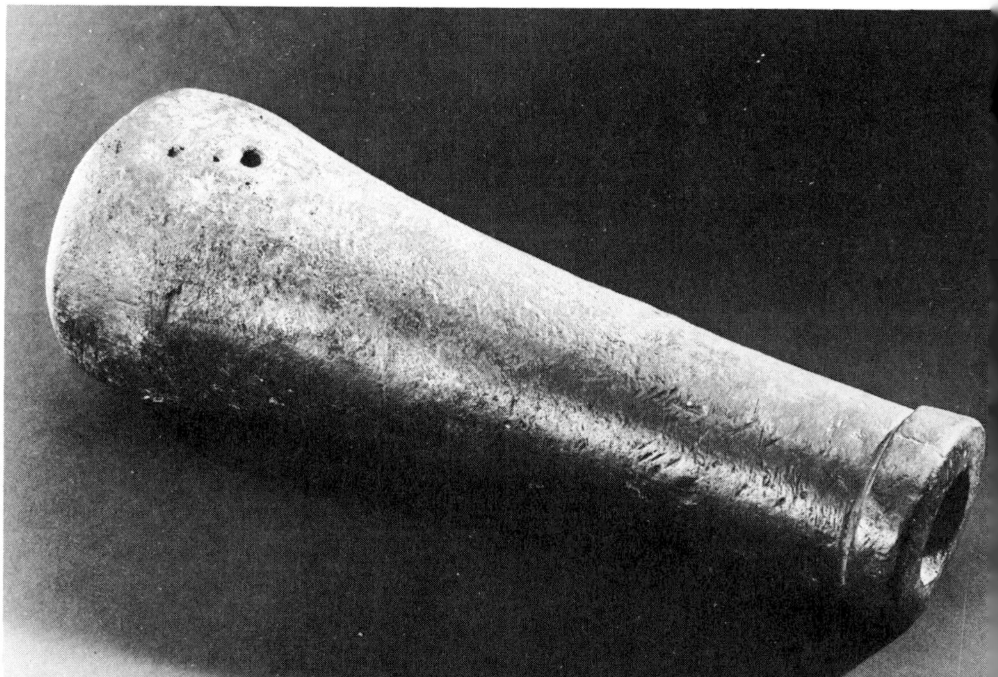

awe) and other more conventional objects such as rocks and boulders could be thrown into a besieged fortress.

**The Advent of Gunpowder**

During this period, the most important innovation since the use of metal appeared. Gunpowder began to make its first appearances in the armies of the West. It seems likely that gunpowder reached Europe from China (where it was primarily used not as an explosive but as a slower-burning rocket propellant) via the Arabs and the Moors. Thus its exact provenance remains obscure, as does the date of its arrival in Europe, although this must have been soon before 1300, as there is mention of it in the Amberg Manuscript of 1301 and in a Florentine manuscript of 1326. The correct mixture of the three ingredients, sulphur, charcoal and saltpetre, is critical in making first-class powder, and the desire of those who knew the right proportions to keep their secret, combined with a shortage of saltpetre in Europe, slowed the spread of the use of gunpowder. But by the middle of the fifteenth century a standard proportion of three parts each of charcoal and sulphur to eight parts of saltpetre was generally approved, and guns were becoming fairly common in the armies of Europe.

The Turks won Constantinople in 1453 thanks to their 100 heavy guns, whilst in the same year Jean Bureau won the last battle of the Hundred Years' War, Castillon, by his use of artillery. It is thought that the English used some cannon as early as Crécy (1346). If so, this was probably the first appearance of gunpowder on a European battlefield, but its use cannot be said to have affected the outcome.

**The First Artillery Weapons**

Early guns were of the muzzle-loading type. They were made of copper or copper alloys and were cast in one piece. The earliest known illustration of a gun shows a small vase-shaped weapon loaded with an arrow which protrudes from the barrel. By the end of the fourteenth century Europeans had discovered how to melt and cast iron, and it became possible to make larger and stronger weapons, which then took on the familiar cylindrical shape. Moreover, not only could larger pieces be made, their powder charges could also be increased and this gave the weapons substantial increases in range.

For the larger pieces – bombards and other cannon – wrought iron was used for the manufacture of the barrel, and a breech-loading mechanism was introduced. Barrels were made by taking strips of wrought iron and placing them tightly round a specially made core of the desired calibre. Rings of hot wrought iron were then slipped over the rods and, shrinking as they cooled, compressed the rods firmly into place. The core was then removed, leaving a barrel which then had to be fitted with a specially forged breech. The problem here was to make the joint between the barrel and breech gas-tight, as any escape of

The dawning of gunpowder wars. **far left** The vase-shaped Milemete gun: this is the earliest known picture of a gun, and comes from Walter de Milemete's manuscript of 1326. **left** A bronze vase gun from Sweden, probably fourteenth century. **below left** A fifteenth-century handgun from Majorca. **below right** A German ribeaudequin or war chariot, *c.* 1505.

**right** A 2-inch petarara-type gun of the late fifteenth century is shown mounted on an early carriage. Breech-loading guns were later almost universally abandoned in favour of muzzle-loaders. This happened because gunmakers were unable before the nineteenth century to produce a gas-tight fit between the barrel and the separately loaded chamber and the barrel.

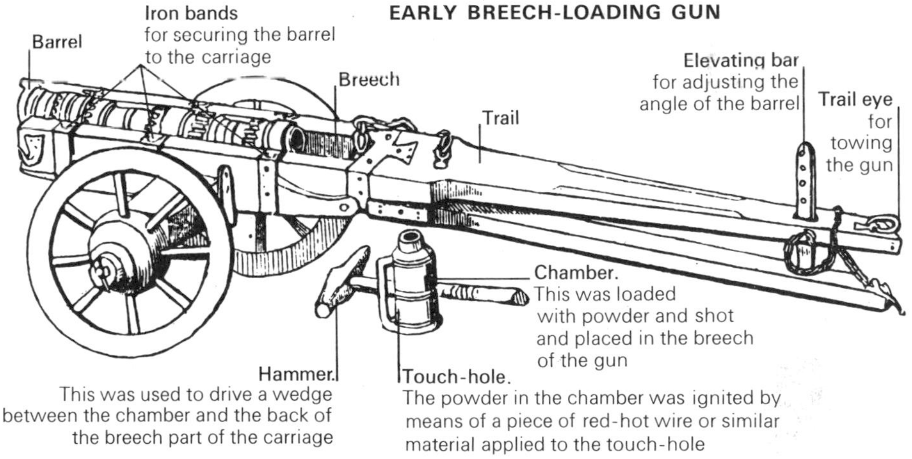

EARLY BREECH-LOADING GUN
Barrel
Iron bands
for securing the barrel to the carriage
Breech
Trail
Elevating bar
for adjusting the angle of the barrel
Trail eye
for towing the gun
Chamber.
This was loaded with powder and shot and placed in the breech of the gun
Hammer.
This was used to drive a wedge between the chamber and the back of the breech part of the carriage
Touch-hole.
The powder in the chamber was ignited by means of a piece of red-hot wire or similar material applied to the touch-hole

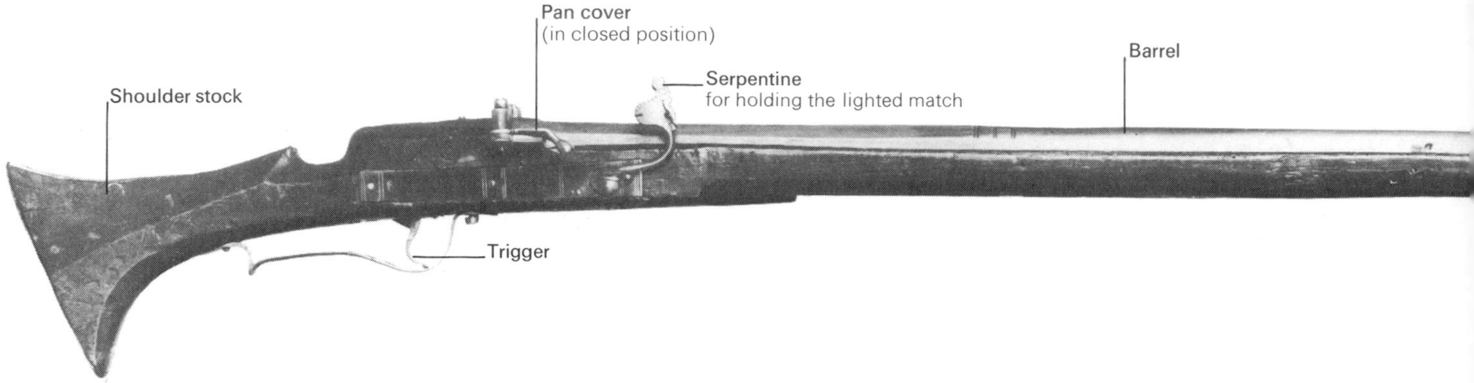
Pan cover
(in closed position)
Barrel
Serpentine
for holding the lighted match
Shoulder stock
Trigger

gas on firing was wasteful of the expensive gunpowder's propellant capabilities – as well as being dangerous.

These early pieces were of little use as field guns because they were not provided with carriages. Their real value was in siege warfare, where platforms of logs or packed earth were erected for them. Since there was also no method of absorbing recoil, the gun had to be relaid or repositioned after each shot. This severely curtailed the rate of fire.

The commonest types of early guns had fairly short barrels – longer barrels being difficult to manufacture – and fired solid spherical projectiles of stone or metal. The one type that fired an explosive projectile was the mortar, a German invention of about 1450. The need for such a piece had been seen fairly early in the gun's career as a siege weapon, for ordinary cannon could only batter at the thick protective walls, whereas a weapon with a higher trajectory could drop projectiles over the walls and onto the defenders. However, although the notion was sound, to practise it was rather different since the nature of the explosive bomb made the process of firing the piece more than slightly hazardous. First the gunner had to light the fuse leading from the bomb and then the powder in the touch-hole at the base of the mortar. The penalties of too tardy a move to the latter can be imagined. That is not to say that the firing of ordinary pieces was not also without its dangers. Guns were prone to blow up, and even after the advent of the linstock – a pole which held the burning match at one end – gunners were by no means immune.

The technique of casting iron guns had spread all over Europe by about the year 1400. This led to a general lightening in their weight because an iron gun, being stronger, could fire a projectile with greater velocity and therefore the same hitting power as a bronze piece of rather larger calibre.

### Gun Carriages

By about 1440 the French had taken the lead in the development of artillery, and had become the first nation to attempt to standardize their guns; this also had the

The musket shown above comes from Sweden and was made in about 1615. The first match-locks were in use almost 200 years before, and were fitted to the musket's heavier predecessor, the arquebus. The system of operation, however, remained much the same. To fire his weapon the musketeer first primed and loaded his piece with powder, shot and wad. Then he drew back the pan cover protecting the priming powder, took aim and pulled the trigger. This activated the serpentine which swung over and a lighted match was pressed against the powder in the pan. (Full instructions, taken from a seventeenth-century drill book, on how to load and fire a musket appear on pages 46–7.)

A fortified camp illustrating the principle of the Hussite wagon laager – a tactical formation that was perfected for use against cavalry by Jan Zizka (*c.* 1360–1424). Zizka's wagons were chained together in a circle and defended by gun and crossbow; then, as the enemy grew dispirited, Zizka let loose his light cavalry and pikemen to finish the affair.

effect of reducing the logistical backing needed for a field army. The French consolidated their superiority in the reign of Charles VIII (1483–98), who was among the first to introduce true field artillery. As was said earlier, the first cannon were not mounted on carriages. When the latter were introduced in about 1400, they were more like wagons in appearance than the later gun-carriages; they were also very large and were pulled by oxen. As such they were inadequate for Charles VIII, who was contemplating a descent on Italy and who realized that if he was to operate successfully so far from his home bases, he needed handy and manoeuvrable field-pieces. To this end he laid down that barrels were not to exceed eight feet in length; the guns were then fitted onto light but sturdy two-wheeled carriages drawn by horses. At the same time the trunnions, twin projections at about the centre of gravity of the gun, were introduced. Apart from providing a means of fixing the gun to the carriage, they allowed the gun to be elevated or depressed on its carriage by means of wedges inserted under the breech. Thus variations in range could be ensured in a far speedier manner than had previously been possible. Charles VIII also made extensive use of a new type of gun, the culverin, a light piece of small calibre and a long barrel, which made for more accurate fire.

### Early Handguns

So far no mention has been made of handguns. These proved difficult to manufacture initially and were developed later than their larger cousins. Further problems of how they should be held, aimed and fired also took a long time to solve. The earliest handguns appeared just after the middle of the fourteenth century and were little more than miniature versions of the cannon then in use. They were mounted on wooden handles which were stuck into the ground or rested on the shoulder while the firer applied his match to the touch-hole. As can be imagined, the accuracy of such weapons left much to be desired.

But in the middle of the first half of the fifteenth century there appeared the match-lock, a device attached to the side of the gun. This held a piece of match at the upper end and a handle at the lower, on either side of a central pivot. By pulling the handle towards himself, the firer swung the match smoothly onto the touch-hole. Soon a mechanical means was found to perform the action – a spring operated by a trigger – and the firer could use both hands to hold and aim his weapon. Aiming was facilitated by fitting a shoulder-stock similar to that fitted on crossbows. The weight of the gun was so great, however, that a forked rest had to be provided on which the soldier could rest the barrel of his arquebus, as the weapon was called. The rate of fire was very slow, and the arquebusier needed pikemen to protect him while he reloaded. For this reason the arquebus did not at first find general favour: in England, for example, the longbow still had its advocates as late as the reign of Elizabeth I (ruled 1558–1603).

### The Wagon Laager

Among the first to use the arquebus were the Swiss, who supplied them to their skirmishers in place of crossbows. But the first man fully to recognize the value of handguns in conjunction with small cannon and pikemen was Jan Zizka (*c.* 1360–1424). Zizka, a Bohemian, invented the third of the great medieval counters to cavalry – the Hussite wagon laager.[1] He had served as a mercenary in Poland and western Russia and had seen the good defensive tactics of the Russians against the Poles, the Tartars and the Teutonic Knights. They drew their wagons up into a circle or laager impervious to the onslaughts of light cavalry. Zizka expanded the idea into an eccentric but remarkably successful system of his own.

His followers, operating from a secure base at Mount Tabor in the mountains south of Prague, roamed about Czechoslovakia in armoured wagons. Their raids naturally provoked reaction: then, at the first sign of danger, the armoured wagons formed a circle and were chained together. Bombards were placed between the wagons. As the attackers charged, they were met by the fire of the bombards and by handguns and crossbows aimed through loopholes in the sides of the wagons, while pikemen defended the gaps between the wagons. Many such circles were also protected by a ditch. Zizka let his enemies charge as often as they liked, but at the first sign of a crack in their order or discipline a body of light cavalry, supported by pikemen, rushed out from the *wagenburg* to inflict a fierce assault on the wilting opposition. This odd defensive-offensive tactic worked admirably under Zizka, even though he was totally blind for the last three years of his life; but after his death in 1424, the system began to fail under the less inspired leadership of his successors.

For a comparatively brief period, beginning at about the time of Crécy (1346), infantrymen had enjoyed superiority in the field. This phase came to an end with the Battle of Marignano in 1515, when the French under Francis I finally broke the power of the Swiss pikemen. Time and time again the Swiss charged, but the French artillery, which the Swiss had disdained for their own use, mowed them down in hundreds. Infantry superiority was over, to be replaced by the dominance of a mixed infantry, cavalry and artillery army, of a type whose first exponents were the French. In the field of siegecraft, too, the gun had completely ousted torsion and counterweight weapons.

[1] Hussite is the generic term for the followers of Jan Hus (*c.* 1369–1415), whose religious ideas were condemned as heretical by the Catholics and whose execution in 1415 led to the Hussite Wars (1419–36).

REVIEWING MILITARY ORGANIZATION
AS HE FOUND IT, GUSTAVUS SAW CLEARLY THAT THE DAY
OF THE NATIONAL ARMY HAD DAWNED,
AND THAT THE MASTER-WEAPON
WAS THE MUSKET

*MAJOR-GENERAL J. F. C. FULLER, 1939*

## CHAPTER 3

# *The 16th and 17th Centuries*

Musketeers of the seventeenth century: each is equipped with a musket, powder, shot and a lighted match – and a sword should his musket fail him.

The wheel-lock was devised in the early years of the sixteenth century. When the trigger was squeezed a piece of iron pyrites held in the jaws of the dog (or cock) was brought into contact with the rough edge of the wheel as the latter span round. Sparks were produced which fell into the pan containing the priming powder.

Progress in the art of artillery and handgun manufacture had been somewhat haphazard during the first 200 years of the gun's life, but the changes heralded by Charles VIII's attempts at standardization bore fruit in the sixteenth century. The main problems holding back the development of the handgun had revolved around the method of firing and the sheer weight of the weapon. For its shot to pierce armour the gun had to be of a fairly large calibre, hence the problems of weight. The trouble with the method of firing was the lack of a substitute for match, which was still inadequate even after the introduction of the match-lock. The first of these two problems was solved at about the time of Marignano (1515), when the wheel-lock was invented in Germany.

### The Wheel-lock

The wheel-lock worked on much the same principle as the spark-producing mechanism of a modern cigarette lighter: when the trigger was pulled, a tightly wound spring revolved a small rough-edged wheel against some form of spark-producing substance such as iron pyrites. By positioning the lock on the side of the gun near the touch-hole and the pan containing the priming powder, gunmakers ensured that the powder would be set off. Thus the main drawback of the match-lock, the fact that it was easily extinguished in wet conditions, was overcome – though at the price of fresh problems. First and foremost, the wheel-lock was costly to produce, and could not therefore be issued to every ordinary infantryman. Secondly, all the spark-producing agents available tended to crumble, and the need to change them in the heat of action could have disastrous consequences. Thirdly, the mechanism had to be wound up before each shot. These difficulties were not normally enough to commend the retention of the match-lock rather than the wheel-lock; even so, the latter was clearly not ideal for the larger, arquebus-type weapon. Where the wheel-lock was of considerable importance was in the manufacture of one-handed guns – pistols – for use by cavalry. Experiments carried out with match-lock pistols had proved unsuccessful. With the wheel-lock, however, the pistol for cavalry use was a practical proposition, and soon most cavalrymen were equipped with two pistols each, which they carried when not in use in holsters on either side of the saddle.

Because the wheel-lock was considered too expensive and delicate for ordinary infantry use, the match-lock continued for a time in general service. Then a wheel-lock mechanism was fitted to the weapon that superseded the arquebus, the musket. This was at first heavier than its predecessor, but had a somewhat longer range. It could kill at 300 yards though it was not accurate at much more than sixty. Meanwhile the inadequacies of the wheel-lock mechanism were not ignored, and a search continued for a better way of igniting the musket's powder propellant.

### Flint-lock Weapons

The first successful solution was the Dutch snaphance, introduced in about 1580, but this again had a number of disadvantages that were not rectified until the advent of the flint-lock, a French innovation, in about 1615. Both locks worked on the principle of a spring, which was automatically wound by the action of cocking the piece. When the trigger was pulled the spring drove a flint, held in a pair of adjustable jaws, against a roughened steel hammer positioned above the priming powder. The hammer lifted on contact and sparks fell into the powder. This, given the technology of the day, was a good solution. The flint was not prone to crumbling, the lock did not need winding by hand and it was simple and therefore inexpensive to make.

The match-lock nevertheless remained an adequate weapon in the opinion of most military leaders, and so the flint-lock was slow to enter service in any other than the sporting field. The first French unit was equipped with it in 1670, and its military advantages were then so obvious that all European armies had introduced the weapon by the turn of the century. The new lock was also introduced on pistols. During the English Civil Wars the majority of the musketeers carried match-locks, but companies equipped with safer 'fire-locks' were assigned to guard the train of artillery, since it was not wise to have men with lighted matches in the vicinity of the budge-barrels from which the gunners ladled their black powder. These companies were the forerunners of the Royal Fusiliers Regiment, which was formed in 1685.

### Cartridges and Bayonets

The principal disadvantages of the arquebus and the early musket had been their size and weight, which had made it necessary to fire the pieces from a rest. The man responsible for altering this state of affairs was one of the great military geniuses of all time, Gustavus Adolphus II (1594–1632) of Sweden. He reduced the weight of the musket by half, bringing it down to little over ten pounds, but still retained the rest as a means of obtaining accuracy of fire. He also increased the rate of fire by introducing into widespread service the cartridge and cartridge pouch. The pouch enabled the musketeer quickly to extract a cartridge (a paper container with powder and shot in it) and load it with much greater convenience, since all that had to be done was to tear open the cartridge, pour the measured amount of powder into the barrel, follow it with the ball and finally ram the paper cartridge down on top to act as a wad.

But even after the introduction of the cartridge the rate of fire attainable by the musket remained low, leaving the musketeer defenceless while he reloaded – unless he was protected by a pikeman. But an invention that was at last to render the pikeman obsolete was very slowly gaining acceptance. This was the bayonet, which seems to have been invented in France shortly before 1640. The

The finely ornamented pistol shown here is one of a pair made in Germany in 1600.

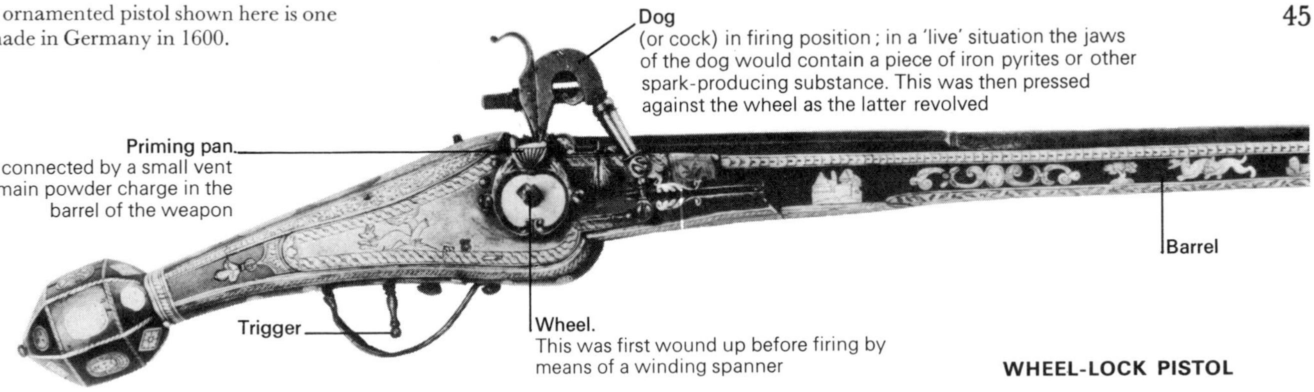
Dog
(or cock) in firing position; in a 'live' situation the jaws of the dog would contain a piece of iron pyrites or other spark-producing substance. This was then pressed against the wheel as the latter revolved
Priming pan
This was connected by a small vent to the main powder charge in the barrel of the weapon
Barrel
Trigger
Wheel.
This was first wound up before firing by means of a winding spanner
WHEEL-LOCK PISTOL

first bayonets offered only a temporary solution, because they had to be 'plugged' into the muzzle of the musket, leaving the soldier unable to fire – an arrangement that contributed to General Hugh MacKay's defeat at the Battle of Killiecrankie (1689). An interim answer to this problem was the introduction, in the 1690s, of the ring bayonet. This was a bayonet with a length of tubing fixed to its handle: the tubing slid over the muzzle of the musket and so left the weapon free to fire. This too had its disadvantages – among them a tendency to slip off the gun – which were solved by the invention of the type of bayonet still in service today, in which the blade is attached to the side of the barrel by the locking of a socket in its handle onto a stud on the barrel. The latter version was in widespread service by the end of the seventeenth century. The musketeer had become his own pikeman, and the pike disappeared from use.

### Artillery Improvements

Despite the attempts mentioned earlier of Charles VIII of France to achieve some measure of standardization in artillery types, the problem of combining the most destructive type of gun with mobility continued to evade solution. Gunmakers experimented continually with different combinations of length and thickness of wall in the barrel, weight of shot, calibre, powder charge and all the features that go to make an artillery piece, without overcoming their chief difficulties.

By this time the best gunmakers in Europe were no longer the French but the Germans and Dutch. In particular the Germans achieved an improvement in the accuracy of gun founding (the process of casting the metal). This allowed the powder charge to be reduced as a result of increased efficiency bestowed by rounder shot and smoother surfaces inside the barrel. The discovery of an improved type of powder also enabled barrel lengths to be reduced, with a consequent saving in weight. The main Dutch contribution was to invent a means of igniting the charge of an explosive projectile in the course of firing the master-gun. This of course disposed of the old dangers attached to lighting the fuse of a shell at the muzzle of the gun and then moving back to fire the piece itself. In the Dutch device the fuse was ignited when the gun's propellant charge was detonated.

The lead in the manufacture and use of artillery was next taken over by the Spaniards. Charles I of Spain, perhaps better known as the Holy Roman Emperor Charles V (1500–58), decreed in 1544 that the logistical demands imposed by the multitude of different types of gun in service were impossible to cope with; he therefore ordered that gun types were to be restricted to seven. The French were not slow to see the possibilities opened up by Charles I's decree and they followed suit in 1550, restricting the number of types then employed in their own army to six.

The larger illustration is of a Scottish flint-lock gun of 1690. Inset is a separate lock, showing the hammer pushed forward. The flint-lock mechanism improved on the wheel- and match-locks in several ways: the flint was hard and not given to crumbling (as iron pyrites did), the lock did not need winding and it was comparatively inexpensive to make.

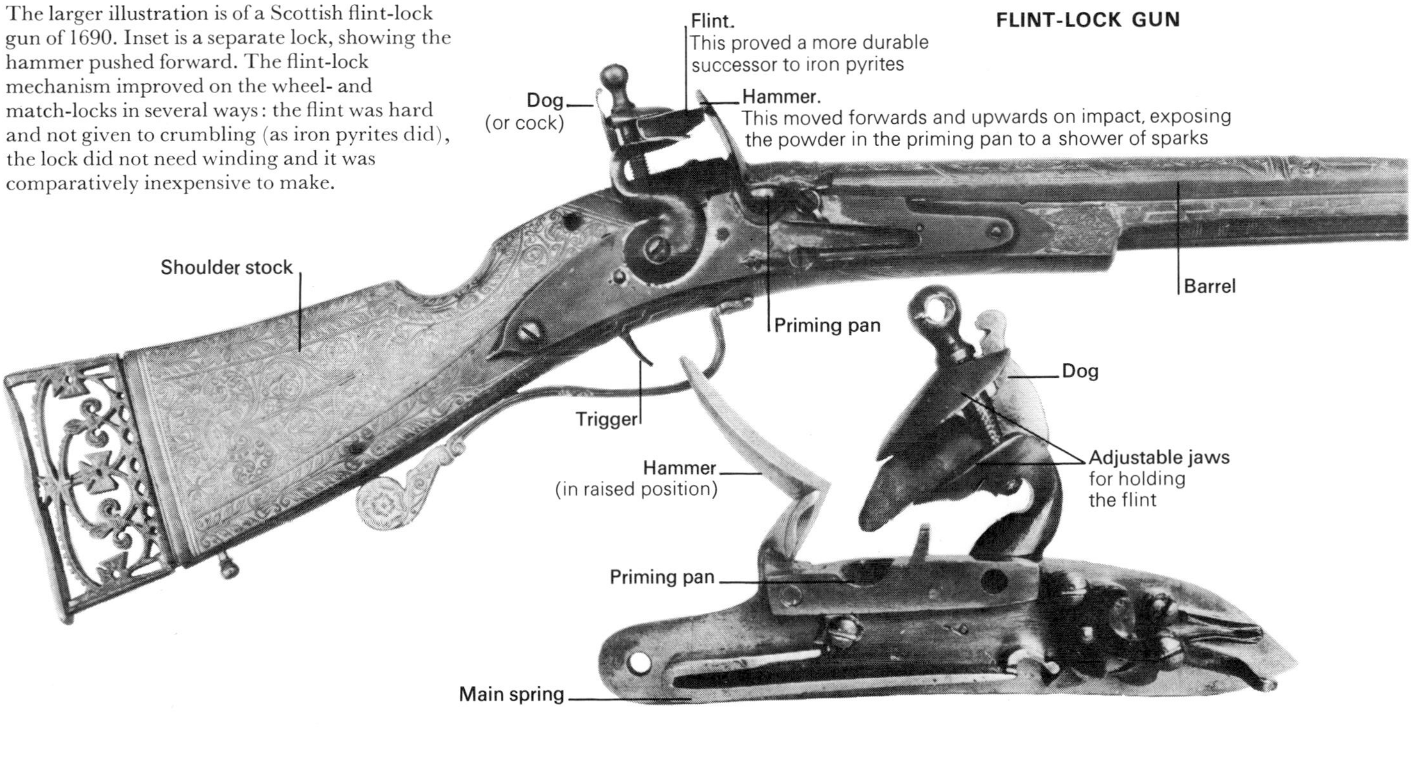
Flint.
This proved a more durable successor to iron pyrites
FLINT-LOCK GUN
Dog
(or cock)
Hammer.
This moved forwards and upwards on impact, exposing the powder in the priming pan to a shower of sparks
Shoulder stock
Barrel
Priming pan
Dog
Trigger
Adjustable jaws for holding the flint
Hammer
(in raised position)
Priming pan
Main spring

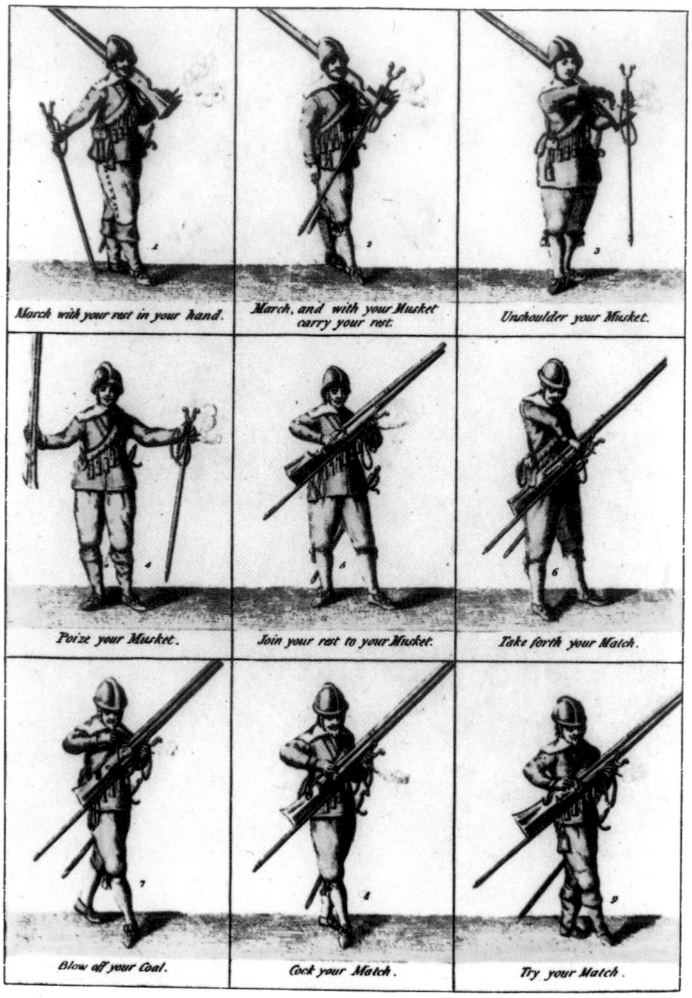

March with your rest in your hand.

March, and with your Musket carry your rest.

Unshoulder your Musket.

Poize your Musket.

Join your rest to your Musket.

Take forth your Match.

Blow off your Coal.

Cock your Match.

Try your Match.

Guard, blow and open your pan.

Present.

Give Fire.

Dismount your musket.

Uncock your match.

Return your match

Clear your pan.

Prime your pan.

Shut your pan.

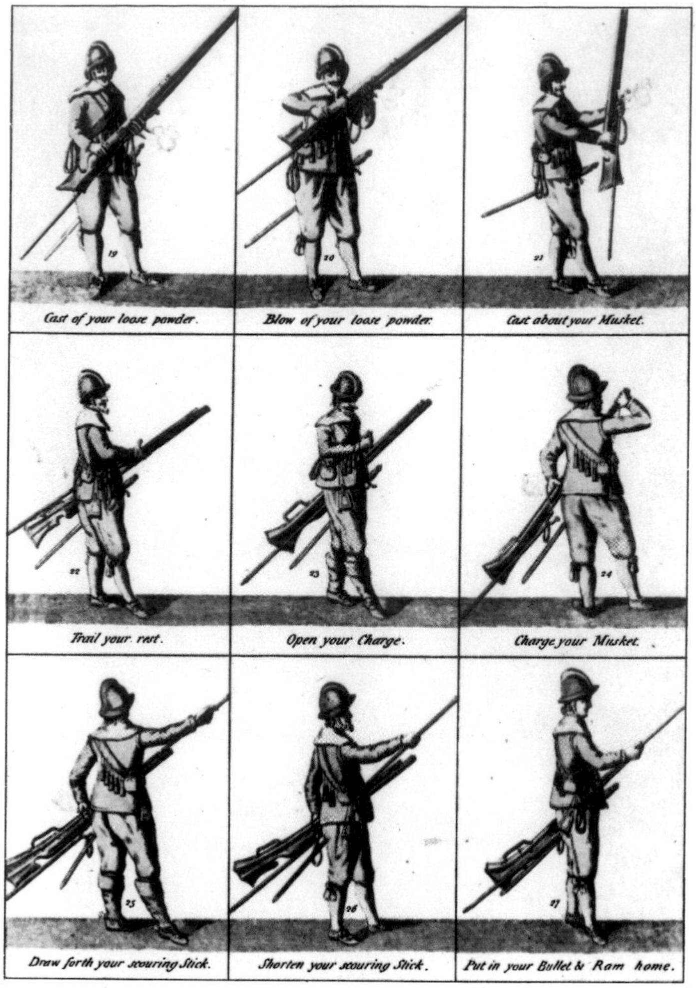

Cast of your loose powder.

Blow of your loose powder.

Cast about your Musket.

Trail your rest.

Open your Charge.

Charge your Musket.

Draw forth your scouring Stick.

Shorten your scouring Stick.

Put in your Bullet & Ram home.

Withdraw your scouring stick.

Shorten your scouring stick.

Return your scouring stick.

Recover your Musket.

Poize your Musket and recover your Rest

Rest your Musket.

Draw out your match.

Blow your match.

Cock your match.

Try your match.
Guard your pan.
Present.
Give Fire.
Come up to your Musket.
Return your match.
Take up your rest.
Blow of your loose Powder and cast about your Musket.
Trail your rest & open your charge.

Bring up your Musket.
Poize your Musket & recover your Rest.
Shoulder your Musket.
Serjeant.
Drummer.
Fifer.
Recover your Halbert.
Advance your Halbert.
Shoulder your Halbert.

**left** Musket drill as it was taught in the seventeenth century. The sequence illustrated covers a cycle beginning with (1) marching to the firing point, then halting, firing, reloading, firing and shouldering the musket again (48). Also shown, from the same drill book, are a 'serjeant', a drummer, a fife-player, and three frames of halberd drill. **below** A musketeer bites the cap off a charge-holder before pouring the contents into the barrel of his musket.

**The Fruits of Standardization**

By the end of the sixteenth century, standardization had spread to much of Europe, and artillery pieces were by then divided into four categories based on the Spanish reorganizations of 1544. First and largest, approximating to the modern gun and having a barrel length of between 24 and 45 calibres, were the culverins; these had thick walls and a considerable range (up to 7,000 yards with 6½-inch pieces). Then came the cannons, having a barrel length of between 15 and 25 calibres and thick walls; approximating to modern howitzers, their largest types were capable of firing a projectile of up to 90 pounds in weight about 4,000 yards. Third were the pedreros, also having some of the characteristics of the modern howitzer, but shorter (10 to 15 calibres) and thinner-walled than the cannons; they could fire a 60-pound projectile up to 2,000 yards. Last were the mortars, 3 to 5 calibres in length and capable of sending a 200-pound shell up to 2,500 yards. The howitzer as we know it today was a Dutch invention of 1693; it combined the best characteristics of the cannon and the pedrero in one weapon. The functions of the types were as follows: culverin – long-range, accurate, flat-trajectory fire; cannon – shorter-range, accurate, heavier fire; pedrero – short-range, less accurate but heavier fire; mortar – very short-range, heavy, plunging fire.

These types remained standard, in their muzzle-loading form, until the advent of rifled, breech-loading pieces. Advances were made not so much in the basic design of the weapons, but in lightening them, fitting them onto better carriages and utilizing better manufacturing techniques to produce more economical and accurate pieces. Various experiments aimed at increasing mobility were also carried out to try and make artillery from materials other than metal. The British tried wooden guns and Gustavus Adolphus developed a tube of thin copper strengthened by a casing of thick leather. The latter's guns weighed under 100 pounds and were extraordinarily manoeuvrable, but cooling proved an insuperable problem and the experiment was soon dropped. Another innovation brought about by Gustavus Adolphus was the formation of artillery units in his army. Up till then the art of gunlaying and operation had been so skilled that contract civilians had been employed for the task, but their conservatism had exerted a dampening influence on the introduction of improved techniques. Gustavus sacked his civilians and introduced artillery regiments operating a standard gun, of which there were only three types: the 24-pounder, the 12-pounder and the 3-pounder; the last was the true forerunner of modern light field artillery. In leaving the field of artillery technology in the sixteenth and seventeenth centuries, it would be well also to note an important advance in the science of ballistics. This is attributable to Niccolo Tartaglia (1500–57). Thanks to him, later gunners were able to lay their guns with a

E
E
E
E
E
C
A
O
F
G
N
N
N
N

**above** One of the leather-clad guns introduced by Gustavus Adolphus II of Sweden in an effort to lighten his artillery pieces. The leather covering was shrunk onto a central tube of copper. **below** Inside the gun foundry. On the left the master founder supervises his men feeding the furnace with metal (centre) and replenishing its fires with wood (right).

M
C
I
N
N
D
L
H
H

previously unheard-of accuracy by using the gunner's quadrant that he introduced.

### Guns Determine Infantry Tactics

The problem of infantry tactics in the sixteenth century was how to adapt prevailing infantry tactics to get the best out of the new gunpowder weapons that were being developed. As we have seen, the demise of unsupported infantry was ensured at Marignano in 1515, when the French combinations of artillery salvoes combined with cavalry charges, supported by pike- and arquebus-armed infantry, showed its superiority. However, a few years earlier the French had not been so successful against a Spanish army led by Gonzalo de Córdoba '*El Gran Capitán*' (1453–1515). He had been able to defeat the more numerous French by protecting his arquebusiers behind field fortifications, so that they might reload without fear of attack. In this way he was able to stretch his men over a greater frontage than the French and outmanoeuvre them, using the firepower of the arquebusiers to disrupt the French and allow his pikemen, who still formed the majority of his infantry, to move out and inflict the final defeat, as in the Battle of Cerignola in 1503. Córdoba's tactics were thus based on the steadiness of his pikemen and the protection of field fortifications supported by the firepower of his arquebusiers and the final shock action of the pikemen.

Córdoba's army opened a new era of Spanish dominance in Europe. This began on a wave of success as the Spaniards finally ousted the Moors from Spain with the recapture of Granada (1492) after three centuries of Arab encroachment. Then, as the sixteenth century progressed, the Spanish grew in confidence and their campaigns brought them ever greater rewards.

By then firearms had become more plentiful, and the Spaniards were able to replace many of their pikemen with arquebusiers, who were formed into separate units which served alongside the remaining pikemen. The Spanish Square, as it came to be called, was a mixed unit of pikemen and arquebusiers (and later of musketeers, as we shall see), which presented the enemy with steady pikes and the firepower of its small arms.

The core of the Square was made up of pikemen, surrounded by a protective screen of arquebusiers; further bastions of arquebusiers fortified each corner of the Square, whose total strength varied between 1,500 and 2,000 men. Its effectiveness was further increased by the novel tactic of having the arquebusiers in the front rank retire to the rear of their unit after discharging their weapons; the second rank moved up to the front to discharge their guns almost immediately after the first, while the latter had time to reload at the rear. By these means the Spaniards were able to deliver an almost uninterrupted volume of fire, causing disruption in the enemy lines; the Spanish pikemen then advanced to mop up the remnants. Later in the century the Spaniards were able to double their firepower by having the men of the front rank kneel and fire, while the second rank fired over their heads. Both ranks then retired to reload while the third and fourth ranks repeated the performance.

Further changes in infantry tactics came about towards the end of the sixteenth century as the musket replaced the arquebus. Although Gustavus Adolphus was soon to revolutionize infantry warfare in a far more substantial and enduring way, an important interim development occurred before he came to power. This was independently introduced, or so it now seems, at more or less the same time by Alexander, Duke of Parma (1545–92) and Maurice of Nassau (1567–1625). Under their separate commands the sizes of individual units were reduced and the arquebusier was shifted from the heart of the infantry and took on new duties as a skirmisher.

These moves are significant, for both these great generals were advocates of mobile warfare, moving their troops about at great speed by all available methods – Maurice doing especially well with his use of barges in the Dutch flatlands. He it also was who accelerated the hitherto long and arduous siege process by a skilful combination of concentrated fire and diplomacy. By these means he brilliantly captured a chain of Spanish-held fortresses in 1590–1. Once a breech had been made, the defenders were induced to surrender with promises that they would receive the full honours of war. Pillage was forbidden, and the time taken to secure an enemy stronghold was thereby reduced to about six days – a wondrously short period for those times.

### The Cavalry Makes a Come-back

Cavalry, particularly the heavy cavalry, had been in decline for some time. But, as armour became lighter and riders more mobile, cavalry's usefulness increased and it enjoyed a gradual resurgence during the sixteenth century. After a disastrous defeat at Pavia in 1525, when the concentrated fire of the Spanish arquebusiers shattered their cavalry, even the French had conceded that the old medieval type of knight was outmoded, and experiments were carried out with a view to finding the right combination of light and heavy cavalry that could successfully resist and outmanoeuvre infantry using the new firearms.

The first people to find a type of cavalry useful to the new age were the Germans; they came up with the *Schwarzreiter*. These were heavy cavalry armed with the newly developed wheel-lock pistol. Their defensive armour at first consisted of mail, but this was soon replaced by helmet, breast-plate and heavy thigh boots. Their tactics were a combination of firepower and shock. As the body of cavalry moved against the enemy at a trot, the front rank fired its pistols and then swung away

Detail of an English flint-lock musket of 0.796-inch calibre, made at the time of William III (reigned 1689–1702).

to the rear to reload, while the second rank moved up to fire. They were something of a cavalry counterpart to the Spanish Square (although the *Schwarzreiter* had the advantage of being equipped with three pistols each). By these tactics the cavalry could keep up a constant fire on the enemy, attempting to create breeches in their line that could be exploited by infantry supporting the *Reiter*. The whole process of advancing, firing, peeling off and then reforming at the rear was difficult to execute and required much skill, and the system was not copied outside Germany. The *Reiter* themselves, however, were in great demand as mercenaries throughout Europe.

The pre-eminence of the German cavalry was overtaken at the end of the sixteenth century by the French. They did so with tactics in which firepower and shock were exercised by the same body, rather than by separate bodies of cavalry and infantry, as in the German system. The French charged in lines three deep and fired their pistols at the last moment before engaging the enemy with the sword; their massed pistol fire was usually enough to throw the infantry into sufficient confusion to allow the cavalry to close with minimum casualties and maximum shock. The tactic was copied all over western Europe, and the lance was discarded as the prime cavalry weapon by all but the Poles and the Spaniards and, to some extent, the Scots.

At the same time, continued conflict with the Turks to the east had made it apparent to Europeans that there was a need for light cavalry for reconnaissance purposes. The first to adopt the idea were the Venetians and the Spaniards, but they were soon copied and overtaken by the Germans and Hungarians. The latter developed an effective type of light cavalry in which each man was armed with a pair of pistols and a light sword, but was completely unarmoured. These men were the first hussars.

### The Reforms of Gustavus Adolphus

Infantry manoeuvres, based on massive columns in the sixteenth century (the Spanish Square), were completely revolutionized by Gustavus Adolphus at the beginning of the seventeenth, when he introduced his linear tactics. These had been made possible by the increased firepower he was able to call upon after his adoption of the cartridge pouch and the lightened musket. Pikemen, who needed to form up in depth if they were operating alone, became a secondary factor and were replaced by battalions containing many more musketeers. In battle these were arrayed across the field in a series of mobile wedge-shaped regimental formations, each containing the men of three battalions (about 1,500 in all). In the intervals between the regiments were positioned cavalry and artillery, with further cavalry on the flanks to prevent this fairly shallow formation from being turned.

The cavalry was also revitalized by Gustavus to combine the best features of the earlier German and French cavalry. Most important of all, perhaps, was the way in which the three arms were trained to co-operate. This was made possible by the fact that Gustavus was the commander of the first large standing army in latter-day European history. The contract gunners had been dismissed, and the professional nature of the three arms enabled Gustavus to train them to use their weapons efficiently and to co-operate with each other. In battle, for example, the musketeers were formed up in six ranks. When the battle began the front rank of musketeers knelt and fired, and the second rank fired over them. The rearmost four ranks then moved up and a second volley was fired by the next pair of ranks; meanwhile the ranks that had just fired reloaded and joined the rear of their formation. Thus the line advanced under cover of steady volleys of fire until the enemy's lines were sufficiently disorganized to permit the pikemen – still the arm that gave the decisive *coup* – to charge and destroy them. If needed, moreover, Gustavus's Swedes could fire salvoes in the form of a simultaneous three-rank volley. It should be noted that the pikemen in Gustavus's army, unlike those in others, wore light armour, while their pikes were only eleven feet long instead of the then normal length of sixteen feet. The combination of lightly armoured pikemen and heavy firepower made the Swedish infantry the best of the Thirty Years' War (1618–48).

Gustavus's cavalry was not an independent arm but was integrated into the general line of battle. In its fully developed form it charged in three ranks, the front rank firing its pistols as it neared the enemy, the other two ranks holding their fire for emergencies. There was a further refinement: just before the cavalry charged the enemy with the sword, special units of musketeers fired on the enemy line to disrupt it; they then reloaded while the cavalry was engaged, and fired again to cover the cavalry's retreat. The artillery was also expected to support the charges of its cavalry. The latter's role in action was generally to add to and possibly complete the disruption of the enemy's line which had been initiated by earlier infantry and artillery fire. The arrival of the cavalry usually heralded the final infantry onslaught by the pikemen.

As was mentioned above, Gustavus introduced the very light regimental artillery pieces – the 3-pounders – which were the true forerunners of modern light field artillery. These weapons were extremely mobile, accurate over the short distances they were expected to fire and served by able and enthusiastic crews, fully integrated into the three-arm system adopted by their King.

It would be hard to over-emphasize the importance of Gustavus in the evolution of modern tactics and weapons development. Although he was not strictly the inventor of the weapons and tactics he employed so successfully, his genius lay in recognizing that the future lay with the firearm and with combined-arms forces, and in moulding

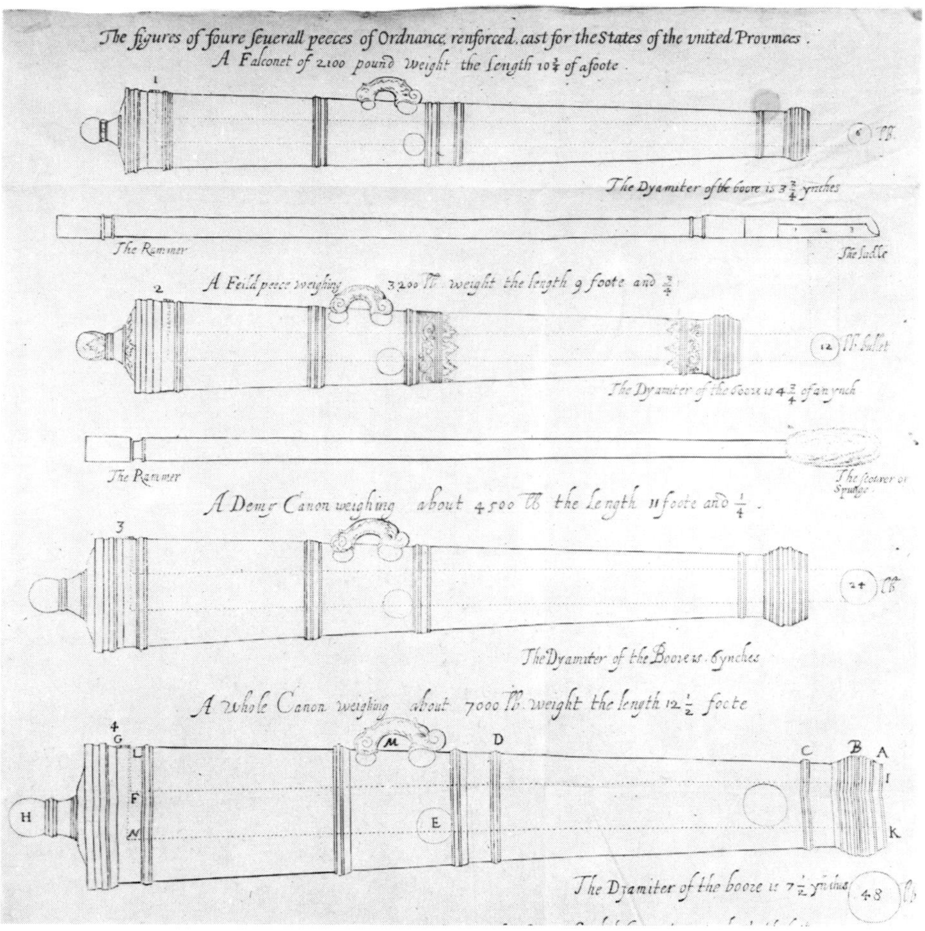
The figures of foure feuerall peeces of Ordnance reinforced, cast for the States of the united Provinces.
A Falconet of 2100 pound weight the length 10¾ of a foote
The Rammer
A Demy Canon weighing about 4500 lb the length 11 foote and ¼
The Dyamiter of the Boore is 6 ynches
A whole Canon weighing about 7000 lb weight the length 12½ foote

**left** A page from Hexham's *Art Militarie* (1639) showing cannon of the day together with a powder ladle and a scourer or 'spunge'. **below** A gathering of Royalist soldiers from the time of the English Civil Wars (1642–51). Personal armour ranged from that of the mounted cuirassier (foreground), who was fully encased from head to knee, to the musketeer (right) who wore none. In between were the dragoons and pikemen; the latter wore a type of half armour consisting of helmet, back- and breast-plates, and in many cases – though not shown here – tassets which covered the hips and thighs. **right** Also from Hexham's book is this mortar fitted with a gunner's quadrant to demonstrate the range of trajectories obtainable with such a weapon. The gunner's quadrant was introduced by Niccolo Tartaglia (1500–57).

his army to those ideas. He realized also that the best army was a professional one, and organized the Swedish Army on that principle. He understood that shock was still the most decisive battle-winning force of his day, and he used pikeman and cavalry for that purpose. But he also saw that the softening-up ability of firepower could make a substantial difference to the course of a battle, and he therefore increased the number of musketeers in his army; to increase their effectiveness he simplified the problems of loading at speed, lightened the weapon itself and devised a tactical disposition that would enable the maximum fire to be brought down on the enemy in the minimum time. And in the field of artillery he worked hard to solve logistical problems, added to the efficiency of his field artillery and worked out a system whereby it was best able to support the decisive arms – the infantry and the cavalry.

### The Army of Louis XIV

The proof of the superlative quality of Gustavus's military thinking is not difficult to find: imitation, then as now, is the sincerest form of flattery, and by the end of the century all the armies of Europe had adopted Gustavus's system, albeit with modifications that were necessitated by the continuing sophistication of weapons and tactical ideas as well as by purely national prejudices. The best of the imitators, and the leading military power of the period after Gustavus, was the

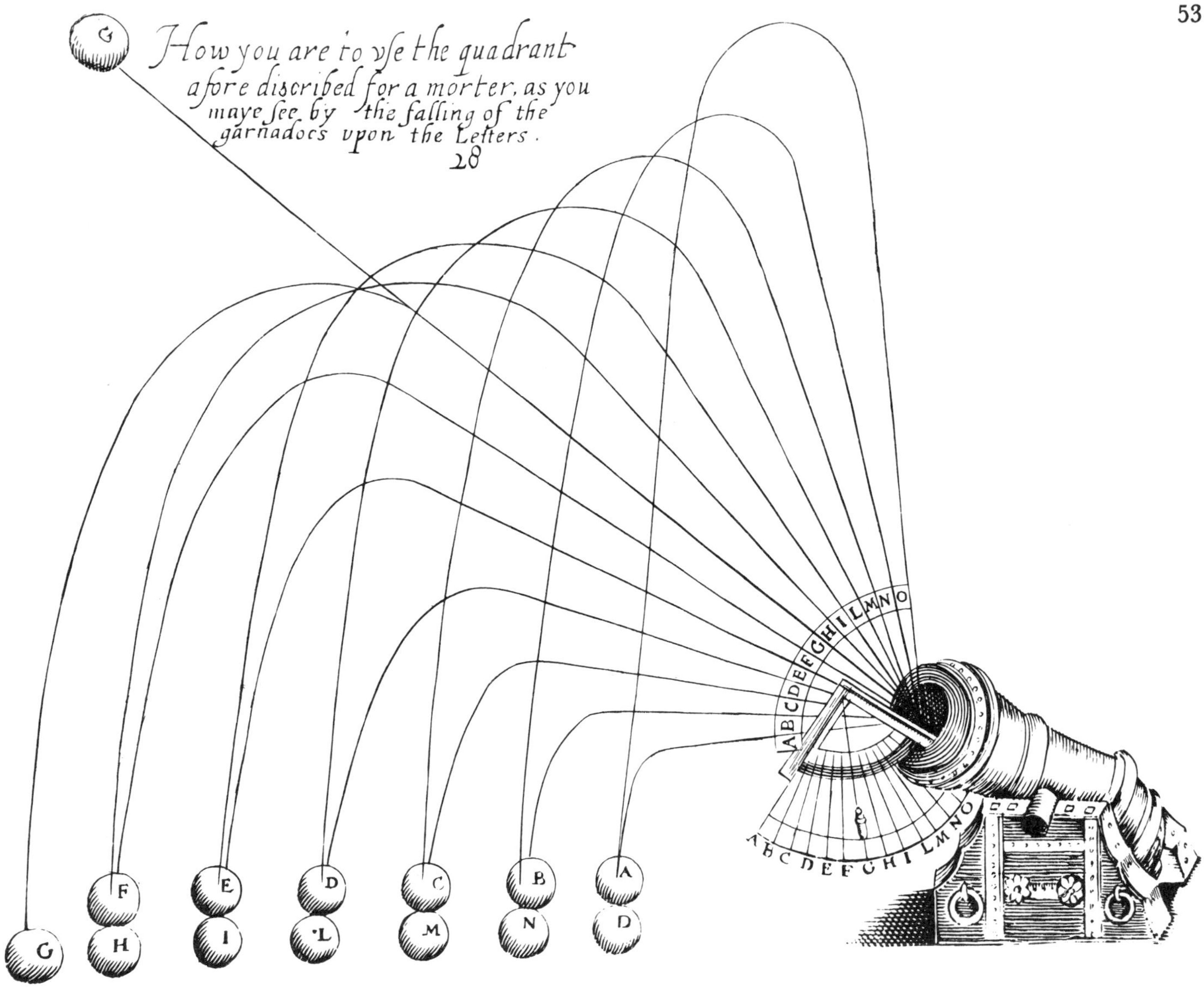
How you are to vse the quadrant afore discribed for a morter, as you maye see by the falling of the garnadoes upon the Letters.
28
G
A
B
C
D
E
F
G
H
I
L
M
N
D
ABCDEFGHILMNO
ABCDEFGHILMNO

French Army of Louis XIV (1638–1714). This army was divided into battalions of about 800 men, two-thirds of whom were musketeers, disposed on the flanks of their battalions as in Gustavus's army. Each battalion, drawn up in six ranks, was part of an expanded chequerboard formation that consisted basically of three lines. Each battalion in the first was separated from its neighbours by a gap of one battalion's width, this gap being covered by the battalions of the second line. Behind the second line, at approximately 600 paces, or twice the distance separating the first and second lines, was the reserve, which formed the third line. Infantry tactics were much the same as those of Gustavus. Those of the cavalry, however, were considerably different, and were derived from patterns set by French cavalry at the end of the preceding century. There were four types: heavy cavalry (gendarmes), carabiniers, light cavalry and dragoons. The gendarmes were similar to the heavy cavalry of 100 years before; the carabiniers were armed with *rifled* carbines (a shorter version of the musket, more handy for use by cavalry), and the light cavalry was similar to Gustavus's except that the men were not armoured. The dragoons, the fourth category, were in effect mounted infantry: each man was armed with a musket and bayonet and equipped with entrenching tools; this produced a very useful combination of infantry firepower and solidity plus cavalry mobility.

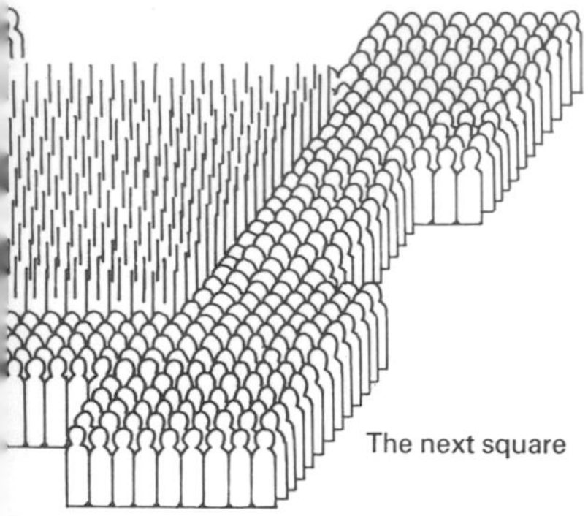
The next square

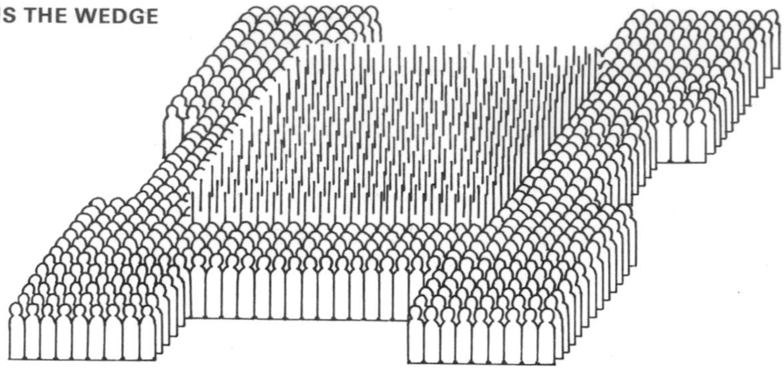

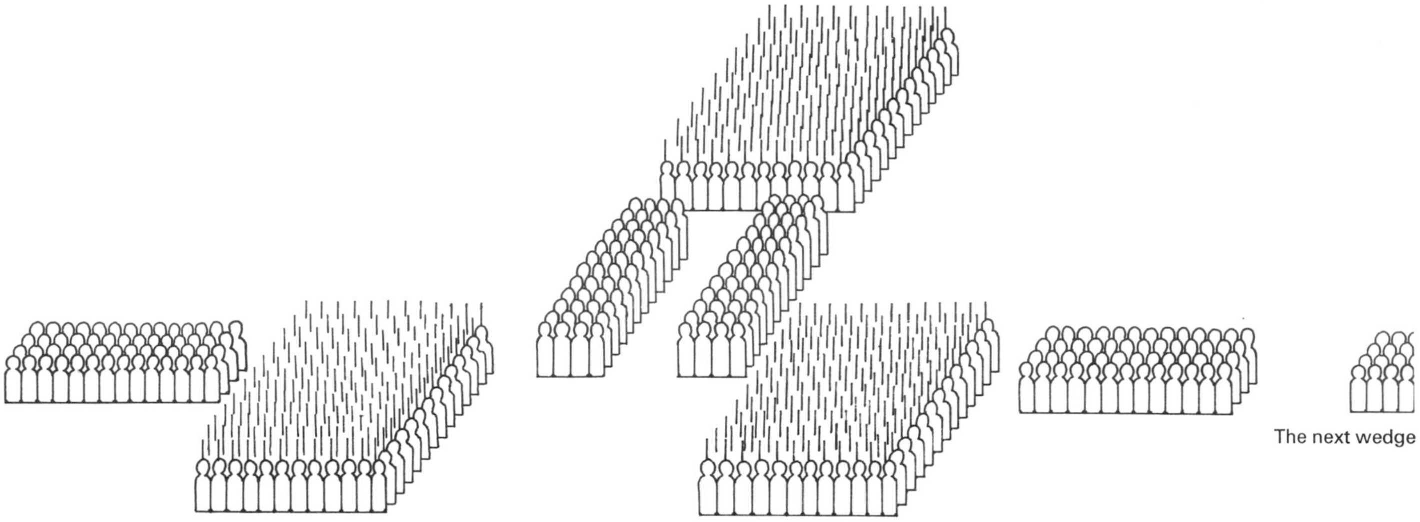
The next wedge

**above** In the Thirty Years' War (1618–48) the heavyweight Spanish Squares or *tercios* (above) consisting of solid blocks of pikemen buttressed by musketeers – about 2–3,000 men in all – were challenged by the more manoeuvrable units of Gustavus Adolphus II, King of Sweden. He devised the wedge formation shown below: co-operation between musketeers and pikemen was much improved by its use, and their respective qualities of firepower and shock effect were also increased.

**far right** An Allied artillery bombardment at the Siege of Tournay (1709), then a French-held town fortified in the Vauban manner (see also overleaf). **below** The closely integrated arms of Gustavus Adolphus II's troops go into action at the Battle of the River Lech (1632).

The sixteenth and seventeenth centuries had seen the growth of the modern state and of standing armies. Their organization was still somewhat crude, however. Staffs were small and there were no permanent formations larger than regiments or brigades. Yet an army was already a balanced force of horse, foot and guns. The cavalry was largely what would in more modern times have been classed as heavy cavalry. But the dragoon regiments were no longer merely mounted infantry. They were capable both of charging in battle and of performing outpost duties. Genuine light cavalry, in the shape of hussars, was beginning to make an impact. The infantry consisted for the most part of musketeers, but companies of grenadiers had been introduced in the French Army in 1667 and in the British during the reign of King Charles II (1660–85). Their weapon, the grenade, had been known at least as early as 1594, and fairly frequent mention is found of it during the English Civil Wars (1624–51), although it was not then considered a missile for specialists. But later, in the siege warfare so common in the long reign of King Louis XIV the grenadier was a real stormtrooper and was in constant demand for the desperate work of trench and mine.

In the wars of the late seventeenth century and early eighteenth century it is possible to count half a dozen sieges for every pitched battle. Roads were still unmetalled and generals depended on rivers and canals to give their heavy siege trains a measure of mobility. Wars tended to develop into methodical campaigns, not unlike games of chess, designed to wrest from the enemy the fortresses which guarded the waterways, and the fortified lines that covered the frontiers of provinces.

**The French Siege-master**

In this context the contribution of the French military engineer, Sébastien de Vauban (1633–1707), deserves more than passing mention. For it was he who radically redeveloped the arts of siegecraft and fortification, bringing to them a spirit of scientific enthusiasm that was wholly in keeping with the age. In the service of his king, Louis XIV, Vauban designed and rebuilt numerous strongholds, including a chain of fortresses to protect France's vulnerable frontiers, notably in the region of the Jura and Vosges mountains. While each fortress was capable of withstanding a heavy and protracted siege, the presence of a chain of such forts also simplified the logistical problems of French armies on the move, enabling them to remain supplied for extended periods.

Lech
Flu:

**below** Grenades, thrown from and into the assault trenches, were a key weapon in siege warfare; from *La Pyrotechnie de Hanzelet Lorrain*, first published in 1620.

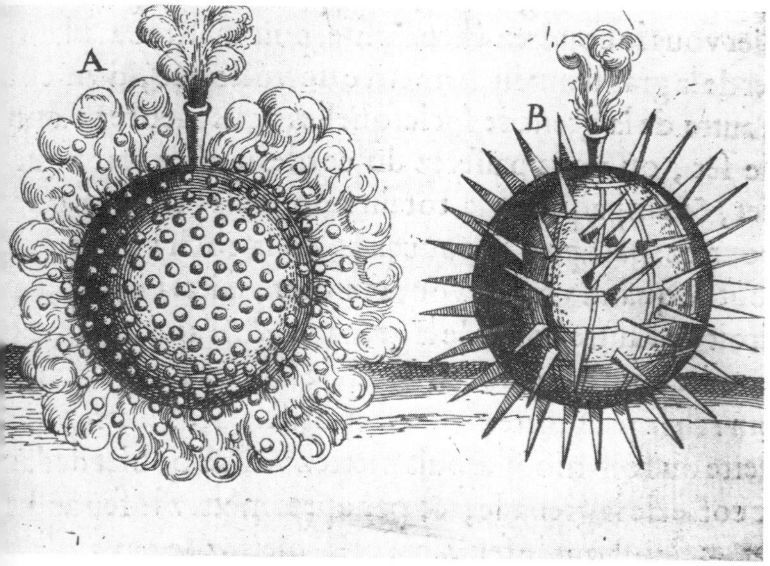
A
B

The fortresses themselves were geometrically precise constructions, designed with angled rather than curved, medieval-style bastions. These gave the defending artillery, positioned in deeply sunken embrasures, a maximum of opportunity to enfilade the enemy's approach works. In his basic groundplan Vauban retained the traditional system of an outer rampart, moat, inner rampart and inner enclosure, which he embellished with advanced strong-points, known as hornworks, and other strong-points sited in the moat, to give added depth to the defences. He also introduced the idea of using earth rather than stone ramparts to avoid the dangers of splintering under fire.

In attack Vauban was also the master of his age, using novel tactics that were to become standard procedures until the nineteenth century. His offensive ideas centred on an ingenious system of parallel trenches linked by a zig-zagging series of saps or approach trenches. The outer or first parallel was sited at a distance of some 600 yards from the fortress. Then, while batteries of siege guns con-

The diagram shows the state of siege warfare in the age of the French military engineer Sébastien de Vauban (1633–1707), and is based on drawings made by him. Not all places were fortified in the same way: Vauban himself insisted that 'one does not fortify by systems but by good sense and experience', in other words the nature of the ground should be allowed to dictate the overall shape of the defences. In general though, forts were built on the pattern shown here, and were attacked by a network of parallel and approach trenches which began about 600 yards from the place under siege and worked inwards. (To avoid undue complication only the attacking side's guns are shown: those of the defending force would in the normal way be directed at the enemy's approach works and gun emplacements.)

**A** Bastion
**B** Half-moon (a type of outwork)
**C** Curtain wall
**D** Ditch
**E** Covered way (an open rampart walk so named because it was covered by fire from the inner defences)
**F** Glacis (the sloping outer rampart)
**G** Third parallel and final assault points
**H** Zig-zag saps or approach trenches linking the three parallels
**I** Second parallel
**J** Redoubt
**K** Gun battery
**L** Mortar battery
**M** First parallel
**N** Passages for the artillery

A
B
C
D
E
F
G
H
I
J
K
L
M
N

centrated their fire on a chosen sector of the wall, teams of engineers protected by gabions (wicker baskets filled with earth) dug their way forwards about 300 yards, where a second parallel was constructed. Artillery was moved up and the process was repeated until a breech was made and the attacking infantry could mount a telling charge on the fort.

### France in Decline

Under Louis XIV the French Army fought four major wars. In their years of success they were guided by several brilliant leaders, benefiting most notably from the generalship of the Vicomte de Turenne (1611–75) and the planning genius of the man who served as the Sun King's Minister of War for twenty-five years, the Marquis de Louvois (1641–91). It was not until the turn of the century, when France was at last showing signs of incipient decay, that this great military nation found herself outthought and outmanoeuvred.

It happened in the War of the Spanish Succession (1701–14), and the two men most responsible for France's downfall were the Duke of Marlborough (1650–1722) and Prince Eugène of Savoy (1663–1736). Both, whether fighting with independent commands or in partnership together, were more than equal to the demands made of them, breaking down the methodical conventions that the French had imposed on warfare up to their arrival. Their success was founded squarely in action. New equipment, with which one army may suddenly surprise another, was not available to them; all the armies in the War of the Spanish Succession had access to more or less similar weapons. But it was Marlborough who added lustre to the profession of arms by his imaginative use of his men. In them he saw a vast potential that others ignored, and the men themselves, well fed and paid with impressive regularity, responded by serving to the utmost of their capabilities the commander they referred to as the 'Old Corporal'.

### Marlborough's Drill and Discipline

One incident may serve to illustrate Marlborough's flair for decisive action – his march to the Danube before the Battle of Blenheim in 1704. Setting out from the Netherlands in conditions of extraordinary secrecy (in order not to disturb not only the French, who were his enemy, but also his over-cautious allies, the Dutch) he moved an army that grew to be 40,000 strong over a distance of 250 miles in five weeks to join the armies of Prince Eugène and Prince Lewis of Baden. In so doing he placed himself dramatically at the heart of a war that was being waged on three widely separated fronts.

By forced marches of this kind, and by the demands he made of them in battle, Marlborough chased his men hard. He drilled his infantry for long hours in a system of platoon-firing in line that was not the accepted model of the age. It required a battalion to be divided into eighteen equal platoons, six of which fired together, then a second six, then a third; by this system one-third of a battalion could be counted on to give fire should an emergency arise. The French, on the other hand, fired in ranks. But the most important point to be made here is that Marlborough did not merely follow current practice: he first studied a range of alternatives, made his choice and then drove his officers and men to make sure that the chosen method was practised with real skill, and that discipline and steadiness under fire were maintained at all times.

He was equally determined to extract the best from his horses and guns, and customarily supervised the laying of individual guns in his main batteries. And in his cavalry tactics he took what others saw as a backward step by virtually banishing the gun in favour of the sword. In his view, however, cavalry was best employed as a shock force and he used it as such: charges were made by massed squadrons moving at a rapid trot (for greater control) and they ended in deadly thrusts of 'cold steel'. This again was not the pattern approved by his French opponents who favoured a round of volleys, delivered at the halt with pistols and carbines, as a means of softening up the enemy before they drew their swords and closed for the *mêlée*. Indeed, in almost every sphere Marlborough's actions were calculated to upset established, French-dominated methods, while his victories effectively concluded a once-grand era in the history of war.

THE BIG GUNS ARE DECISIVE.
TURENNE HAD SEVENTY—
WHAT WOULD HE SAY
TO THE
TWO HUNDRED
WE HAVE GOT?

*FREDERICK THE GREAT (1712-86)*

CHAPTER 4

# *The Age of the Muzzle Loader*

The early part of the eighteenth century was marked, as we have seen, by no spectacular or radical changes in weapons themselves, but rather by an expansion of ideas on how they should be used. To take an extreme but important example from the field of weapons development, the flint-lock musket known in England as the Brown Bess was not only the staple infantry weapon in use throughout Europe during that period, it was to remain so for some 150 years.

The only important innovations in the early decades were both Prussian: the double-ended iron ramrod introduced by Leopold von Anhalt-Dessau *c.* 1719, and the funnel-shaped touch-hole. Earlier wooden ramrods had been prone to snap but the iron ramrod, as much by the confidence it inspired in the user as by its inherent superiority, combined with the well-practised loading drill initiated by Frederick II 'the Great' to give the Prussian infantry twice the rate of fire – at four rounds per minute – of most contemporary armies. The improvement in the rate of fire was also aided by the funnel-shaped touch-hole, which made it considerably easier to prime the musket.

**Frederick the Great**

With one great exception, the faithful and unimaginative adherence of most military leaders to the Gustavan system of infantry tactics, based on severe drill and strict discipline, had a stultifying effect on European armies. They became slow and unwieldy as more emphasis came to be placed on correct dressing in rank and file than on the aims of that dressing. And so manoeuvre became more important than the tactical reasons for the manoeuvre. The exception was Frederick the Great, whose drill was more severe and whose discipline was far

The course of the Battle of Leuthen is shown in its main phases. Frederick the Great's performance at Leuthen was probably his masterpiece. Napoleon said of it: 'Alone it is sufficient to immortalize Frederick, and place him in the rank of the greatest generals.'

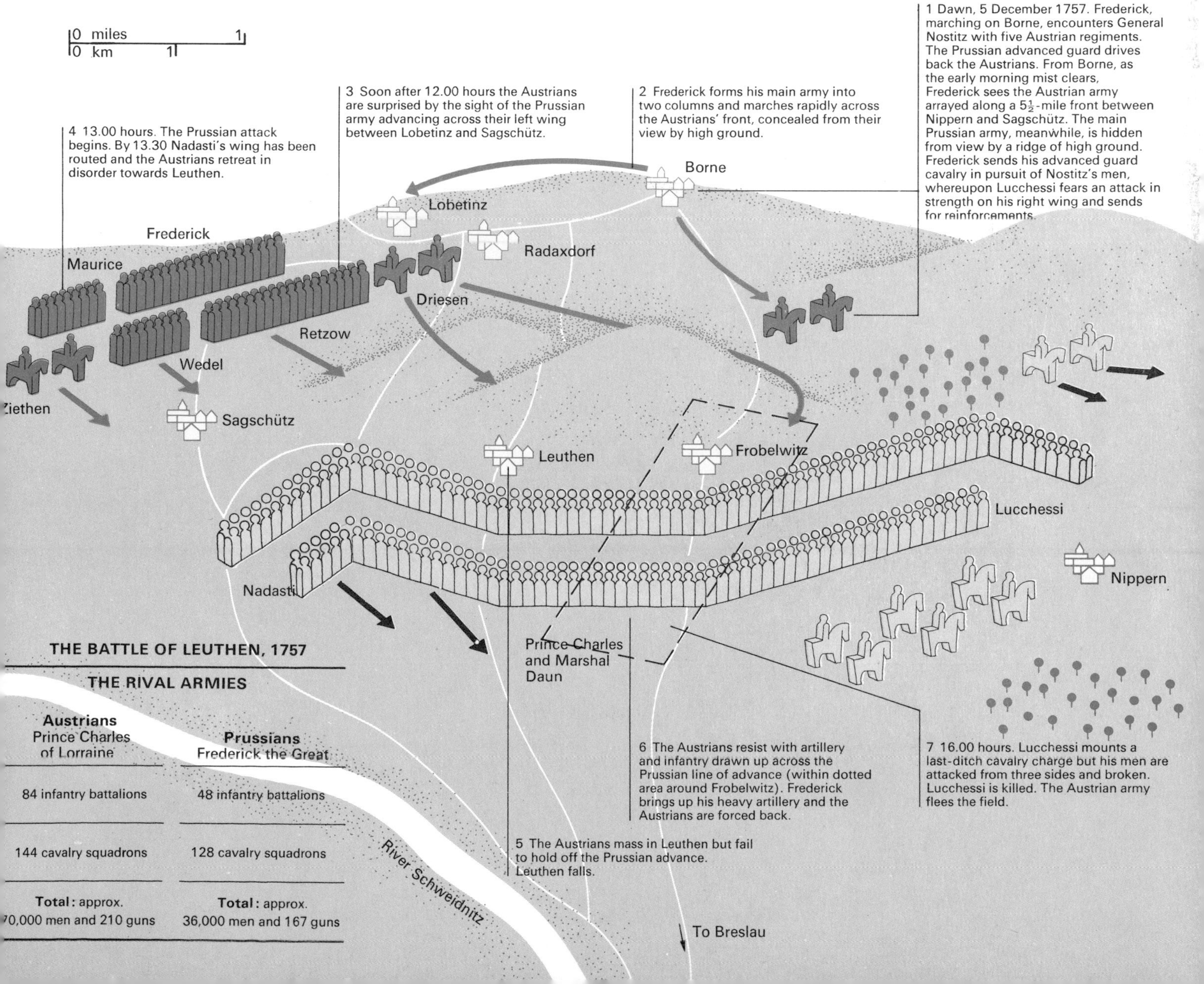
0 miles 1
0 km 1
1 Dawn, 5 December 1757. Frederick, marching on Borne, encounters General Nostitz with five Austrian regiments. The Prussian advanced guard drives back the Austrians. From Borne, as the early morning mist clears, Frederick sees the Austrian army arrayed along a 5½-mile front between Nippern and Sagschütz. The main Prussian army, meanwhile, is hidden from view by a ridge of high ground. Frederick sends his advanced guard cavalry in pursuit of Nostitz's men, whereupon Lucchessi fears an attack in strength on his right wing and sends for reinforcements.
2 Frederick forms his main army into two columns and marches rapidly across the Austrians' front, concealed from their view by high ground.
3 Soon after 12.00 hours the Austrians are surprised by the sight of the Prussian army advancing across their left wing between Lobetinz and Sagschütz.
4 13.00 hours. The Prussian attack begins. By 13.30 Nadasti's wing has been routed and the Austrians retreat in disorder towards Leuthen.
Borne
Lobetinz
Frederick
Maurice
Radaxdorf
Driesen
Retzow
Wedel
Ziethen
Sagschütz
Leuthen
Frobelwitz
Lucchessi
Nippern
Nadasti
Prince Charles and Marshal Daun
5 The Austrians mass in Leuthen but fail to hold off the Prussian advance. Leuthen falls.
6 The Austrians resist with artillery and infantry drawn up across the Prussian line of advance (within dotted area around Frobelwitz). Frederick brings up his heavy artillery and the Austrians are forced back.
7 16.00 hours. Lucchessi mounts a last-ditch cavalry charge but his men are attacked from three sides and broken. Lucchessi is killed. The Austrian army flees the field.
River Schweidnitz
To Breslau

**THE BATTLE OF LEUTHEN, 1757**

**THE RIVAL ARMIES**

| **Austrians** Prince Charles of Lorraine | **Prussians** Frederick the Great |
|---|---|
| 84 infantry battalions | 48 infantry battalions |
| 144 cavalry squadrons | 128 cavalry squadrons |
| **Total:** approx. 70,000 men and 210 guns | **Total:** approx. 36,000 men and 167 guns |

harsher than those of his contemporaries. But Frederick understood the reason for Gustavus's system. What he required was speed and endurance before the battle, and steadiness combined with precision even under the exacting conditions of the battlefield itself. The Prussian Army was admirably suited to this ideal, as the result of the Battle of Leuthen against the Austrians in 1757 clearly indicates. Outnumbered by about two to one, Frederick marched obliquely across his opponents' front at a speed incredible at that time and deployed from the march straight into action against the Austrians' left wing. A total rout followed.

Although Frederick's genius may have been greatest in the field of infantry manoeuvre, his greatest innovations were in the field of horse artillery. He abandoned the idea of horse-drawn field artillery in favour of what we would now call light horse artillery. The distinction is simple: horse-drawn field artillery was pulled to the field of battle by horses, and took up a position in which it usually remained until the day was lost or won. Horse artillery, on the other hand, was moved around the battlefield by horses as the tactical situation demanded. This enabled Frederick to use his light guns with far greater effect than his opponents. He also improved the techniques of howitzer fire, being the first to use it indirectly, that is, to fire on an unseen target, on the far side of a hill or wood.

**above** Two grenadiers. The lower picture shows a British grenadier of the 1st Foot Guards responding to the command 'Blow your match', 1735. In the upper picture is a French *grenadier à pied*, 1812–14. **left** One of Morgan's Riflemen (centre) using the long American rifle that came to prominence in the Revolutionary War (1775–83). **right** James Puckle's machine-gun of 1717. This gun anticipated many features of the Gatling gun introduced over 150 years later. It had a single barrel and a chamber of six or more cylinders that was fixed in the firing position by means of the rear locking handle; in trials it fired sixty-three times in seven minutes – a remarkable rate of fire at that time. The authorities, however, were insufficiently impressed by the gun as a whole and it never went into service.

### Light Infantrymen of Hungary and America

A major innovation that began to affect European armies in the second half of the eighteenth century was the use of the light infantryman. He was discovered almost simultaneously in two widely separated areas, in Hungary and the British colonies in America. For centuries Hungary had been on the borders of the Ottoman Empire, and her eastern frontiersmen were well accustomed to skirmishing with the Turkish light cavalry. During the War of the Austrian Succession (1740–48), shortage of manpower forced the Austrian commanders to call upon the aid of these border Hungarians, and they soon realized the true worth of this novel type of infantry which they had almost unwittingly discovered. Lightly equipped, the Hungarian infantrymen could move quickly and efficiently in front of the main body of the army as skirmishers and scouts, using every advantage offered by the ground. In dress, equipment and discipline they were decidedly irregular, but they were a highly effective fighting force.

The British in the Americas drew much the same conclusions as the Austrians had done shortly before them. In their constant skirmishes with the Indians, they learned that lightly armed irregulars stood a far better chance than the ordinary infantry because they could fight on equal terms with their opponents. Rogers's Rangers was perhaps the most effective British unit in North America during the Seven Years' War (1756–63). Robert Rogers, a New Hampshire man, was a skilled woodsman and former smuggler who recruited others of similar skills and inclination to fight the French and their Indian allies in the thick forests around Lake George and Lake Champlain. Moving with great stealth Rogers's men carried out numerous successful ambushes and raids on enemy forts and outposts. The Rangers showed scant concern for uniform, and were usually armed with a musket, an axe and a hunting knife.

The American Revolutionary War (1775–83) drove the point home with considerable emphasis, when light infantrymen such as Morgan's Riflemen proved as

efficient against the well-drilled if cumbersome British redcoats as they did against the Indians. Soon, light-infantry units were to be found in all the major armies of Europe, gradually replacing the irregulars who had formerly been employed to scout and skirmish. Indeed, the British had light companies in every regiment before the Revolutionary War, but these still wore red coats even though they fought in open order.

**Riflemen and Grenadiers**

About this time a new weapon was introduced to the arsenals of Europe – although it had, nevertheless, been in use as a sporting weapon for two centuries. This was the rifle. Originally a German weapon, the rifle had travelled to America, where a longer version was manufactured by German settlers in Pennsylvania which found favour among woodsmen who valued its accuracy more than the better rate of fire of the musket. Similar to the flint-lock musket in most respects, the rifle had a longer barrel, inside which was a series of grooves spiralling from the firing chamber to the muzzle.

The bullet, which had to be a tight fit, was hammered down the barrel – a slow process – and so was squeezed into the grooves. When the piece was fired, the bullet was spun as it went up the barrel and emerged with sufficient spin to stabilize it in flight for a range of up to 300 yards, giving it an accuracy that the musket, with its smooth bore, could not hope to match. The rifle was not, clearly, the weapon for line infantry, but it was admirably suited to the tactics of the light-infantry regiments that were just being introduced.

In his reorganizations of the French Army in the latter part of the seventeenth century the Marquis de Louvois had put his grenadiers into special corps; as was mentioned earlier, these specialist storm troops had made an important contribution to siege tactics in the Vauban era. A century later the British Army tried the unsuccessful experiment, soon abandoned, of concentrating its grenadier companies, which belonged one to each regiment, in battalions. This, however, deprived units of their best men and was a vicious arrangement that was discontinued in the following generation.

The grenade, which had been introduced in the British Army in 1677, was a hollow-cast shell filled with gunpowder and ignited by a fuse on the top. The original versions had been upwards of three pounds in weight, and needed the largest men in the regiment to throw them. And although the grenade had been lightened considerably by the second half of the eighteenth century, the grenadier companies still retained the status of élite units from the days when they had needed the strongest men in the regiment for their use.

**Changing Role of Cavalry**

Cavalry tactics had perhaps undergone something of a retrograde step at the hands of Gustavus Adolphus, for he seems to have integrated the cavalry into his three-

Maintenance activities in the artillery park at Toulon: a detail from *Le Port de Toulon* by Claude-Joseph Vernet (1714–89), who was commissioned by Louis XV to produce a series of paintings of the sea ports of France.

arm forces almost too closely. Co-operation with infantry and artillery had resulted in the cavalry losing certainly one of its most important assets, mobility, and sometimes another, speed. By rigorous training and the use of relatively small bodies of cavalry Gustavus had obviated the worst potential evil of the system – that the three arms, with their different speeds, might become hopelessly entangled at a critical moment – but his system was clearly not ideal. The proper function of cavalry was to mass independently of the other arms, though always in concert with the tactical requirements governing all three.

Most armies slavishly copying the successful Swedish example failed to capitalize on the cavalry's vital rôle as a shock weapon. Instead they armed their cavalry with pistols, carbines and muskets and used them as mounted infantry, their highest charging speed being the trot. The obvious failings of the system of mixing cavalry and infantry were brought home for the last time at Minden in 1759, when the British infantry broke the French combined cavalry and infantry line. Frederick the Great had recognized the limitations of the Gustavan system before this, however, and reorganized his cavalry on more traditional lines as scouting and shock forces. Firearms were forbidden to all except the dragoons, who preserved their nature as mounted infantry, and cavalry tactics under Frederick consisted of charges, sword in hand, at the gallop. Before him Marlborough, while restricting the speed of his charges to a fast trot, had also cut down on the use of firearms in his cavalry, allowing his men only three charges of powder per campaign and this for use on outpost duty. At the beginning of the eighteenth century he had taught his cavalry to rely upon the sword, and its success at Ramillies (1706) and elsewhere had underlined the importance of leaving the cavalry free and comparatively unencumbered by arms. Elsewhere though, armies were generally slow to modify the earlier cavalry tactics of Gustavus.

### De Gribeauval's Artillery Improvements

The design of artillery had been fairly static for some time now, and was to remain so until the advent of rifling

1737

and breech-loading, but considerable improvements in current types were effected by a Frenchman, Jean Baptiste de Gribeauval (1715–89), from 1765 onwards. Artillery types were further reduced to four (4-, 8- and 12-pounders and 6-inch howitzers, all cast from iron or bronze and designed as smooth-bore muzzle-loaders), thus further simplifying logistical problems.

But the perpetual difficulty with artillery was its lack of mobility, and here de Gribeauval made considerable advances. He further improved upon the lightening of guns begun by Gustavus Adolphus, and placed them on stronger carriages, so that they could be moved across country at higher speeds. To help in this de Gribeauval introduced the system of harnessing the horses in pairs instead of tandem; he also made caissons (ammunition chests) and limbers (the detachable fore-parts of gun carriages) integral parts of each gun's equipment. Thus a piece could be moved to a desired point quickly and brought into action immediately, without having to wait for a supply of ready ammunition, powder, etc., to be brought up. Gunlaying scales were standardized and improved, and all pieces were fitted with elevating screws in place of the wedges, little changed from medieval times, that some of them were still using.

Finally, de Gribeauval insisted that all gun-crews should be military men, and dismissed the last contract drivers from the French Army. All these reforms had

**above** Casting cannon balls *c.* 1803; from a contemporary work by W. H. Pyne. **below** French cannon mounted on a field carriage, 1803. Following the artillery reforms begun by de Gribeauval in 1765, gun types were rationalized and mobility was also much improved.

1.

been foreshadowed elsewhere, but de Gribeauval was the man who brought them all together in the artillery arm of one country, and also trained that arm to a high state of efficiency. It was in this remodelled artillery that Napoleon Bonaparte first served, and so acquired his deadly knowledge of how best to use it.

**Ammunition, Balloons and Rockets**

By the end of the eighteenth century ammunition had also been standardized into four types among European armies: solid shot, explosive shell, grapeshot, and canister or shrapnel. Grapeshot was in effect an open tubular rack containing a number of small balls of iron, which spread out in flight to form a wall of projectiles for use against targets such as cavalry and artillery. Canister or shrapnel was invented in Britain in 1784 by Lieutenant (later Captain) Henry Shrapnel (1761–1842): it consisted of a tubular canister filled with musket balls and a bursting charge which detonated the projectile in the air and showered the enemy troops below with a massive hail of musket balls. The idea of shrapnel was not, it should be noted, a new one, the Venetians having used a similar device, in which the exploding charge broke up the casing to send out large numbers of jagged splinters, in 1376. Shrapnel was first used in action at the taking of Surinam by the British in 1804.

The only entirely new 'weapon' was the balloon, which was used for observation purposes at the Battle of Fleurus in 1794, but soon afterwards fell out of favour with Napoleon and was forgotten for sixty years. Another weapon, the rocket, made its first significant appearance in Europe during the early part of the Napoleonic wars – although it had been in use in China for centuries. The Congreve rocket, so named after its developer, Colonel Sir William Congreve (1772–1828), was inaccurate and short-ranged (about a mile), but was used sometimes to supplement the light artillery of which the British had too little. When fired in salvoes its lack of accuracy was more than compensated for by its rate of fire and incendiary capabilities, as was proved by the razing of Copenhagen in a fire started by 25,000 rockets in 1807. Rockets were used at the passage of the Adour and at Leipzig (1813) and also in the Waterloo campaign. However, their popularity was shortlived and they did not long survive the Napoleonic period. They seem to have been used for the last time in the Burmese campaign of 1825–6.

**Tactics: From Frederick to Napoleon**

Tactics remained for the most part based on the pattern introduced by Frederick the Great, and no important new weapon appeared that could have radically disturbed that system. Increased rate of fire, the result of better drilling and improved loading methods, meant that the infantry line could be further thinned to two men. The exception to this was the French Army, where the resort to the *levée en masse*, with its consequent large numbers of poorly trained troops, necessitated tactics

**bottom left** A picture painted in a letter to his father by a Belgian gunner in Napoleon's army. **below** Members of the British Royal Horse Artillery firing a Congreve rocket. **bottom** Warfare with rockets as it was envisaged in Congreve's day (early nineteenth century). In practice though, his rockets fell from use soon after the Napoleonic Wars.

based on the column during the Revolutionary Wars. These were not always true columns but often consisted of units echelonned in depth, which induced a feeling of solidarity and also allowed the deployment of the army onto any front straight from the line of march. Other than this, and the use of highly mobile artillery on the de Gribeauval system to give massed fire at the decisive point, there was nothing particularly novel about Napoleon's tactics. His successes were gained mainly by strategic means, by organization, and by choosing the right ground for battle. One notable tactical innovation adopted by all armies, but especially Wellington's, was the increased use of cover not only during the approach to a battle, but in the battle itself. The reason for it is not hard to find: the volume of fire that could by now be produced by artillery and infantry was so great that casualties would have been immense if cover had not been used.

By the end of the eighteenth century an army clearly needed to be a well-balanced force of horse, foot and guns. It was very rare for cavalry to break steady infantry formed in square; but by threatening to charge cavalry could compel infantry to adopt that formation and thus offer the best possible target to artillery. Although cavalry could overrun a battery, without the support of foot it could not keep what it had won.

It cannot be said that either missile or shock action changed very much between the days of Marlborough and those of Napoleon. Although equipment grew lighter and means of traction more efficient, the ranges and rates of fire of cannon and musket had not changed so much as to alter what might be called the Rules of the War Game. The main body of an army still fought in close order, and few regiments wore uniforms that made any concession to the need for concealment.

### The Elaboration of Armies

Army staffs, especially Napoleon's, became larger and more efficient. The maps, telescopes, time-pieces and other tools of the staff officer's trade were also much improved. In general the organization of armies underwent changes which made them far handier. Armies were now organized in permanent divisions and army corps. The latter, consisting of troops of all arms, could hold out for long periods without support. This was a development of the greatest importance and one which Napoleon himself pioneered when, between 1800 and 1805, he built up his Grand Army – the force that was the basis of his power and whose eventual destruction in 1815 coincided with his own.

The armies of the Napoleonic Wars were considerably more elaborate, not only in their dress, than those operating in the days of Marlborough or Frederick. The cavalry, once composed merely of cuirassiers, ordinary cavalrymen and dragoons, was now organized in three classes of heavy, medium and light cavalry that included horse grenadiers, carabiniers, cuirassiers, dragoons, lancers, mounted chasseurs, hussars and light dragoons. Infantry included grenadiers, riflemen, light infantry and musketeers, to name only the main categories. Engineers, pontoon trains, ambulances, wagon trains and staff corps were also to be found (though not necessarily all for the first time) in the days of Napoleon. Even the least important of these changes in the make-up of armies had their particular significance, while the improvements in organization and staff duties were of prime importance.

Napoleon's Campaign of 1815 was fought over country well-trodden by the armies of Marlborough's day. Yet the pattern of war had utterly changed. Gone were the tedious sieges of the War of the Spanish Succession. Instead of stately and cautious movements Napoleon concentrated with a speed and advanced with a suddenness that would have astonished his compatriot, the Duc de Villeroi, a century before as much as the *blitzkrieg* of 1940 was to amaze the Allied commander-in-chief, General Gamelin.

Ever since the Industrial Revolution, which began in about 1760, a subtle change had come over the more

populous parts of Europe. While equipment had been improved and lightened, roads too had become far better and it was no longer necessary to campaign up and down the waterways. The great fortresses of Vauban might scarcely have existed for all the effect they had on the campaign that led to Waterloo. But it was not only the Industrial Revolution that had changed the face of war. The French Revolution, too, had played its part, breathing into it a spirit of violence that would have seemed positively shocking to the generals of the Old Regime, men like Lord Stair, the Prince de Soubise or Marshal Daun.

The great Prussian general and military theorist Karl von Clausewitz (1780–1831) observed this change and wrote: 'Let us not hear of generals who conquer without bloodshed. If a bloody slaughter is a horrible sight, then that is a ground for paying more respect to war, but not for making the sword we wear blunter and blunter by degrees from feelings of humanity, until someone steps in with a sword that is sharp and lops off the arm from our body.' However, despite the unpleasant images conjured up by von Clausewitz, the Great Powers were still far from beginning to suspect that war might, one day, become too dangerous a way of advancing the ends of state policy.

**left** A military balloon, used to observe enemy movements at the Battle of Fleurus, 1794.
**below** A scene from the Battle of Austerlitz (1805), where Napoleon achieved one of his most crushing victories. Although developments in weapons were few, the armies of this period were larger and more elaborately organized than before and contained many more specialist units.

Inventors of the breech-loading age and some of the weapons which they brought into being. **above** Sir Hiram Maxim; he is also seen with King Edward VII, who is trying out a Maxim machine-gun. **right** Alfred Krupp, who began manufacturing heavy guns at the family works in Essen *c.* 1847; also shown is his 1,000-pounder gun, which was featured at the Paris Exhibition of 1867. **far right** A portrait of Dr Richard Gatling, and an action scene in which the Gatling gun is being fired (centre) by a detachment of the 26th Middlesex Cyclists. Military cycling, incidentally, was first taken up in 1875 in Italy; the gun shown here was carried on four 'safeties', joined together and ridden by four men.

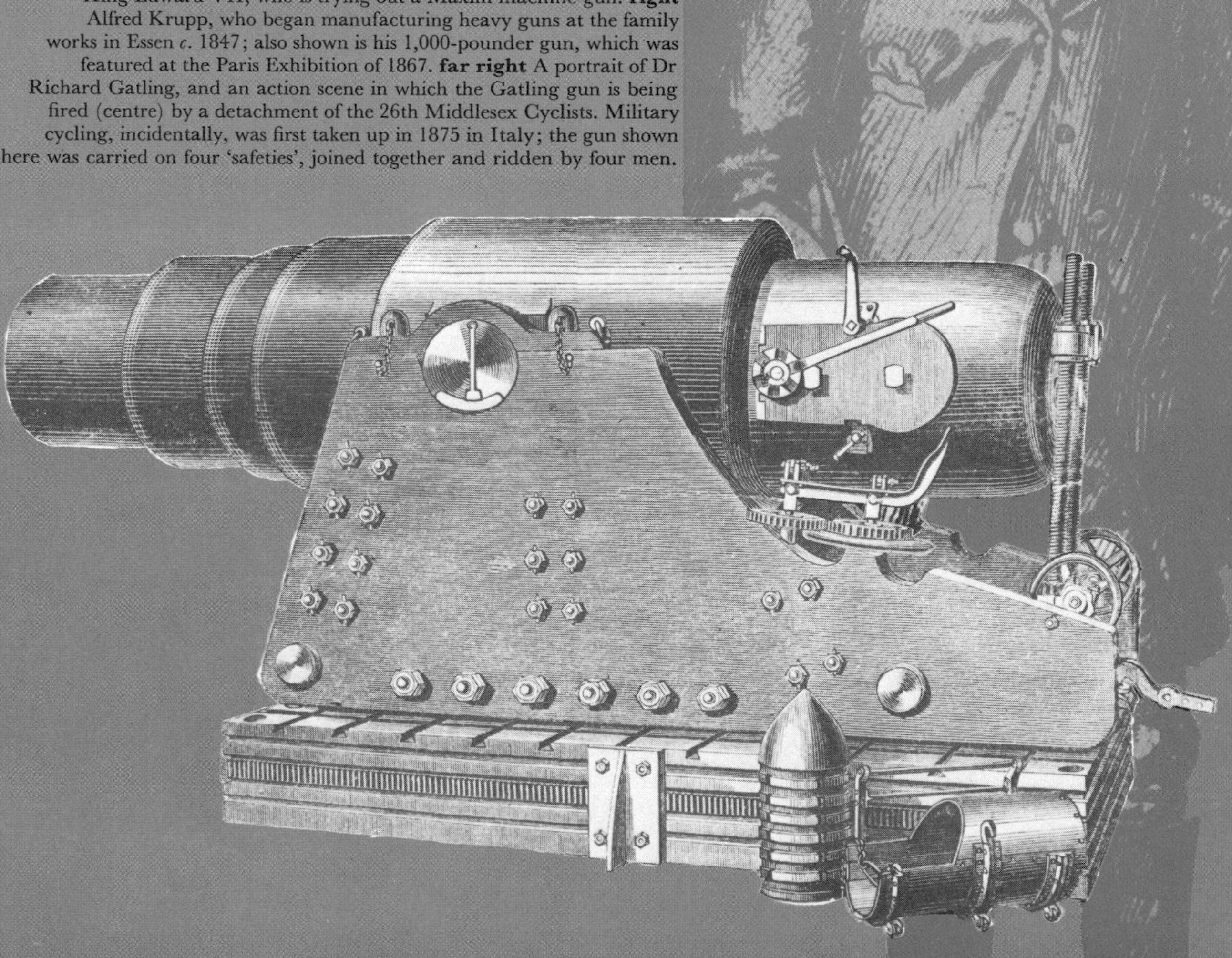

CHAPTER 5

# *The Age of the Breech-Loader*

INVENTIONS
HAVE ALL BEEN INVENTED
OVER AND OVER
FIFTY TIMES.

*RALPH WALDO EMERSON* (*1803-82*)

The breech-loading of firearms and artillery had been attempted from the time of their invention, but every gunmaker had stumbled on the same difficulty: the state of metal-working simply did not permit the manufacture of a mechanism that would close tightly enough to stop obturation – the escape of gases round the badly fitting joint between breech and breech-block.

The chief incentive to use this method of loading is obvious: if the gun is fired from behind cover the crew gathered at the breech end can open the breech and load directly without exposing themselves by walking round to the muzzle to ram powder and shot down the barrel. If a means of producing tightly fitting parts and an adequate breech-locking system had been available from the beginning, breech-loaders might well have come immediately to the fore and stayed there. But, as we have seen, the idea was impractical in those early times. Later, as gunmakers grew more skilful at casting guns in one piece, the desire for a breech-loading mechanism waned – at least on the manufacturing side since it would have meant cutting the one-piece casting to make a breech-block.

The makers of handguns also tried to invent some form of breech-loading mechanism, usually derived from the efforts of their predecessors with artillery. The earliest efforts centred around a breech-block that screwed into the chamber after the latter had been loaded; a hinged mechanism with a lock to hold it in position when loaded, and finally a hole in the barrel, through which powder and ball could be inserted, the hole then being sealed by a screwed-in plug. The major difficulty was still the problem of sealing the breech adequately, but the early inventors were faced with another hindrance to their efforts in the loose nature of the powder and shot. At that time the conventional muzzle-loading pistol or musket proved the best solution because the powder could be dropped into the barrel, rammed down and followed by the ball and finally by the wad, which held powder and ball firmly together in the firing chamber. Had it been possible to invent some form of cartridge earlier, *i.e.* an all-in-one container for powder and shot, inventors might have had more success with breech-loading mechanisms. However, that was not to be. The development of breech-loaders was slow and had to be preceded by several notable inventions, which were finally combined to make the modern breech-loader an efficient weapon.

Perhaps the most important of these inventions was the development of mass production by Eli Whitney, an American who invented the cotton gin in 1793. The invention was not new, being known in France as early as 1775, but the credit must go to Whitney for making mass production a workable industrial technique. Using it, armaments manufacturers could achieve regular tolerances in their weapons, which enabled parts to be easily

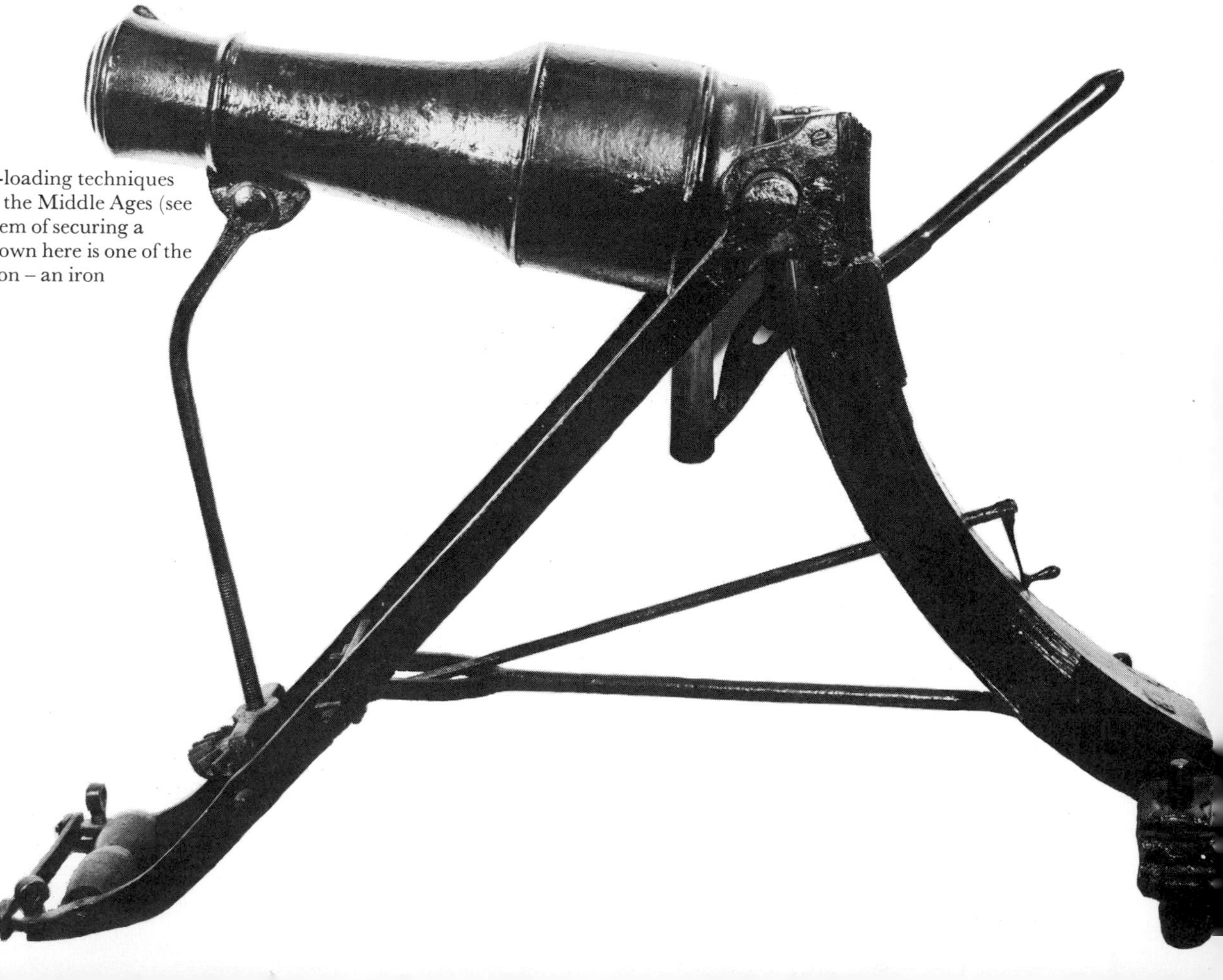

Experiments with breech-loading techniques had been carried on since the Middle Ages (see Chapter 2), but the problem of securing a gas-tight fit remained. Shown here is one of the many attempts at a solution – an iron breech-loader of 1740.

**above** Three percussion pistols. From top to bottom are: a US Navy model Colt .36-inch single-action revolver, 1851; a British .577-inch muzzle-loading cavalry pistol, 1856; and a British Adams .50-inch double-action revolver. **below** Some products of the cartridge revolution. 1 Maynard's patent ignition cartridge of 1865. 2 Pin-fire cartridge for a Lefaucheux revolver. 3 Rim-fire cartridge for a Gatling gun. 4 A paper combustible cartridge for an Enfield (Pattern 1853). 5 A cartridge covered with greased paper and incorporating a felt wad. 6 A paper cartridge tied with string. 7 A paper-covered brass foil Gallagher cartridge (fired with a separate percussion cap). 8 An early American (Burnside) brass-cased cartridge. 9 A selection of ignition tubes containing the explosive agent, the fulminate of mercury; these were usually made of thin copper and were fitted into the vent leading to the chamber. 10 Various types of percussion cap: these small containers, filled with fulminate of mercury and fitted over a nipple on the gun, were struck by the (trigger-operated) hammer; this exploded the fulminate, which detonated the main charge.

interchanged; they could, moreover, produce smoothly moving actions and tightly closing joints, the last two of which were to prove very important in the introduction of breech-loaders.

Then, in 1807, a Scottish clergyman named Forsyth obtained a patent for a percussion cap that he had invented, and the military authorities of the world were quick to adopt a version of it as the means of setting off the powder in the firing chamber of their muskets and pistols. The military percussion cap was simple: it consisted of a small copper container of fulminate of mercury with a detonator at the bottom of it. This container, shaped like a cap, was fitted over a nipple with a vent leading to the chamber. When struck by the trigger-operated hammer (which replaced the jaws holding the flint on the flint-lock musket), the fulminate of mercury exploded, setting off the detonator, which in turn set off the powder in the chamber via the vent. The beauty of the system was in its simplicity: the musketeer no longer had to prime his weapon, keep its priming pan dry and make sure that the flint was in good condition; instead he merely loaded his powder and shot and fitted the percussion cap over the nipple.

### Von Dreyse's Needle-gun

The next step in the evolution of the breech-loader was the invention of the self-contained cartridge, including in one package the bullet, powder and detonator. The

1
2
3
4
5
6
7
8
9
10

**top** Claude Minié (1814–79), who brought greater accuracy to his guns with a system of rifling allied to a bullet with protruding rings which expanded on firing to produce a gas-tight fit against the walls of the barrel. **above** Johann von Dreyse (1787–1867), inventor of the world's first breech-loading bolt-action gun, known as the needle-gun after its long firing-pin.

first to achieve this and to interest the authorities was a Prussian named Johann von Dreyse (1787–1867), who in 1827 persuaded the Prussian military hierarchy of the advantages they would gain from the adoption of his gun and cartridge. The cartridge was of paper, with the powder at the rear, the bullet at the front and the detonator between the two. The gun used to fire it was a muzzle-loading smooth-bore, but the first true breech-loader appeared in 1837, when von Dreyse introduced his needle-gun, which used the same cartridge as the earlier weapon.

The reasoning behind the design of this extraordinary gun, the firing-pin of which resembled a long needle (hence the name) was the idea then current that the way to stop, or at least cut down, obturation was to start the propellant charge burning at the front. The percussion cap was accordingly placed there, and had to be struck by the firing-pin after it had travelled through the propellant. The action of the bolt was simple, and modern bolt-action rifles are still based on the same principle. As the bolt was pulled back, exposing the breech to the chamber, the firing-pin and the spring to drive it forward were also drawn back. The cartridge was then inserted and the bolt pushed forward to close the breech, and turned to lock it against lugs on the main body of the breech. As the bolt was pushed forward, the firing-pin, its spring fully compressed, was held back by a sear until the trigger was

**above** Some critical stages in the gun's progress during the nineteenth century. From top to bottom are: a flint-lock musket of the kind that had been in service since Marlborough's day; next to it is one of von Dreyse's needle-guns, followed by a French *chassepot* – the first military breech-loading rifle, introduced in 1866 – and a Minié rifle.

pulled; then the sear was disengaged and the pin driven forward by the spring through the propellant and into the percussion cap.

Here, then, was the world's first successful breech-loading bolt-action gun. Severe problems of obturation remained, for which reason it was turned down by the British and French Armies, but it proved its worth in the Austro-Prussian War of 1866 and in the Franco-Prussian War of 1870–1, despite the fact that the needle-like firing pin broke under the stresses of ordinary service use after the gun had fired only a few hundred rounds.

Meanwhile the solutions to the problems of obturation and the long firing-pin were being found. In 1847 a Frenchman, Houiller, produced his pin-fire cartridge, based on the work of his compatriot, Casimir Lefaucheux, eleven years earlier. This was a cartridge with the percussion cap in its base – but at the side. This second idea was a retrograde one, as it meant that the action of the gun had to be directed to drive a pin through the side of the cartridge to fire it. In the same year, however, another Frenchman, Flobert, introduced the rim-fire cartridge: the percussion cap was still at the side of the base but now was placed right round the flanged rim of the bullet. (The flange was intended to engage the rear of the chamber, and so prevent the bullet sliding down the barrel.) In Flobert's version, too, the action of the gun was allowed to operate in the most obvious axis, the longitudinal one. A still better solution, the centre-fire cartridge, which had the percussion cap in the centre of the cartridge's base, where it could be struck by a firing pin travelling directly forwards, was invented by yet another Frenchman, Pottet, in 1857, and further developed in 1861 by Schneider. Colonel Boxer of the Royal Laboratory at Woolwich, London, next refined the centre-

**top** Four rifles which made their appearance in the latter part of the nineteenth century. From left to right are an Enfield, a Lee Metford, a Lebel and a Mauser. **left** Profile of a .65-inch Gatling gun on a heavy naval mounting.

fire cartridge by giving it an iron base and coiled brass wire walls, while the last word in basic design came from the armaments manufacturer, Kynoch British. He introduced the type of cartridge we still use today – a centre-fire cartridge made entirely of brass. This finally solved the obturation problem: the walls of the cartridge case were of a metal thin enough to be expanded by the detonation of the propellant, and were thus pushed against the sides of the chamber with sufficient force to make a gas-tight joint.

The first bolt-action weapon, von Dreyse's needle-gun, was still unrifled and suffered from the congenital deficiency of the type, namely a lack of accuracy at long range. The obvious step was the introduction of rifling, which should have proved a comparatively easy step after the introduction of one-piece cartridges, since the bullet would no longer have to be screwed down the barrel. The introduction of rifling was slow, however, not beginning until 1849 with the Minié bullet – and this was used with a muzzle-loading rifle. The Minié bullet was of lead and had a pointed nose, a hollow base and protruding rings around its base. When the rifle was fired, the expanding gas inside the hollow base of the bullet forced the sides out against the walls of the barrel, pushing the rings round the base into the rifling and providing a gas-tight seal.

The muzzle-loading gun was on the way out, however, and the first military breech-loading rifle was the French *chassepot*, introduced in 1866. This was a better weapon than the Prussian needle-gun, but was not available in large enough numbers in 1870. Its superiority is attested by the fact that captured *chassepots* were used by the Prussians as snipers' weapons. Then, in 1874, there appeared the true forerunner of the modern rifle, the French Gras rifle, which used a bolt action and a metal centre-fire cartridge.

**Rapid Fire**

The rate of fire now attainable with modern rifles was high enough for it to be a hindrance to have to load each round by hand. The answer was the magazine; this was placed under the rifle where it did not obscure the sighting arrangements. First came the American Lee box-magazine of 1879. This was a box, which might hold up to ten rounds, placed under the rifle between the forward end of the bolt in the open position and the rear of the chamber. A spring at the bottom of the magazine pushed the rounds upward, and they were held by the lips at the top of the magazine until the bolt pushed the top round forward and up past the lips of the magazine into the chamber. After the round had been fired, the opening of the bolt brought an extractor into play to pull the empty cartridge-case from the chamber and eject it, leaving the chamber empty for the next round. Variations on the box-magazine were produced by Nagant in Belgium, Mauser in Germany and Mannlicher in Austria-Hungary.

**NORDENFELT MACHINE-GUN**

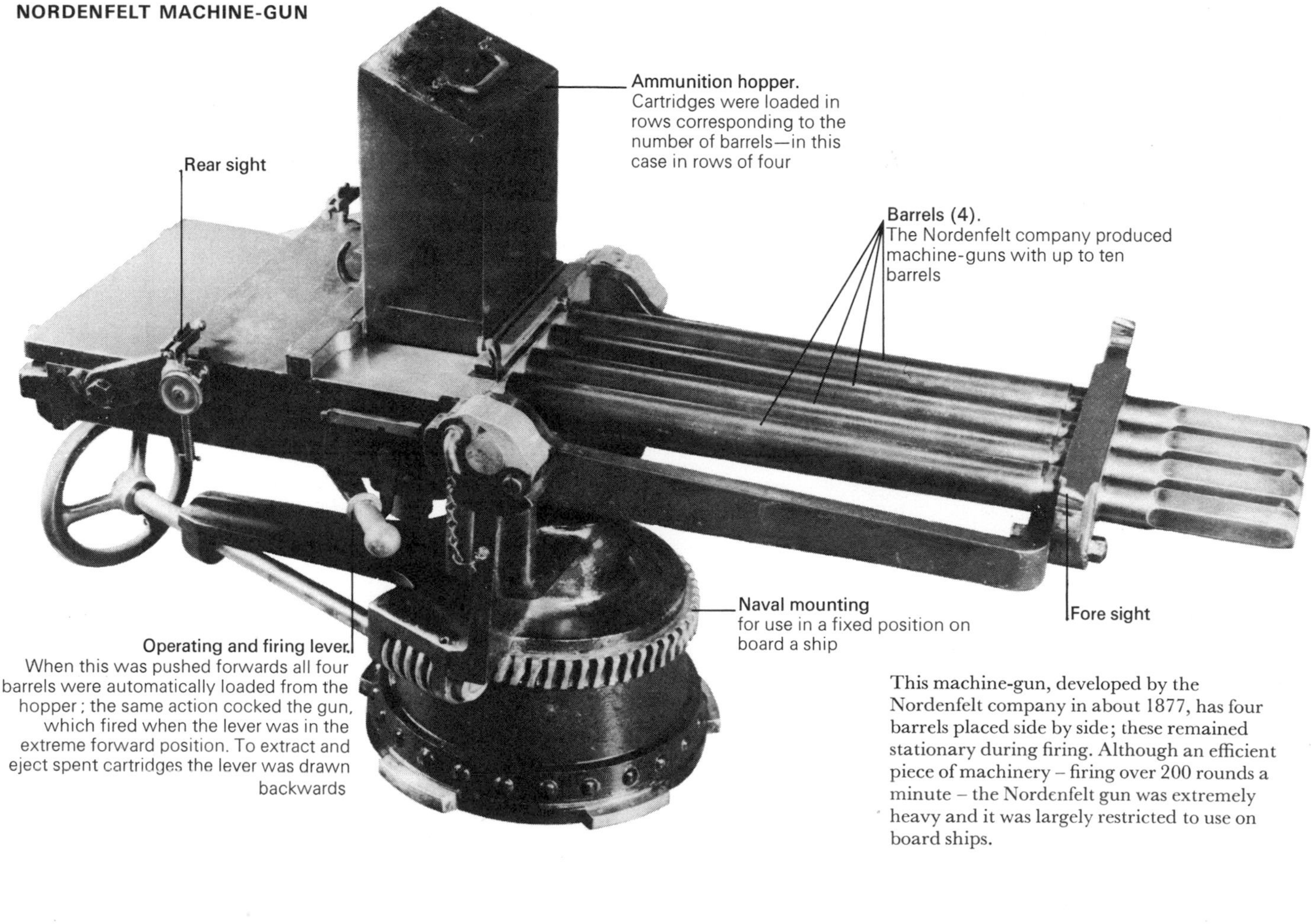
Ammunition hopper.
Cartridges were loaded in rows corresponding to the number of barrels—in this case in rows of four
Rear sight
Barrels (4).
The Nordenfelt company produced machine-guns with up to ten barrels
Naval mounting
for use in a fixed position on board a ship
Fore sight
Operating and firing lever.
When this was pushed forwards all four barrels were automatically loaded from the hopper; the same action cocked the gun, which fired when the lever was in the extreme forward position. To extract and eject spent cartridges the lever was drawn backwards

This machine-gun, developed by the Nordenfelt company in about 1877, has four barrels placed side by side; these remained stationary during firing. Although an efficient piece of machinery – firing over 200 rounds a minute – the Nordenfelt gun was extremely heavy and it was largely restricted to use on board ships.

The other type of magazine to find favour was a tubular one, in which the rounds were stored one in front of the other in a spring-loaded tube running under the barrel. The spring forced the line of rounds back onto a vertical spring, from where they were chambered as in the box-magazine.

The French were particularly taken with the tubular magazine, introducing it in their army with the Lebel rifle of 1886. The main failing of this latter system was that any jam that might occur in the magazine was difficult to clear, whereas with a box-magazine the whole unit could be removed easily for repairs. Finally in the development of the modern rifle came the introduction of an excellent system of rifling, the Enfield, which is still used today, and the invention in 1887 of a smokeless propellant by a Frenchman, Paul Vieille. This new propellant was more powerful than gunpowder and gave the infantry rifle an accurate range of up to 1,000 yards. Shooting accurately at long ranges was made easier by the smokeless powder because no longer was there a fog-like cloud of black smoke hanging over the field. Vieille's invention was quickly overtaken by another in the same line, however, the development by the Swedish inventor, Alfred Nobel, of cordite, which was easier to handle and was still more powerful than Vieille's propellant.

The way was now open to the realization of the infantryman's greatest desire: an automatic weapon with a high rate of fire – the machine-gun. As with all the major innovations, experiments had been carried out before but had been unsuccessful because of technological inadequacies at the time. The two original types of machine-gun had consisted of, firstly, a single barrel loaded with charges and rounds one in front of the other, and secondly of a number of barrels each loaded with one round. These could be fired in one of two ways, either by firing each particular round individually by means of a separate touch-hole for each or by firing the first and then letting a powder-train leading from that set off the second, then the third, and so on.

Experiments continued with little success until the arrival of the all-in-one cartridge, which made possible the first quick-firing weapon, the revolver-pistol. This contained a circular magazine of five or six rounds, a new round being brought into the barrel by the cocking of the hammer after the firing of the previous round. The advances contained in the revolver were enough to make it an important weapon in its own right – once it had been fully developed by men such as Samuel Colt in the late 1830s. But it was not the answer to heavy battlefield fire since it was both inaccurate, except at short ranges, and lower-powered than a rifle. Even so, during the American Civil War (1861–5) the Confederate cavalry preferred to put their trust in a pair of revolvers rather than an old-fashioned sabre when they closed for the *mêlée*.

**Early Machine-guns**

The first successful machine-gun was created as a result of the demands of the American Civil War. This was the Gatling gun, named after its designer, Richard Gatling, which had anything between six and ten barrels arranged to revolve around a central axis. Ammunition was fed from a large magazine above the weapon: as each barrel, turned by a crank, reached the top of the circle, its firing mechanism loaded a round, fired it and ejected it as it continued round, allowing the next barrel to move into position. It was an important and useful first step, but the gun was too heavy and clumsy, and had to be mounted on a field-gun carriage.

The French also produced a machine-gun, the *mitrailleuse*, which had between twenty-five and thirty-seven barrels, with a breech-plate holding the correct number of rounds, the plates being capable of being changed twelve times a minute. But in the Franco-Prussian War (1870–1) the weapon was used incorrectly, in small groups and at too great a range. Its lack of success went far to discourage many otherwise enthusiastic supporters of the weapon from pressing for its introduction in other armies – with dire consequences for the Allied armies, which were grossly deficient in machine-guns when the First World War broke out in 1914.

Another type of machine-gun, with up to ten stationary barrels placed side by side, was invented by the Nordenfelt company in about 1875, but this was even heavier than the Gatling, and so found use only on ships where a stationary mounting of considerable weight was no particular disadvantage. The same basic design was improved by Captain William Gardner in the United States to the extent that the number of barrels was eventually reduced to one, but the weight, with 1,000 rounds of ammunition, was still a formidable 200 pounds.

The first, truly successful, portable machine-gun was invented by an American working in Britain, Hiram Maxim. His gun appeared in 1884, but did not work satisfactorily until the advent of more powerful smokeless propellants three years later. Maxim used the recoil of the bullet's detonation to send the breech mechanism forward at high speed to chamber a round, fire it and recoil again. The process continued until the firer released the trigger, which allowed a sear to stop the mechanism, or until the ammunition ran out. The weapon's rate of fire was so high that it had to be water-cooled. Manufacture of Maxim's design was taken over by the firm of Vickers, which then produced what became known as the Vickers gun – a brilliantly thought-out, reliable weapon which with very few modifications remained in service with several armies for over seventy years.

Two other machine-guns appeared shortly after the Maxim. These were the American Hotchkiss and Browning models, which had slower rates of fire and could therefore be air-cooled and consequently lighter. They had slower rates of fire because whereas the Maxim gun's mechanism started the process for loading and firing the next round the moment the first round was fired, the Hotchkiss and Browning guns were both gas-operated. In gas-operated guns the breech mechanism is not operated by recoil, but by the propellant gas, part of which is bled off near the muzzle through a hole in the barrel wall. After passing through the hole, the gas is turned through another 90 degrees and then forces back a piston, which in turn drives the breech mechanism back against its spring. The firing of the next round then follows the same course as in the Maxim. Since the mechanism is not operated until the bullet has passed the hole in the barrel wall allowing the gas to be bled off, the rate of fire is necessarily slower.

The chief failing of the Browning and Hotchkiss designs was that although they needed no coolant for short bursts of fire, sustained fire caused the heat to mount and the barrel to expand, which seriously lowered the efficiency of the gun. An attempt to resolve this difficulty was made by Colonel Isaac Lewis of the United States with his gas-operated design. The Lewis gun provided its own cooling air by forcing a fast draught past the barrel: the passage of the bullets beyond a special fixture on the muzzle forced air down sixteen channels along the barrel to carry off the excess heat. This design was successful – despite a high number of 'stoppages' – and became the standard light machine-gun of the British in the First World War. It was succeeded in 1938 by the Bren, a very reliable LMG, which saw the British through the Second World War.

**The Big Guns**

The development of artillery did not for a time keep pace with that of small arms. But if the first half of the nineteenth century belonged to small arms, the second half belonged to the big guns. In an effort to make cannon more accurate, muzzle-loading rifled pieces were coming into service by the mid-1850s. This development, combined with a new type of shell, introduced by the Frenchman, Henri Paixhans, which was intended to penetrate the object fired at before exploding, rather than detonating on impact, made artillery an accurate and devastating weapon at previously unheard-of ranges. The effect of this combination on the navies of the world, at a time when they were about to introduce the Ironclad, was considerable, and all artillery was considerably advanced by the prodigious efforts of the various navies to produce guns that could outrange, without loss of accuracy, those of their rivals. The first advance made was in the evolution of projectiles with better ballistic qualities. The type evolved was of conoidal shape at the nose, and was fitted with copper driving bands to fit into the grooves of the rifling. These bands, like the rings on the Minié bullet, were forced into the grooves by the detonation of the pro-

**below left** The *mitrailleuse*. In 1870, when the Prussians still lacked a machine-gun, the French produced the *mitrailleuse*; up to then it has been a secret weapon, so secret in fact that little thought had been given to its tactical employment. As a result the French tended to use it, artillery-style, in batteries instead of well forward in support of the front-line infantry – which certainly reduced the weapon's effectiveness. **above** A .303-inch Lewis gun, Mark I, introduced in 1915. Its inventor, Colonel Isaac Lewis of the USA, successfully resolved problems of overheating with a gas-operated system that forced cooling air along the barrel. The Lewis became the standard light machine-gun of the British Army in the First World War. **below** A .303-inch Maxim machine-gun. This was the first truly successful, portable machine-gun; its rate of fire was so high that it had to be water-cooled. The Maxim gun first appeared in 1884.

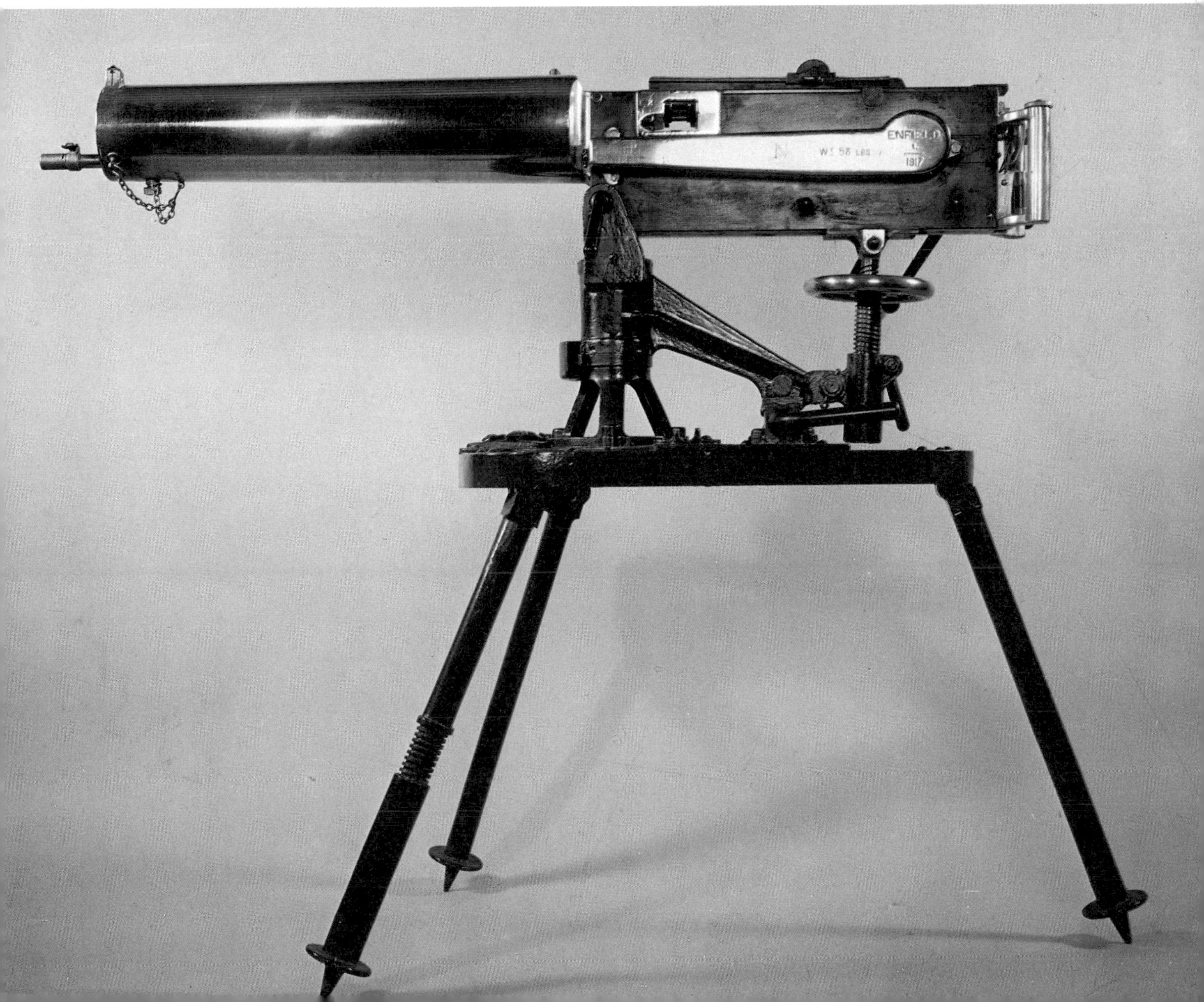

pellant and drove the shell round as it moved up the barrel.

With the improvements in shells and rifling, the usefulness of cast iron as a gun material was at an end. The result was the re-introduction of built-up guns, in which an inner tube carried the rifling, wound in miles of wire and covered by an outer tube. At first wrought iron was used, but this was quickly superseded by cast steel and finally by forged steel. As guns increased in calibre, both for naval and military uses, muzzle-loading was becoming very nearly impossible, and was extremely hazardous. Attempts to design breech-loading guns had proved unsuccessful in the past, but a solution was found in Germany by the Krupp Works in Essen shortly after the Crimean War (1853–6). This was the sliding wedge, a tapered wedge of steel which gave access to the breech when it had been moved to the right, and shut it off when it was moved again to the left.

By the time of the Franco-Prussian War, much of the German artillery had been re-equipped with breech-loaders and had a clear superiority over its French counterpart. After this lesson had been brought forcibly home by her defeat in 1871, France turned to the modernization of her artillery, and became the first nation in Europe to adopt for widespread service an American breech mechanism – the interrupted screw. In this system the outside of the breech-block and the inside of the breech have threads, with portions cut away from each so that when the gap in one part is matched against the threaded part in the other, the block can be swung open or shut on its hinges. All that is necessary to lock the block into place is to turn it a quarter of a turn so that the threads on breech and block mesh. Turning the block back unlocks the mechanism and allows the spent case to be extracted and a fresh round loaded.

The French then developed a variant, the eccentric screw, in which the centres of barrel and block are not on the same longitudinal axis. In this, there is only one position in which the hole in the block matches up to the breech, allowing a shell to be loaded. Any movement from this position locks the mechanism ready for firing.

**Problems of Recoil**

Another problem that was encountered as a result of the increase in calibre and power of heavy guns was that of recoil. All guns had to be relaid after each shot, since the recoil moved the gun slightly, but the problem of moving large guns back into position and relaying them promised to be a difficult and lengthy process, with a resultant loss in accuracy and rate of fire. Some system of overcoming recoil had to be found. The old type of muzzle-loaders had been held against recoil by blocks and tackles attached to stakes driven into the ground, but this was impractical in view of the tremendous forces generated by the newer breech-loading pieces.

above The breech mechanism that finally provided artillery weapons with a gas-tight fit. Known as the interrupted screw, it worked by fitting together the threads and flat portions of block and breech. **below** 'The Dictator', a giant mortar used by the Union Army from the beginning of 1865. This was the biggest gun made in the American Civil War.

The answer was simple in theory but more difficult in practice. Instead of mounting the gun rigidly on its carriage, so that the shock of recoil was transmitted from the gun to the carriage, it was found that by fitting a recoil mechanism which allowed the gun, or rather the barrel, to recoil on its own, relaying became unnecessary. This recoil mechanism took the form of an hydraulic cylinder, usually assisted by a spring, fixed rigidly to the carriage, with the piston attached to the gun barrel; as the barrel recoiled, the forces generated were used up in compressing the fluid in the cylinder, and little was transmitted to the carriage. There was, too, an added bonus in that as the recoil spent itself, the barrel was pushed back to its proper position by the fluid as it expanded again. As the technique became more sophisticated, the recoil action was used to open the breech and eject the spent case ready for the next round.

As guns developed, so did their shells. We have already mentioned the evolution of the shell from a generally round shape into a long, streamlined, conoidal form, with better ballistic qualities. At the same time the explosive used in shells was undergoing rapid changes. In 1882 the now-outdated black gunpowder was replaced as the explosive component of shells by picric acid, known variously as melanite and lyddite. But, being an acid, the explosive attacked the casings of shells and caused them very quickly to deteriorate. Picric acid was soon replaced by trinitrotoluene (TNT), a similar explosive but one which was more stable and did not attack the shell casings. In a period of merely forty years these advances, combined with the new smokeless propellants, altered artillery out of all recognition.

### Progress in Communications

During the middle period of the nineteenth century a number of innovations brought the techniques of communication firmly into the industrial age. Their revitalization took two principal forms. Firstly, the widespread growth of railways meant that armies could be moved and concentrated at far greater speeds than had been possible before; this advance also had far-reaching repercussions in the manner in which armies could be supplied, and railhead depots became an integral part of supply networks. Secondly, the introduction of the electric telegraph made instant contact possible over much greater distances: commanders could in future expect greater control in combat areas, and the latter in turn could be considerably increased in size without, necessarily, any sacrifice to efficiency.

The changes in signalling methods came about gradually. Up to the Crimean War commanders had to rely on drum and bugle to transmit their orders. Then came more sophisticated methods that involved semaphore flags and the heliograph – an instrument that used flashes of sunlight to send messages. In time the electric telegraph, invented by Samuel Morse in 1832, was

adopted by railway companies and cable lines were established across Europe and America. In its early days the field telegraph at the front was a less ambitious but nevertheless effective piece of machinery: in the Crimea, for example, Allied communications were set up by means of pairs of horse-drawn wagons, each equipped with batteries, telegraphic apparatus and enough wire to establish contact over ten or twelve miles. But by the end of the American Civil War the telegraph was widely used as part of an intricate communications network that extended even to reconnaissance balloons, now linked to the ground by telegraph wires.

All this progress did create some fresh pitfalls, however. Commanders, for instance, now found themselves for the first time at the end of a direct line to their political overlords; and there were some who thought this an unattractive proposition.

### The Changing Face of War

The Napoleonic Wars had been followed by a fairly long period of peace in Europe. The Dynasts, having re-established themselves through the Congress of Vienna (1814–15), were in no hurry to upset the old order by warring among themselves, and it is significant that their first use of force on a serious scale was in the suppression of a series of popular, if misguided, uprisings which marked the year 1848.

When a major war did come, in the Crimea, neither side displayed such efficiency or achieved such success as to encourage fresh exploits in the application of force. British administration and Russian tactics had not improved since 1812, and if the French did marginally better their showing at their next outing – the Italian campaign of 1859 – was unimpressive. It is true that they achieved their strategic concentration by railway, a move which

The big guns come of age. **above** A Prussian battery firing on Paris during the four-month siege of 1870–1. **right** British 4.7-inch naval guns in action at Colenso in the Boer War, 1899.

the great Napoleon would, one feels, have approved, but the bloodbaths of Magenta and Solferino were evidence of gallantry rather than tactical skill.

The American Civil War, a long slogging-match between improvised armies, seemed to demonstrate that while strategy – with its new adjuncts, the electric telegraph and the railway – was becoming swifter and surer, the art of tactics was becoming infernally difficult. The effects of long-range rifle fire on troops who still clung to the close-order formations of Waterloo were devastating. Now men resorted to the axe and the spade, and though the fortifications they constructed were rudimentary compared to those of the present century, they effectively slowed down the forward movements of formations that on occasions outnumbered the defenders by as much as three to one.

Just when Mars seemed in fact to be losing his touch, modern Prussia emerged with her first versions of the *blitzkrieg*. The 1864 campaign against so feeble a military power as Denmark proved but little, but the swift blows by which Prussia then won the leadership of Germany at Sadowa (Königgratz) in 1866, and consolidated the German Empire on the battlefields of 1870, showed that the disciples of von Clausewitz could still further their policies with an efficiency and a speed which made war seem worthwhile.

At Sedan, where Napoleon III and a French army of 83,000 surrendered, the Germans felt, not without reason, that they had achieved a new breakthrough in the sphere of rapid conquest. But other governments and peoples were already beginning to look askance at the size and expense of their armies and their navies, as well as at the uncertain results which the wars of that century had brought. They were beginning to wonder whether violence in the conduct of international affairs was still a useful instrument, one which statesmen could reasonably hope to employ with any real and lasting advantage to the peoples they governed.

NO PLAN OF OPERATIONS
WAS EVER PUT IN WRITING . . .
I HAD NO PRECONCEIVED IDEA
BEYOND A COMPLETE DETERMINATION
TO TAKE UP THE OFFENSIVE
WITH ALL MY FORCES.

*MARSHAL JOSEPH JOFFRE, 1914*

**CHAPTER 6**

# *The Great War*

In August 1914 a major European war broke out for the first time in forty years. By the time it ended just over four years later, it had involved nations all over the earth and had become the greatest conflict in the history of mankind, changing the political, economic and social conditions of victors and vanquished alike – and few of them for the better.

Militarily, the Great War was the proving ground for the weapons developed since the Crimean War sixty years earlier, and the forcing ground for the invention of a whole new range of military hardware.

The war opened with a devastating German sweep into France, made possible by the meticulous planning of the German Chief of Staff, Field Marshal von Schlieffen, by an efficient mobilization scheme and by the high state of preparedness of the German Army. The weapon that ensured the success of that first advance was sheer impetus, the fact that the Germans kept up their onslaught, never giving the Allies a chance to recover their balance until they had reached the Marne south and east of Paris. But the Germans failed in their strategic aim of encircling Paris and forcing the French to capitulate, and their subsequent defeat on the Marne compelled them to fall back and consolidate a line, albeit still in France, while they prepared their next moves. Mobile warfare ended at that point, to be replaced by the drudgery of trench warfare.

**New Weapons**

Much of the new hardware that jointed its first war in 1914–18 had been made possible by the invention of the petrol-driven engine by Gottlieb Daimler in 1882. So-called 'motor war cars' were already in existence by the turn of the century, and a semi-armoured *automitrailleuse* (machine-gun car), built by Charron, Girardot & Voigt, was displayed at the 1902 Paris Motor Show. Later, in the years leading up to the war, numerous experimental armoured vehicles were built: these consisted in broad terms of modified passenger cars or light trucks armed with a machine-gun and fitted with armour-plating and a revolving turret to give all-round fire.

By 1914 automobile manufacturers were alive to the enormous scope for their machines as assault vehicles (though still largely road-bound and unequal to cross-country operation), as mobile anti-aircraft weapons and as troop transports and general supply vehicles, Indeed, three months after the outbreak of war vast numbers of these new machines – perhaps as many as 20,000 – had been pressed into service on the Allied side as supply and transport vehicles. However, as the war became bogged down in the stalemate of its first winter, few motor vehicles proved capable of churning through the mud that surrounded the combat area. In such circumstances – although armoured cars were used throughout the war in the Middle Eastern theatre – the horse remained universally in demand for purposes of cavalry action and for the transport of artillery and supplies at the front.

**The Flying Arm**

Meanwhile, in an altogether different and equally novel sphere, great progress had been made since Orville Wright had first taken to the air in 1903 in his historic *Flyer*. At first, though, the 400-foot airships of Count Ferdinand von Zeppelin had seemed to many people to be potentially the most useful form of military aircraft, to be employed for observing troop and fleet movements and for dropping bombs. In the event, however, these lighter-than-air craft proved unacceptably easy targets once they were in range of enemy guns and they were also unreliable in poor weather conditions; of the sixty-one airships originally commissioned by Germany only ten survived the war.

Nevertheless conventional or heavier-than-air machines made great leaps forward in the years between 1903 and 1914, and on the outbreak of war the British had fifty-five aircraft in service, the French 155 and the Germans 260. These early military aircraft were used solely for reconnaissance purposes, photographing the enemy's defences and putting its own artillery on target by means of Morse-code radio messages – another new development in warfare that had been made possible by Guglielmo Marconi's pioneering work in wireless telegraphy.

In due course aircraft were armed with machine-guns in an effort to prevent enemy flyers from carrying out their reconnaissance work and for self-protection. The guns were usually operated by the observer, who was seated either in front of the pilot in the nose or behind him to guard the tail. Eventually it became possible for the pilot to become his own gunner, firing his machine-gun directly forwards through the propellor-blades, which were fitted at first with special deflector-plates and then with an interrupter gear which stopped the gun from firing when a propellor-blade passed in front of the muzzle. Using the latter device Fokker monoplanes swept every rival from the sky in the so-called 'Fokker Scourge', which began in October 1915 and lasted until May 1916.

Later in the war aircraft were developed that did more than reconnoitre and fight each other. Bombers had existed since 1914, when Sopwith Tabloids carried out valuable raids on Cologne and Düsseldorf armed with light 20-pound bombs. But these were small-scale operations. However, by the autumn of 1918 the British firm of Handley Page had twin-engined machines able to carry a 1,650-pound bomb or an equivalent weight of smaller bombs.

But, for all their later progress, in the winter of 1914 aircraft could do no more than provide a reconnaissance service to the armies on the ground, while the petrol-driven vehicles mentioned above were equally incapable of influencing the *impasse* in the trenches. That was where the Great War was doomed to be fought and, eventually, decided.

### The Trench War: Tactics and Weapons

The chief tactical lesson to be learned from the opening campaign was simple: attacks by infantry in close order were suicidal, for firepower was now so great that the attackers were mown down before they had a chance of closing with the enemy. The lesson was well learned by the Germans, but not by the French, who were to continue close-order assaults for at least another two years, relying on the false hope that *élan* was everything, and that the bayonet was the supreme weapon of the battlefield. The price of this romantic illusion was hundreds of thousands of lives.

The only army to emerge with credit from this first campaign was the British. The Boer War (1899–1902) had taught it the value of aimed firepower and of open-order combat tactics, and with these it inflicted considerable tactical defeats on numerically superior German forces. But that was not enough, and in the winter of 1914, after the Race to the Sea and the First Battle of Ypres, the combatants settled down to a form of latter-day siege warfare in trenches which ran from the sea near Nieuport on the Belgian coast to the Swiss frontier south of Belfort. The trenches, defended by barbed wire and machine-guns, were to remain along much the same line for the next four years: to break it was the tactical problem that now became the main aim of weapons development.

Unfortunately for the assaulting units the first attacks on fortified trench systems were undertaken with the same weapons that had been in service at the beginning of the war. The infantry went over the top with rifle and bayonet, and was covered by the fire of machine-guns sited in its own front line. Artillery support was provided by the relatively light field artillery of the day – the French 75-mm, the German 7.7-cm and the British 18-pounder – although, significantly, the Germans had a larger proportion of medium pieces than either the British or French. The defending infantry had almost exactly the same weapons, with belts of barbed wire in front of its trenches to check the assault waves; these were launched at ranges so close that men armed with Brown Bess could still have hit their opponents (in some British zones the opposing trenches were no more than twenty-five yards apart).

Tactics were simple. First came an artillery bombardment, more or less prolonged according to the state of ammunition supply, and intended to blow gaps in the barbed wire and drive the defenders down into the dug-outs which soon became an integral part of a well-prepared trench system. Then the artillery barrage lifted, and the infantrymen went in. Often they were cut down by rifle and machine-gun fire before they had reached the enemy's wire. When they did reach it they were likely to find that the wire had not been cut: this was because most of the artillery had been firing shrapnel, which was useless against wire, high explosive being in short supply. Even when HE (high explosive) was employed, the small amount used in a field-gun shell was insufficient to make much of an impression on an extensive belt of barbed wire. Finally, if the attackers did succeed in getting to the wire and through it, they had to assault the front-line trench itself. The defenders, who on the whole did not suffer heavy casualties as a result of the bombardments, knew when the barrage lifted the exact timing of the enemy offensive; when it came they were standing-to, their fingers on the trigger. And if the attackers managed to take the front trench, there were two or three more beyond containing the defenders' reserves, who by then would be preparing to counter-attack.

#### Slaughter by Machine-gun

The main weapon of defence was the machine-gun. All the armies had been short of them at the beginning of the war – the Germans less so than the others – but the lessons of the first trench attacks brought home how indispensable they were. Sited in well-positioned, carefully

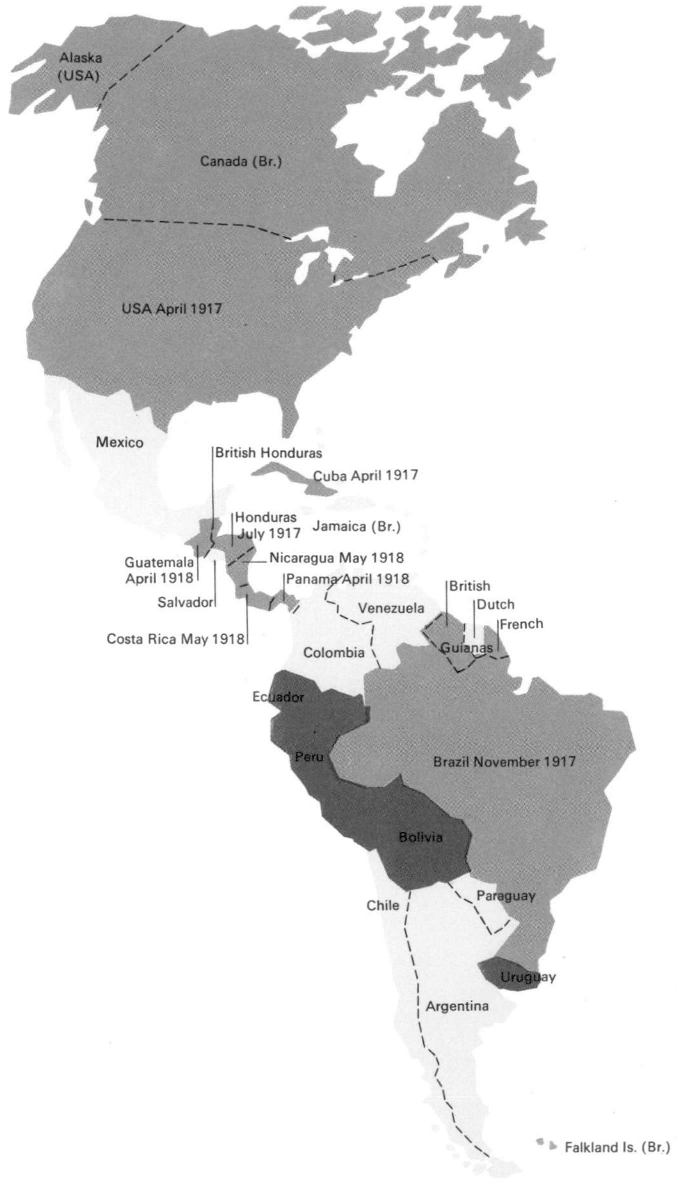
Alaska (USA)
Canada (Br.)
USA April 1917
Mexico
British Honduras
Cuba April 1917
Honduras July 1917
Jamaica (Br.)
Guatemala April 1918
Nicaragua May 1918
Panama April 1918
Salvador
Costa Rica May 1918
Venezuela
British
Dutch
French
Guianas
Colombia
Ecuador
Peru
Brazil November 1917
Bolivia
Chile
Paraguay
Uruguay
Argentina
Falkland Is. (Br.)

protected emplacements in the front line, the machine-guns, supplied with ample stocks of ammunition and interlocking fields of fire, could enfilade the advancing infantry and reap a terrible toll. What is more remarkable is that the lessons of trench warfare were not even novel. Fifty years before, in the American Civil War, the same factors had applied, and then there had not even been machine-guns and magazine-rifles. Both the Confederacy and the Union had learned the futility of frontal attacks on a dug-in position. Furthermore, the conditions under which the First World War was fought had been rehearsed only ten years earlier in the Russo-Japanese War (1904–5). All the Western powers had sent observers, and they had clearly seen the incredible cost in lives that had to be paid in frontal assaults against modern firepower. French, German and British generals had largely ignored the tactical lessons of these two wars, or, if not, had failed to think out solutions to them. For this their men were to pay with their lives.

The first to have a glimpse of the light were the Germans, who launched only two major frontal assaults after the end of the Second Battle of Ypres in 1915: these were at Verdun in 1916, an offensive calculated to 'bleed the French army to death', and in their five-act offensive in the spring and early summer of 1918. But they had other fronts to the east – in East Prussia and Poland, and later in the Ukraine, until the collapse of Russia in 1917 – where manoeuvre was still possible. The British and French continued with their costly and unsuccessful 'pushes' throughout the period; of these only the last series, from 8 August to the Armistice on 11 November 1918, was successful. And even that success may be attributed to massive American reinforcements and German exhaustion rather than to any overwhelming technical or tactical superiority on the part of the Allies.

### Grenades and Mortars

In the meantime the men in the front line shaped their own methods of assault and survival. Mud-filled trenches became their homes, grenades and mortars their principal weapons. The latter had proved very successful

THE FIRST WORLD WAR

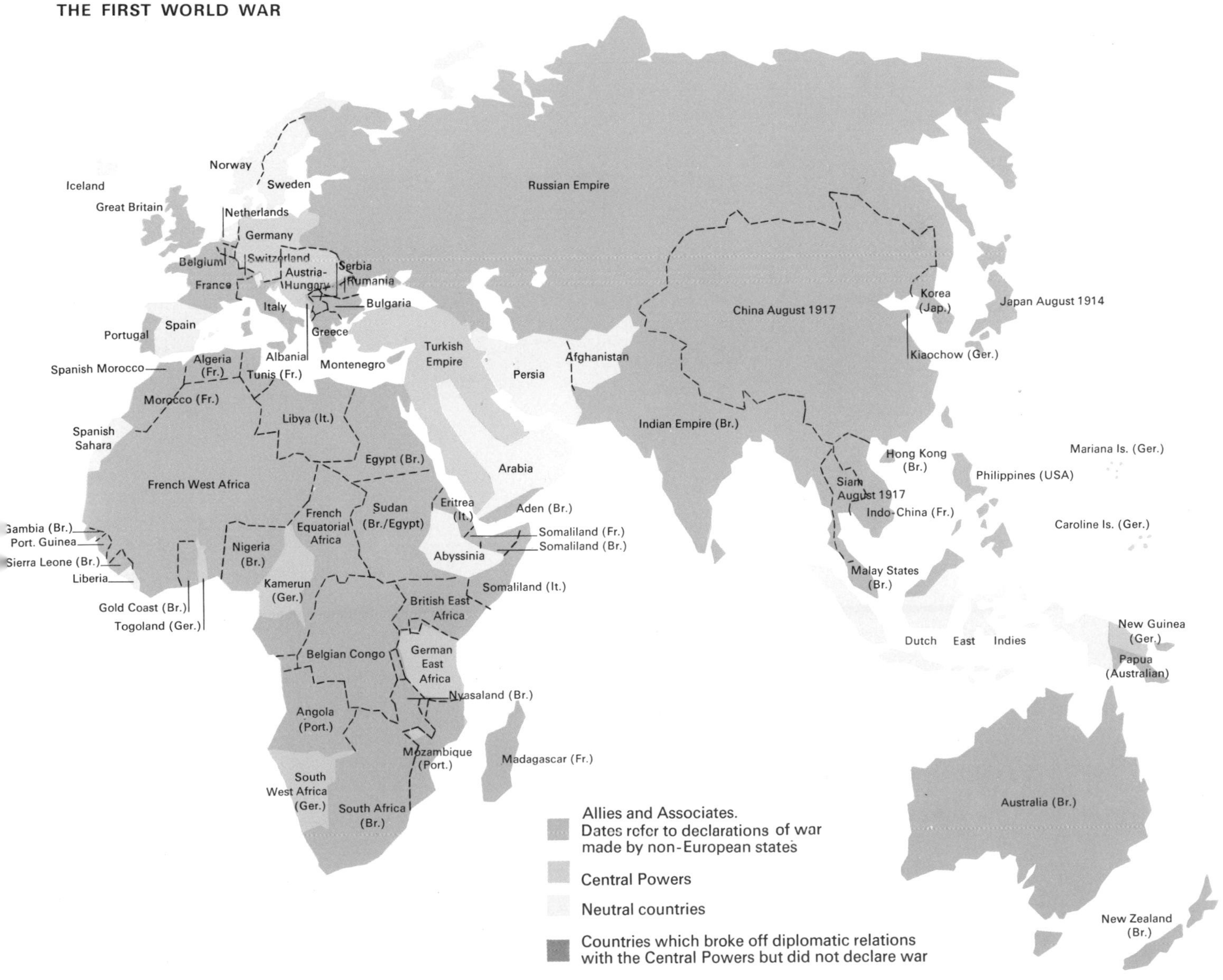
Iceland
Great Britain
Norway
Sweden
Russian Empire
Netherlands
Germany
Belgium
Switzerland
Austria-Hungary
Serbia
Rumania
France
Italy
Bulgaria
Portugal
Spain
Greece
Albania
Montenegro
Turkish Empire
Afghanistan
Persia
Spanish Morocco
Algeria (Fr.)
Tunis (Fr.)
Morocco (Fr.)
Libya (It.)
Spanish Sahara
Egypt (Br.)
Arabia
French West Africa
French Equatorial Africa
Sudan (Br./Egypt)
Eritrea (It.)
Aden (Br.)
Somaliland (Fr.)
Somaliland (Br.)
Abyssinia
Gambia (Br.)
Port. Guinea
Sierra Leone (Br.)
Liberia
Nigeria (Br.)
Kamerun (Ger.)
Somaliland (It.)
Gold Coast (Br.)
Togoland (Ger.)
British East Africa
Belgian Congo
German East Africa
Nyasaland (Br.)
Angola (Port.)
Mozambique (Port.)
Madagascar (Fr.)
South West Africa (Ger.)
South Africa (Br.)
China August 1917
Korea (Jap.)
Japan August 1914
Kiaochow (Ger.)
Indian Empire (Br.)
Hong Kong (Br.)
Mariana Is. (Ger.)
Philippines (USA)
Siam August 1917
Indo-China (Fr.)
Caroline Is. (Ger.)
Malay States (Br.)
Dutch East Indies
New Guinea (Ger.)
Papua (Australian)
Australia (Br.)
New Zealand (Br.)
Allies and Associates.
Dates refer to declarations of war made by non-European states
Central Powers
Neutral countries
Countries which broke off diplomatic relations with the Central Powers but did not declare war

in the American Civil War; the former had not been seen much since the eighteenth century – except in the hands of the assassin! Both sides spent the winter of 1914–15 devising home-made weapons of this sort. Ordinary jam tins filled with explosive were used as grenades; lengths of pipe were turned into mortars to hurl home-made bombs into the enemy's trenches and machine-gun emplacements, where artillery shells, because of their relatively flat trajectory, could only do damage by a direct hit. Special knives and clubs and armour were evolved for trench conditions as well as methods of aiming and firing rifles over the top of the parapet while the marksman remained in the safety of his trench. In time these individual, haphazard inventions were taken up, improved and put into mass production, especially the grenade and the trench mortar.

The two most famous grenades were the German stick grenade, which kept the jam-jar shape for the explosive part and added a handle at the base with which to throw the whole contraption, and the British Mills bomb, a

Military hardware tested for the first time in the Great War. **right** Peerless armoured cars, fitted with twin machine-gun turrets, 1918. These and other predominantly road-bound vehicles like them could only come into their own once the great trench *impasse* had given way to periods of comparatively mobile war. **below** One of Count von Zeppelin's lighter-than-air craft with (inset) a British Royal Naval Air Service pilot aiming a bomb over the side of his machine.

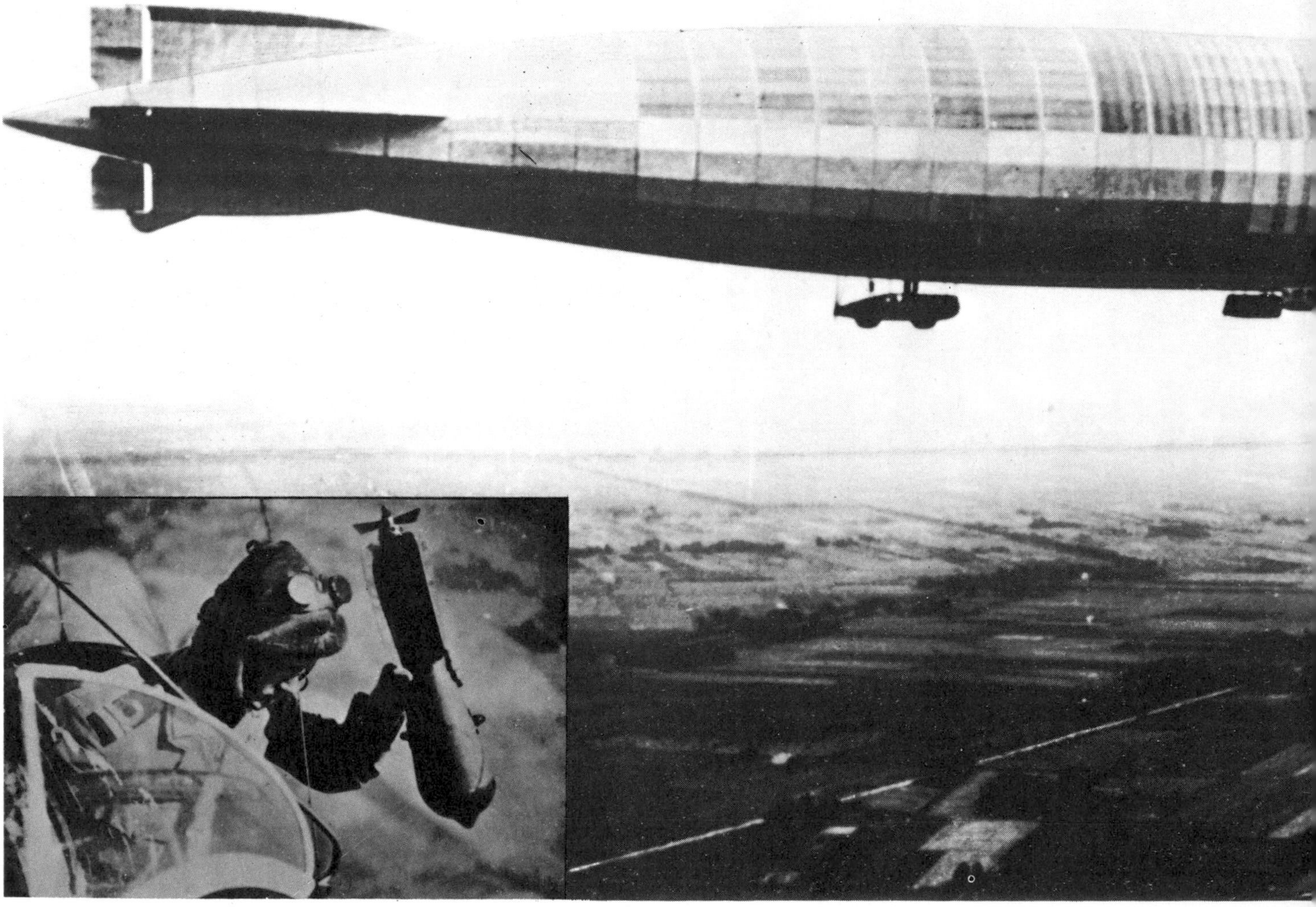

small ovaloid grenade, the walls of which were segmented to break up into a dozen or so shrapnel fragments on explosion. Both the German and British bombs had delayed-action fuses of between four and seven seconds in duration. The Mills bomb was filled with a new high explosive, amatol, which was being introduced for shells and grenades by the British in 1915. This was a derivative of TNT which had more oxygen in it, giving it a greater explosive power. It was so successful that the Germans started to manufacture it as well.

**Experiments with Gas**

Early in 1915 the Germans were developing new weapons. The first of these was poison gas. After a trial run in Russia, it was used for the first time on the Western Front on 22 April 1915, when a cloud of chlorine gas was released from cylinders in the German front line to float down on an easterly wind to the Allied trenches. Its tactical success was considerable. All along the front on which the gas had been released the Germans made what were by First World War standards extensive gains. But they could not effect a breakthrough because the Allied defence positions in depth were unaffected by the gas as it dispersed in the wind – and the German troops, not surprisingly, displayed some reluctance to walk into it. Gas cylinders were also vulnerable to counter-battery fire. Not only did the wind tend to disperse the gas very swiftly, but the prevailing wind on the Western Front during most of the year was westerly and favoured the use of gas clouds by the Allies!

The Germans, having been too clever by half, now found that the best solution was to deliver the gas by shell, for though the quantity delivered was smaller, it did at least arrive without waste at the desired spot. Soon the Allies developed masks to give some protection against the growing number of poison gases employed by the Germans. The gases for the most part attacked the respiratory tract and the nervous system; later in the war the Germans introduced mustard gas, which incapacitated men by producing blisters on whatever part of the body it touched. To this there was no effective counter, but luckily for them the Allies won the war soon after its introduction. The Allies themselves also produced gas in vast quantities and used it with similar success against the Germans. If this singularly unpleasant weapon was not used in the Second World War it was not due to any humanity on the part of the contestants but more to its relative ineffectiveness as a battle-winner.

**The Flamethrower**

Another new weapon was first used by the Germans in July 1915 – the flamethrower. This was a cylinder strapped to the back of its operator which contained an oil-derived combustible fluid, the propellant force being supplied by compressed gas kept in the same container as the fluid. As it emerged from the nozzle at the end of the tube leading from the container, the oil was ignited by an automatic device, and sprayed a jet of flaming fluid up to a range of about twenty yards.

The flamethrower was first used at Hooge and scored a tactical surprise, but its use was at first limited as only small numbers were ready for service. In time the device was improved considerably and produced a jet of flame shooting some forty yards with a continuous duration of up to two minutes. But even the later apparatus was bulky and heavy, and prevented the flamethrower from becoming anything more than a useful adjunct to infantry attacks, especially on pillboxes and dugouts.

**More and More Hard Pounding!**

Meanwhile, army staffs continued to work on ways of breaking through the trench systems of the Western Front. The Germans were waiting, building up their strength for the decisive blow, but the Allies kept hammering away at the German defences in attack after costly attack. The only solution the conservatively minded staff could think of was increased artillery preparation before the infantry went in. Surely, their reasoning ran, if we increase the number and calibre of the shells fired, there will come a point when the Germans must be overwhelmed? Following this doctrine, preliminary artillery bombardments were gradually lengthened until they were anything up to a week in duration with several thousand guns, ranging from the 18-pounders to monstrous 16-inch pieces, taking part. The result was as before. At the first sign of a heavy bombardment, the Germans pulled back from their front line, letting the millions of shells rain down on thinly held positions, which they reoccupied as the barrage lifted, in good time to slaughter the approaching infantry. And even after this sort of enormous artillery barrage, the infantry often found that the wire had not been cut.

**Assault by Mining**

Another method tried to break through defence lines was mining. The idea was started – or rather revived – by the British, but was soon adopted by both sides. The theory, as is so often the case, was simple: all one had to do was dig a tunnel under the enemy's line, enlarge it to a large cavern at the end, fill this with explosive and then blow the enemy's trench line to pieces. The infantry could then exploit the gap in the enemy's line to start an offensive action.

In practice matters were entirely different. The tunnel-digging often had to be performed in the wrong sort of soil and in wet conditions where the danger of cave-ins was considerable. An alert enemy would be listening for activity under the surface, and would try either to blow in the tunnel from one of its own or break into it, kill the enemy's miners and exploit the tunnel for its own use. But nevertheless the system worked. At Messines (7 June 1917) the British Second Army under General Herbert Plumer put mines containing over one million pounds of explosive under the German front line and blew holes

**above** A Vickers Gunbus, a two-seater biplane with a 'pusher' engine and propeller situated behind the wings. The gunner-observer sat in the nose and was armed with a .303-inch Lewis machine-gun. Air combat was later revolutionized by the interrupter gear, a device which made it possible for pilots to fire through the front propeller without striking the blades.

The big guns of the First World War. **above left** A German 42-cm heavy mortar. **left** A French rail gun booms across the cornfields. **above** The Paris Gun, a gigantic weapon used by the Germans in 1918 to shell Paris from a range of over sixty-seven miles. **below** An Allied 60-pounder battery at Cape Helles during the Dardanelles expedition.

several hundred feet wide and over a hundred feet deep in places, with a blast that could be felt as far away as London. Plumer's victory was the greatest the British had won so far. But the problem was still exploitation.

It was here that the Allied High Command made one of its major errors, for it assumed that the cavalry waiting behind the lines could move up quickly and pour through the gap. This never came off. The Germans had usually sealed off the breach by the time the cavalry arrived at the front, where it could hardly move as a result of the devastation caused by massed artillery fire. Even if the cavalry had managed to pass through the breach, it then had to face dug-in positions equipped with machine-guns and defended by barbed wire. Given such conditions, cavalry could clearly not be expected to offer a lasting solution to the deadlock on the Western Front.

### A Prelude to Armour: the First Tanks

The potential answer to the problem appeared late in 1916. This was the tank, a tracked and armoured vehicle, mounting light guns and machine-guns, and able to move around with comparative freedom in the face of rifle and machine-gun fire. In the tank armoured protection, firepower and a measure of mobility were combined. It could, moreover, dispense with artillery support to knock down barbed wire and subdue pill-boxes and other machine-gun emplacements, since it was able to trample down the former itself, ignore the latter and advance over trench systems with little fear of being stopped before it reached the open country beyond.

Here, then, was the ideal weapon both for creating and exploiting the breakthrough. But the Allied High Command, impatient for success, insisted on using the first models in penny-packets as soon as they arrived in France. Had those whose decision it was waited for the teething troubles to be ironed out and for a large number of tanks to be produced, a decisive attack might have been mounted on a wide front by hundreds of the new vehicles. In the event tanks performed useful service at the end of the Battle of the Somme, but suffered heavy losses as a result of the inexperience of their crews and the mechanical unreliability of their engines and transmissions. More important still, in the short term, the Germans learned of the tank and started to develop first an anti-tank rifle and then an anti-tank gun.

A vital problem affecting the success of these early tanks was their dependence on heavy armour at the expense of mobility. The reason for this order of priorities is to be found in the very nature of the stalemate situation in the trenches that the tank was designed to break. After two years of static war, the officers of the High Command had been almost literally sucked into the quagmire which they had created, and as a result few were able to see beyond the limits of siege warfare. Thus, when the first Allied tanks loomed up before an astonished enemy on the Somme, they were envisaged by their inventors as a form of special siege vehicle, a modern 'sow', rather than a weapons carrier. The tank was immune to machine-gun fire and could therefore break into the enemy front line to clear a way for the infantry: it was not generally visualized that the vehicle might have any wider, more far-ranging use.

The first tank to go into action (15 September 1916) was the Mark I or 'Mother'. The now-familiar lozenge shape was the direct result of the requirement for a vehicle able to cross an eight-foot ditch. In fact 'Mother' could tackle a ten-foot gap, but she had many disadvantages, not least being the need to employ no less than four of her eight-man crew on driving her – the commander, who co-ordinated the operation, one man to change the main gears and one man to control each track. Another disadvantage lay in the bulky side sponsons or half-turrets carrying the guns (a centrally mounted rotating turret would have increased the overall height to an unacceptable level). In addition, the poor power-to-weight ratio gave a speed of only 3.7 miles per hour to this 28-ton vehicle. Furthermore, despite the fact that armour protection received perhaps rather more than its share of emphasis in the design, the 10mm of protection was barely adequate against machine-gun fire and was certainly not proof against a direct hit from a high-explosive shell. This meant that she was vulnerable to the normal field-gun. Nevertheless the vehicle was a workable proposition, and if the original tactics failed to make the best use of her, at least a different dimension had been added to the battlefield.

Despite 'Mother's evident shortcomings, the British continued to develop the basic design. At the same time, though, they were developing a faster, lighter model, the medium tank, which was designed with a lower hull and had its armament mounted in a rudimentary turret on the hull top. The two different types were the origin of a fallacious idea that was to dog British tank design until the middle of the Second World War twenty-five years later. This was that two types of tank were necessary, one to co-operate with the infantry, which needed heavy armour and armament but no great speed, and one to act in the cavalry role, with lighter armament but a much higher speed. The French were also designing tanks along the same lines and fell into the same trap as the British. It was to be left, ironically, to the defeated Germans to realize where the future of the tank really lay.

### Cambrai: a Turning-point

After their début in September 1916 and throughout most of 1917, British tanks continued to be used in driblets and in support of the infantry. It was not until the great Passchendaele offensive of that year had ground to a halt in the mud, with very heavy casualties and very little success, that the pleas of the Tank Corps staff for a mass attack on ground favourable to tanks were listened to. The attack, largely the product of Colonel J. F. C.

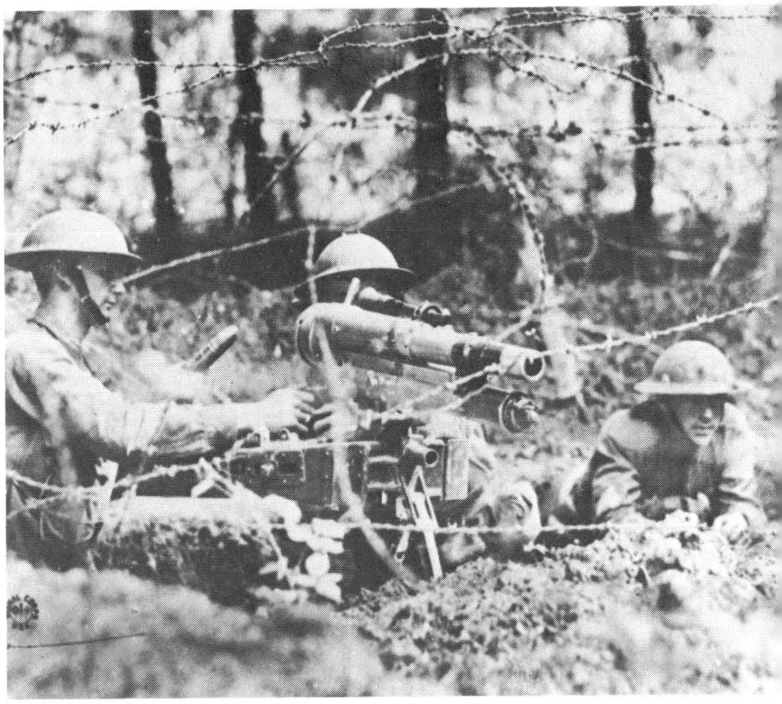

The sheer firepower of the machine-gun forced the armies of both sides belatedly to revise their infantry tactics. **above** A German machine-gun post in the hills. **right** American gunners dug in behind barbed wire in Alsace, 1918. **below** British Lewis-armed motor-cycle units in training, 1916.

3.4

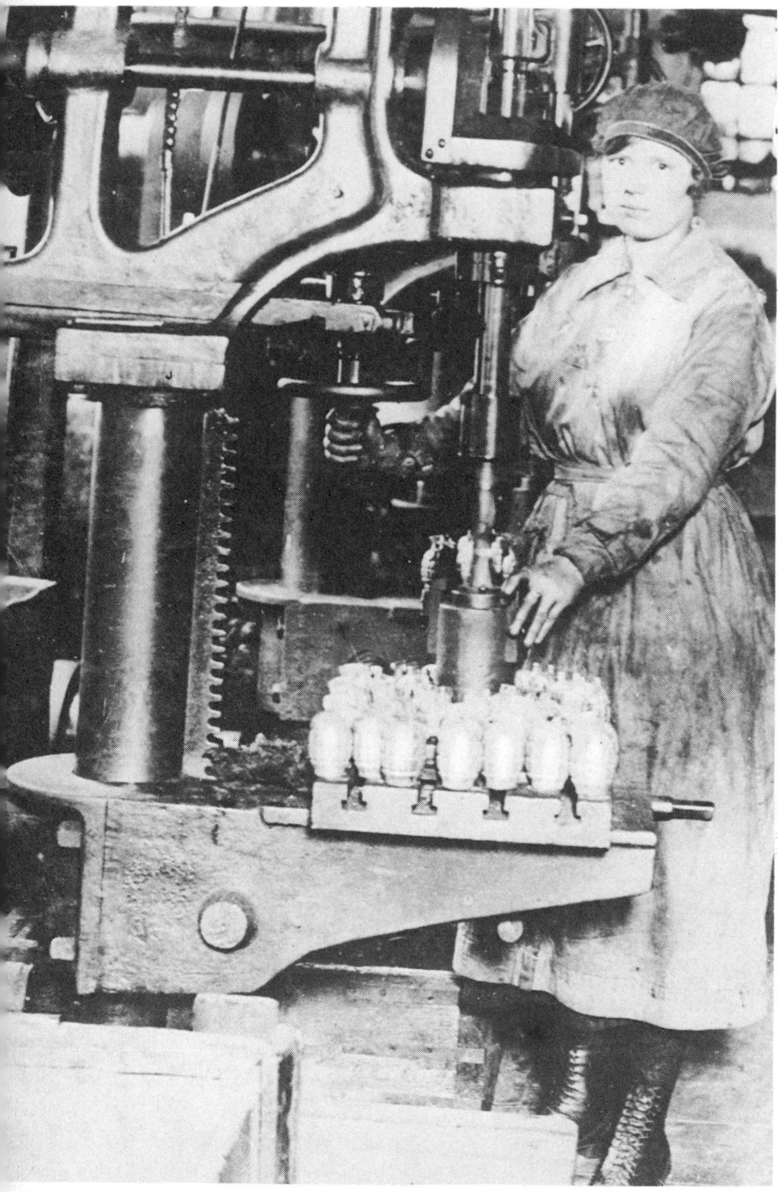

Girl in a grenade factory. Industrially manufactured grenades were in short supply during the first winter of the war, and until production caught up with demand the men in the trenches improvised with jam-tin bombs and other home-made devices.

Fuller's active mind, began on 20 November 1917 at Cambrai and proved to be a turning-point as far as the use of tanks in the First World War was concerned. The Tank Corps staff insisted on absolute surprise – hence no artillery bombardment – and the Germans were faced at the outset and without warning by a large number of tanks tearing a gap in their wire. These tanks, once through, quickly shot up the German front-line trenches, while others carrying fascines (large bundles of palings) dropped them in the trenches and crossed over on top of them. Infantry poured through the gaps to clear up pockets of resistance whilst overhead aircraft co-operated by bombing and machine-gunning opportunity targets in the battle area. A massive breakthrough was achieved and with minimal British casualties.

Success at Cambrai would have been complete had it been possible to exploit the initial breakthrough. But this proved unattainable: most of the horsed cavalry held in reserve for this task was unable to get through the mud, wire and chaos of the battle area; those that did were quickly held up by German machine-gun fire. Thus Cambrai demonstrated the fallacy of the current idea that provided the trench system could be gapped, mobile warfare would automatically follow. Since the cavalry was unable to follow up the advantages gained by the use of tanks, the question posed by these early actions was how armoured vehicles could best be used, not only to break through enemy defences but also to exploit such preliminary successes.

The Mark IV tank which took the field at Cambrai was an improvement on the Mark I, though of the same fundamental layout and with the same armament of two 6-pounders and four machine-guns; there was also a so-called 'female' version, armed only with machine-guns, which had thicker armour. However, the limited speed and endurance of these vehicles prevented their use for exploiting a breakthrough and the development of a lighter, faster tank for this purpose was demanded. The British solution was the Whippet, a tank of some fourteen tons mounting four machine-guns and capable of eight miles per hour. The Whippet first saw action in 1918 as the so-called 'cavalry' tank and proved its worth at Amiens.

### German Counter-moves with Stormtroopers

The German answer to the tank was not to reply in kind. Her general staff as yet saw no great merit in these vehicles and only some twenty German-designed tanks were built in the whole of the First World War. (This figure compares with approximate totals for the British of 2,630, and 3,870 for the French – most of the latter being Renault light tanks.)

Instead, in the Spring of 1918, the Germans under General Ludendorff launched a series of infantry offensives designed to force the Allies out of the war before the full weight of American reinforcement could make itself

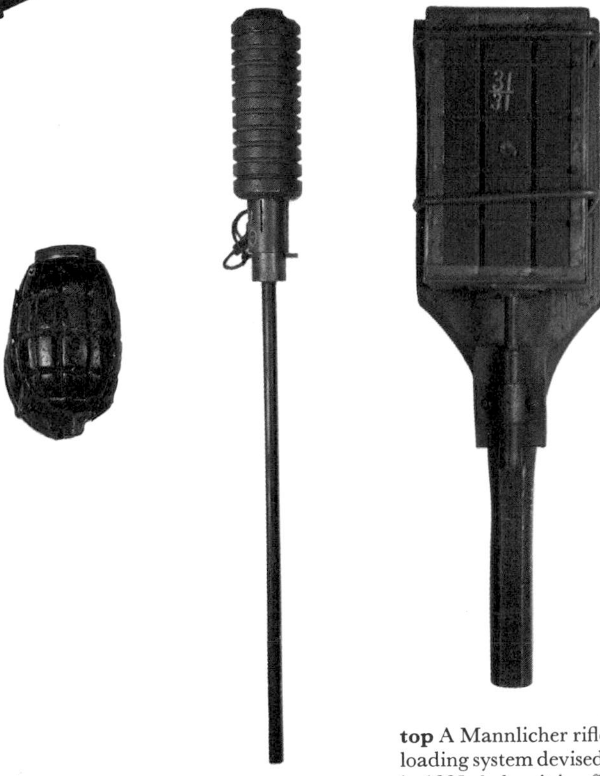

**top** A Mannlicher rifle incorporating the clip loading system devised by Ferdinand Mannlicher in 1885; below it is a Short-Magazine Lee-Enfield rifle fitted with grenade and bayonet. **above** A selection of grenades. From left to right are: a No. 5 Mills bomb; a stick grenade, and a square-box bomb, also propelled by hand like the version (above right) about to be thrown by a German infantryman, who holds the fuse between his teeth. **below** Setting up a light trench mortar. These high-trajectory weapons were ideal for the short-range work of lobbing bombs into the enemy's trenches; they were, in addition, lighter and cheaper to manufacture than conventional varieties of gun or howitzer.

The gas war. **above left** Machine-gunners in gas masks at the Battle of the Somme, 1916. **left** A battery of German 18-cm *Gaswerfer*. **below left** French infantrymen pose defiantly, ready to beat off a gas attack with bayonet and primitive nose pad.

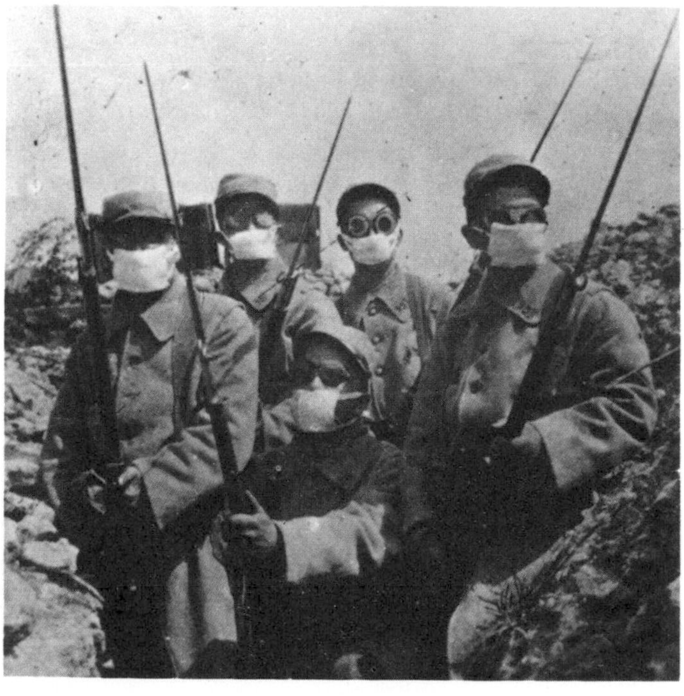

felt. The United States had declared war on Germany in April 1917, but her acute shortage of all military supplies and equipment meant that, as in 1861, her large numbers of men were slow to take the field. When they did, however, their influence became increasingly important to the Allied effort.

In their Spring offensives the Germans introduced the Western Front to new tactics and new weapons. The former are generally referred to as 'Hutier tactics' after General Oscar von Hutier, whose Eighth Army had used them for the first time in September 1917 at Riga against the Russians. (This was, incidentally, two months before Lenin and Trotsky seized power in Russia and three months before the armistice which took her out of the war and brought an end to hostilities on the Eastern Front.) The new method of assault was applied in the West in the following manner: instead of trying to bludgeon a hole in the Allied line with a prolonged artillery bombardment, the Germans used a short sharp barrage from hundreds of guns, which then turned into a creeping barrage, that is, one in which the range is slowly increased. Immediately behind this followed a new type of infantry, the stormtrooper, in many ways similar to the old light infantryman. The stormtroopers were lightly armed and had the task of infiltrating the Allied front, penetrating to the artillery lines and overrunning them, ignoring on their way any pockets of resistance which

above A German flamethrower; this weapon was introduced by the Germans in 1915. below In Palestine, away from the claustrophobic conditions of the Western Front, a different, more traditional war was fought. This photograph shows the 1st Hertfordshire Yeomanry with, to the rear, the Bikari Camel Corps on a reconnaissance mission, 1915.

could be mopped up by the ordinary infantry moving in the stormtroopers' wake. The tactics worked very well at first, but Germany no longer had the strategic means to follow up and exploit the gaps made in the Allied lines in the first three offensives. The last two were disasters because by then the Allies had found an answer to the new German tactics. They pulled back from the front line as soon as the bombardment started and then destroyed the stormtroopers with machine-gun and artillery fire as they advanced.

### The Submachine-gun

A new weapon introduced in 1918 was the Bergmann submachine-gun. This was used by the stormtroopers and was in effect a recoil-operated, air-cooled light machine-gun, adapted for use by one man. Not very accurate, its uses lay in close-quarter fighting, where fire-power was more important than aim. Although this particular weapon was only used in 1918, submachine-guns were of course destined to have a far greater role in future wars; the Bergmann gun was also the forerunner of the Thompson version which was to be the weapon of Dillinger and Capone in the heyday of the Chicago gangster.

### The War Ends

The Allied reply to the German offensive effectively ended the war. On 18 July French tanks and infantry drove the Germans back from Rheims to beyond the Marne. On 8 August (Ludendorff's 'black day of the

German Army') a British tank and infantry force that included ninety-six of the lighter Whippet tanks pushed the enemy away from Amiens and in retreat towards Flanders. Then, on 26 September, the Americans attacked in the south. Fighting continued on all fronts and on 4 October Germany, exhausted, requested an armistice; fighting ceased on 11 November.

### The Lessons of Mass Warfare

The First World War left the world in serious doubt as to the value of modern warfare. It went on too long: it cost too much in blood and suffering, and in treasure. Statesmen thought the generals were a lot of arrogant muddlers who did not know their trade. Generals thought that statesmen were a lot of charlatans who wanted their dirty work done, but were not prepared to provide the tools. But they could not deny that men had been provided, masses of them, and, for the most part, excellent material. The trouble was that in 1914 most of the masses, who were to fight each other for the next four years, were untrained. It followed that they never would be. The volunteers, territorials and conscripts who, for example, followed the original British Expeditionary Force to France would never attain its high all-round standard of training. Keenness and patriotism in themselves were not enough. One simply cannot wield a bludgeon with the delicate precision of a rapier. The spirit of von Clausewitz still inspired the German High Command and von Schlieffen, like the elder von Moltke in 1866 and 1870, had worked to finish the war by a single, swift, deadly campaign. But the addition of the British and the Belgians to the French array had put just enough grit in the works to ensure that a swift victory would elude their aggressors. And so the war dragged on its weary way for four years until at least 8,020,780 soldiers and 6,642,000 civilians of some sixteen nations were dead.

The war left the victorious statesmen, notably Clemenceau and Lloyd George, in a savage mood and all too ready to sow the seeds of future friction. It also left them in grave doubt as to whether anyone could conceive any cause so vital as to warrant resort to war. Never again, surely, they thought, would the youth of Europe go out to battle as eagerly as it had in 1914. Never again would nations mobilize their resources on such a scale. No crusade could be worth it. In the last resort a man might be pushed into fighting for hearth and home, but that was all. The hour of the pacifist was soon to come – and if there is one person as dangerous as the out-and-out warmonger, it is he.

British Mark V tanks being assembled at the Metropolitan Carriage Waggon Company's works in Birmingham. By the end of the war British tank production totalled 2,636; the French had built 3,870 and the Germans 20.

In the Spring offensives of 1918 the Germans introduced new weapons on the Western Front: they created the lightly armed stormtrooper, trained to infiltrate the Allied lines at speed and equipped for close-quarter fighting with the Bergmann submachine-gun shown here.

A British Mark I tank crosses a friendly trench on its way forward, 1916. The rear steering wheels are in the raised position and the side sponson and projecting 6-pounder gun are clearly shown. The speed of these 28-ton rhomboidal monsters was less than 4 mph but their effect on enemy morale was dramatic.

CHAPTER 7

# The Age of Armour

. . . HITLER'S ASTOUNDING
TECHNICAL AND TACTICAL VISION
LED HIM ALSO TO BECOME
THE CREATOR OF MODERN WEAPONRY
FOR THE ARMY.
IT WAS DUE TO HIM PERSONALLY
THAT THE 75-MM ANTI-TANK GUN
REPLACED THE 37-MM AND
50-MM GUNS IN TIME,
AND THAT THE SHORT GUNS
MOUNTED ON THE TANKS
WERE REPLACED WITH THE
LONG 75-MM AND 88-MM GUNS.
THE PANTHER, THE TIGER,
AND THE KONIGSTIGER WERE
DEVELOPED AS MODERN TANKS
ON HITLER'S OWN INITIATIVE.

*ALFRED JODL, GERMAN CHIEF OF STAFF, 1946*

**above** A German self-propelled gun, the Sturmgeschütz III, armed with a 75-mm gun, 1942. **left** The campaign on the Eastern Front: German armour rolls through a Russian village, 1942.

Towards the end of 1918 British and French ideas on armoured warfare had crystallized and offensives were being prepared in which the initial breakthrough would be as at Cambrai – this time using the Mark V tank, which was now coming into service as the first one-man-driven vehicle. Gearbox improvements had done away with the need for separate gearsmen and the commander could concentrate on commanding. Whippets, too, were to be employed, following up the main thrust in the exploitation role.

There emerged from these plans Fuller's famous 'Plan 1919'. This ambitious idea, overtaken by the Armistice of November 1918, was to have involved the deployment of some 10,000 tanks of various types. Having enticed the enemy into reinforcing some ninety miles of front, Fuller proposed that the various enemy headquarters thus concentrated should be attacked without warning by large numbers of fast-moving tanks; the Medium D, which in fact never got beyond the experimental stage, was assigned for this task. Once the enemy had been thrown into confusion, the main assault was to be delivered at selected points on the ninety-mile front by heavy tanks breaking through and fanning out behind the enemy line, followed up by the motorized infantry. Aircraft were to be used extensively, not only to mark the enemy headquarters for the attackers, but also to support the ground troops with bombs and machine-guns. He had conceived a real *blitzkrieg* of the 1939 style!

**Future Plans for Armour**

Although Fuller's revolutionary plan was devised too late to be used, it undoubtedly stimulated the fierce debate which went on after the war between members of the old school who were offended by such ideas for conducting war and those with younger minds who were stimulated by it.

We have seen how the requirement to break the stranglehold of the trenches influenced the tactical use to which tanks were first put and in the French and American armies after the First World War this concept remained; in both armies the tanks became an integral part of the infantry, and when the USSR started to build up a tank force it too followed this precept. Only in Britain, with 'Plan 1919' before its military leaders, did different ideas gradually take shape. In the first place the Royal Tank Corps, as it became, managed, not without opposition, to retain its identity as a separate arm of the service. In 1927 the Royal Tank Corps formed the nucleus of the Experimental Mechanized Force which assembled for manoeuvres on Salisbury Plain – manoeuvres which were to prove a landmark in the development of armoured warfare.

The Experimental Mechanized Force can fairly be said to be the true ancestor of the present-day armoured brigade and division, and the tactical and logistical experiments which it carried out had far-reaching effects. The Force, comprising mechanized units of all arms, consisted of two Royal Tank Corps battalions, an infantry battalion, an artillery field brigade, a light-artillery battery and an engineer field company; in addition air support was available in the shape of an Army co-operation squadron, a fighter squadron and two bomber squadrons.

By this time tank design had progressed beyond the original concept of a barbed-wire-crushing, trench-crossing siege vehicle, and the new Mechanized Force contained a substantial number of the Vickers Medium Mark II tank, first introduced in 1922. This vehicle departed entirely from the old shape and incorporated a rotating turret, capable of a 360-degree traverse, carrying a co-axially-mounted 47-mm gun and a .303-inch machine-gun; the turret layout, getting away from the awkward sponsons of earlier vehicles, was a fundamental advance, concentrating the crew into a single fighting compartment where team-work enabled the vehicle to be fought much more efficiently than before.

The Force followed the basic outlines of Fuller's proposals submitted to the War Office in 1924. In particular this was reflected in the conversion of the 2nd Battalion Somerset Light Infantry into a motorized machine-gun battalion. This arrangement was based on the concept that the infantry's task would be to defend ground won by the tanks. However, an opposing point of view held that ordinary motor-borne infantry should be included, and the 2nd Battalion the Cheshire Regiment took part in some of the trials, equipped with half-track and six-wheeled vehicles. Yet a third view held, among others, by Liddell Hart, was that armoured infantry, that is, infantry carried in armoured vehicles, should form part of the Force to clear obstacles. Unfortunately this concept did not receive sufficient attention in the British Army, although the German armoured forces under General Heinz Guderian learned the lesson and applied it with devastating effect in the early campaigns of the Second World War.

The trials of the Experimental Force finally got under way in the summer of 1927. One great problem was the widely differing types and performance of the vehicles used. To minimize the effect of these differences the Force was divided into a Fast Group (armoured cars with a march rate of twenty-five miles per hour); a Medium Group (light battery, field company, infantry battalion and transport; march rate ten miles per hour), and a Slow Group (tanks, tankettes and field brigade artillery; march rate seven miles per hour). Despite this attempt to compensate for differing speeds, Liddell Hart described the march tests as 'an attempt to drill a mechanical menagerie into a Noah's Ark procession, carried out in ceremonial slow time'. Operational tests revealed an even more limited approach: even attack exercises were carried out in a highly deliberate manner, often preceded by scouts on foot.

**above** British Vickers Medium tanks on manoeuvres between the wars. **below** The diagram shows the composition of the British Experimental Mechanized Force of 1927, set up to examine future possibilities in land warfare using armoured vehicles as the key units. The Force also received air support from an Army co-operation squadron plus one fighter and two bomber squadrons.

EXPERIMENTAL MECHANIZED FORCE, 1927

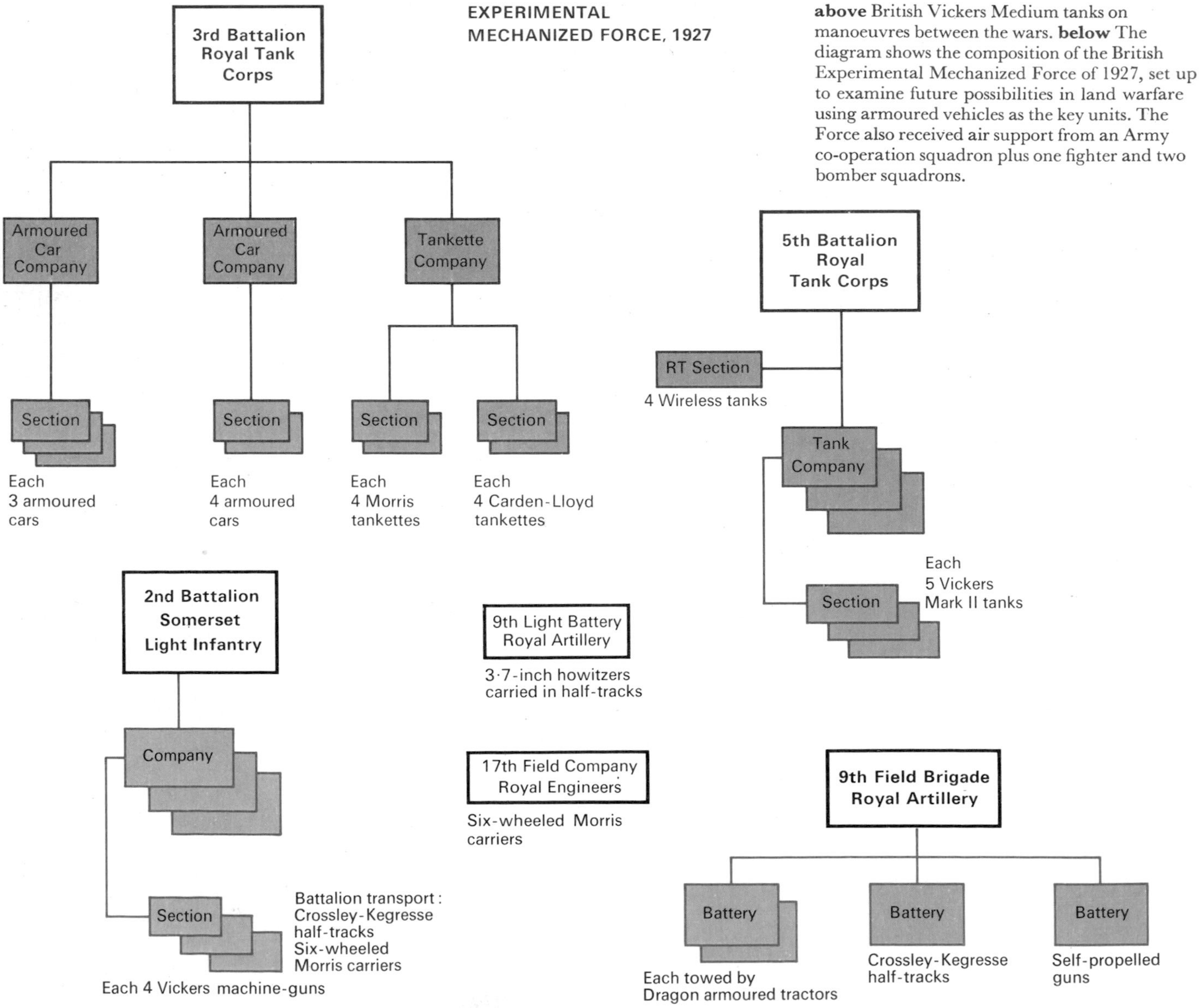
3rd Battalion Royal Tank Corps
Armoured Car Company
Armoured Car Company
Tankette Company
Section
Section
Section
Section
Each 3 armoured cars
Each 4 armoured cars
Each 4 Morris tankettes
Each 4 Carden-Lloyd tankettes
5th Battalion Royal Tank Corps
RT Section
4 Wireless tanks
Tank Company
Section
Each 5 Vickers Mark II tanks
2nd Battalion Somerset Light Infantry
Company
Section
Battalion transport: Crossley-Kegresse half-tracks Six-wheeled Morris carriers
Each 4 Vickers machine-guns
9th Light Battery Royal Artillery
3·7-inch howitzers carried in half-tracks
17th Field Company Royal Engineers
Six-wheeled Morris carriers
9th Field Brigade Royal Artillery
Battery
Battery
Battery
Each towed by Dragon armoured tractors
Crossley-Kegresse half-tracks
Self-propelled guns

While the experimental exercises on Salisbury Plain aroused intense interest abroad, something of a reaction took place in the British Army, where the annual estimates for forage still exceeded those for petrol. However, the trend was unmistakable and in 1931 a properly balanced armoured brigade was formed for the first time. By this time, too, a workable system of inter-communication between crew members was in use and radio between tanks, although not yet entirely reliable, had proved its essential value as a means of control.

The early British efforts to exploit the potential of the armoured fighting vehicle have been described in some detail because they were the real pioneers. The lessons which the exercises brought out were, however, learned most effectively abroad by the resurgent German Army and in particular by General Guderian, architect of the *Wehrmacht*'s armoured forces. Similar experiments to those of the British were carried out in the United States, France, Italy and Russia, and in all these countries tanks fell into two basic classes: the slow moving 'infantry' tank for the assault and the light tank or 'tankette', often little more than a machine-gun carrier, for reconnaissance.

**The Dawn of Blitzkrieg**

To the Germans must go the credit for being the first to do away with these ill-conceived categories, and for realizing that a tank is a tank, however it is used. Guderian created a versatile armoured force combining tanks and armoured infantry in the form of the Panzer Divisions which, supported by Stuka dive-bombers, swept all before them in Poland and France in 1939 and 1940.

The decisive blows delivered by the German *blitzkrieg* radically altered thinking in the opposing armies, particularly when it was appreciated that in 1940 some ten German Panzer divisions had successfully dealt with a total of three French light armoured divisions, four *divisions cuirassées*, a British armoured brigade and a large number of infantry tank battalions. The Allies had had some 3,000 tanks to oppose 2,700 German vehicles; but they had no *masse de manoeuvre* nor did they concentrate their armour.

Both the United States and the British in due course successfully adopted very similar organizations and tac-

**right** A .303-inch Bren machine-gun Mark I; first made in 1937, this weapon was the standard British light machine-gun in the Second World War. **below** A talk during training for members of the British Expeditionary Force to France; the men are mounted in Bren Carriers, developed from the inter-war tankettes to give extra mobility and armoured firepower.

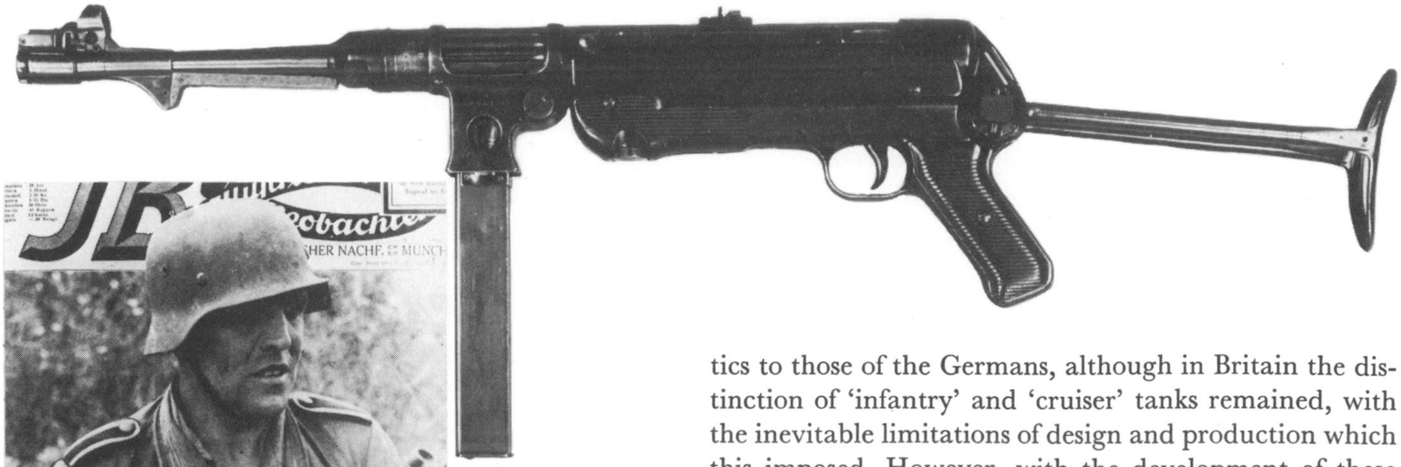

**above** A German 9-mm Schmeisser submachine-gun; the lower picture shows a German corporal holding a Schmeisser at the ready. Submachine-guns were not new weapons in 1939–45, the Germans having introduced the Bergmann version in 1918 (see page 98), but they were better suited to the more mobile fighting conditions of the Second World War.

tics to those of the Germans, although in Britain the distinction of 'infantry' and 'cruiser' tanks remained, with the inevitable limitations of design and production which this imposed. However, with the development of these new techniques, together with increased production of armoured vehicles, the supremacy of armoured forces on the battlefields of the Second World War rapidly became apparent; unsupported infantry, particularly in the desert and in Russia, was rarely able to hold its own against armour unless protected by extensive natural or artificial obstacles. On the other hand in the Battle of Kursk (1943), the greatest tank battle of all time, the Germans were shown to be capable of faulty design. Their ninety Ferdinand guns, monsters though they were, had no machine-guns. Guderian describes what followed:

Once they had broken into the enemy's infantry zone they literally had to go quail-shooting with cannons. They did not manage to neutralize, let alone destroy, the enemy rifles and machine-guns, so that the infantry was unable to follow up behind them. By the time they reached the Russian artillery they were on their own. Despite showing extreme bravery and suffering unheard-of casualties, the

**RUSSIAN TANK T34/76A**

Episcope
Main armament
Two-man turret
Pistol port
Driver's hatch
Headlamp
Secondary armament
Linked track
Sloped armour to reduce penetrative power of missiles aimed against it
Mud shield
Road wheel
Broad tracks for good cross-country performance

**Specifications**
Length 19ft 9ins
Width 10ft 0ins
Weight 26·3 tons
Maximum speed 32 mph
Range (on roads) approx. 250 miles
Armour 45-mm
Armament one 76·2-mm gun; two 7·62-mm machine-guns
Crew 4
Troop-carrying capacity 12

One of the most successful tanks of the Second World War was the Russian T34 which, when it appeared in 1941, outgunned and outmanoeuvred every German vehicle ranged against it. The T34/76A shown here was succeeded by the 76B and 76C models and then by the T34/85, which mounted a heavier 85-mm gun to combat the new German Panthers.

infantry of Weidling's division did not manage to exploit the tanks' success. Model's attack bogged down after some six miles. In the south our successes were somewhat greater but not enough to seal off the salient or to force the Russians to withdraw.

### The New Role of Armour

Once the desert campaigns of 1940–2 were over and tanks were faced with the more limiting conditions of Sicily and Italy, military opinion in Britain and the United States began to see armoured forces once again as being of value only in special conditions and in support of infantry; to some extent this regression was halted by the spectacular armoured advances after the Normandy break-out and during the closing stages of the European war, but by 1945 the general view in the West was that armour was a mobile arm complementary to the infantry, which remained the main striking force. In the German and Soviet armies, on the other hand, armoured forces were seen as the principal striking force, powerful as well as mobile. This attitude may be seen reflected in the undergunned mobility of the Sherman when compared with, for example, the Soviet T34 or the German Panther.

### Heavy Guns and Anti-Tank Weapons

The Second World War was above all the age of the tank, but by no means to the exclusion of other weapons. Indeed in July 1944, after a month in Normandy when doubts began to be raised about the adequacy of the Allied tanks, Field-Marshal Montgomery wrote in a memorandum for the War Office: 'I cannot emphasize too strongly, that victory in battle depends, not on tank action alone, but on the intimate co-operation of all arms; the tank by itself can achieve little.' Military technology followed every line of development that human ingenuity could suggest. Every effort was made not only to devise

**top** A Stuka dive-bomber, one of Hitler's principal assault weapons in the *blitzkrieg* years. **right** A German Panther A tank, designed to take the sting out of the Russian T34s which had dominated the armoured war on the Eastern Front. **below** A German Ferdinand self-propelled gun, first built in 1943 and mounting an 88-mm gun on a Tiger P chassis.

new weapons but to improve upon old ones. The British, for example, were in the process of rearming their field artillery with the 25-pounder gun/howitzer, in place of the 18-pounder, when the war broke out. By 1940 the Germans had developed an assault gun. This was a 105-mm gun mounted on the chassis of an obsolescent tank, which had a shield to protect the crew. The self-propelled gun, of which this was the forerunner, was to play an important part in the Second World War. By 1944 each British armoured division had a regiment of 'Sextons' armed with 25-pounders, and two of the assault regiments on D Day had each a regiment of 'Priests', mounting American 105-mm guns.

Since the weapons most feared in 1939–45 were aircraft and tanks, much thought was given to their destruction. By the time of the Spanish Civil War the Germans had already produced the 88-mm gun, which was to be a real maid-of-all-work from 1937 onwards as an anti-tank gun, an anti-aircraft gun and as a field gun all in one. In 1939 each British brigade had an anti-tank company each armed with twelve 2-pounder anti-tank guns, but these were too small, and had to be replaced first by the 6-pounder, and then by the hard-hitting 17-pounder. Unfortunately the 6-pounder was difficult to conceal in the forward areas, and the size of the 17-pounder made it extremely conspicuous even in the densest country.

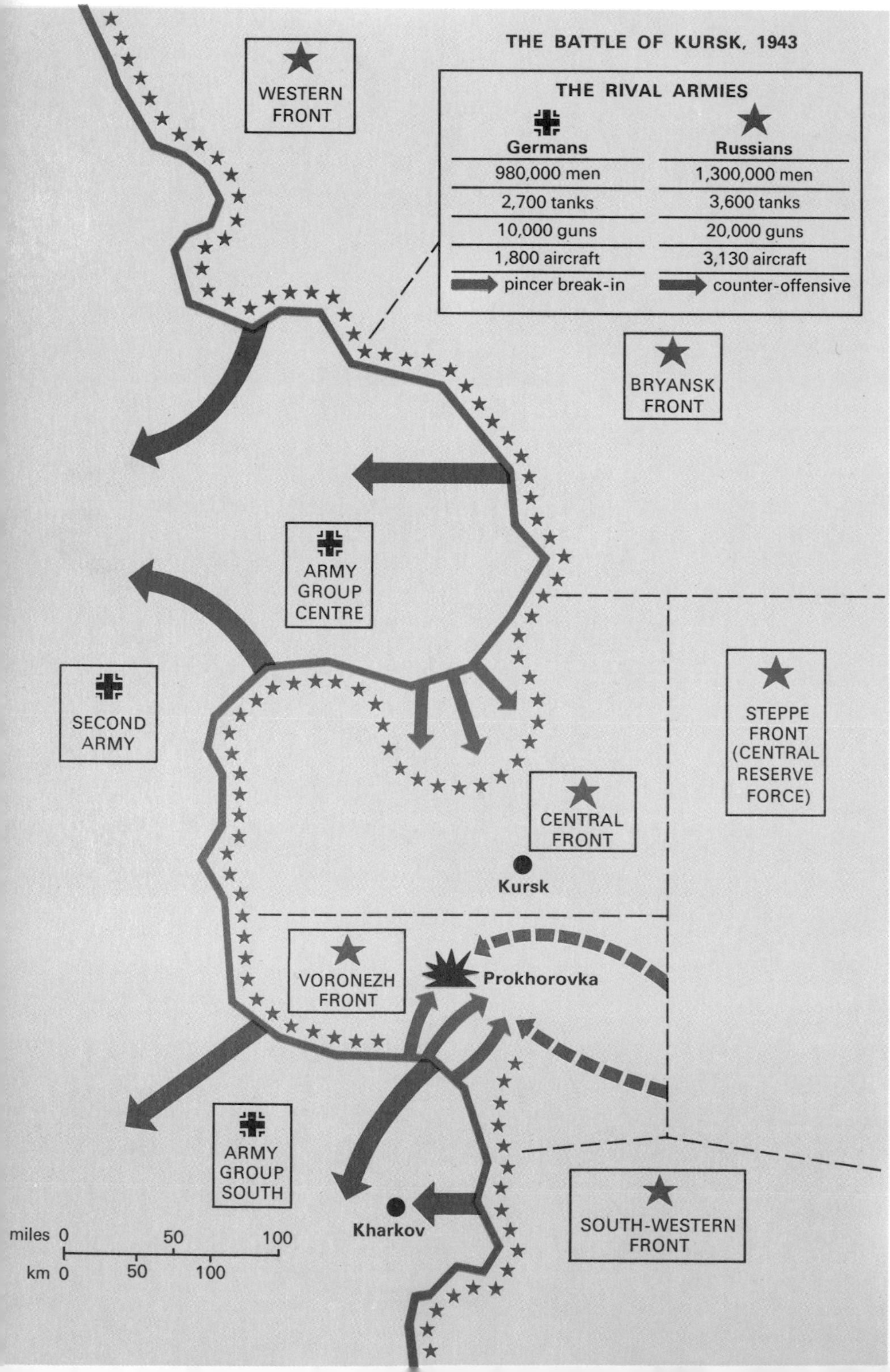
THE BATTLE OF KURSK, 1943
THE RIVAL ARMIES
Germans
Russians
980,000 men
1,300,000 men
2,700 tanks
3,600 tanks
10,000 guns
20,000 guns
1,800 aircraft
3,130 aircraft
pincer break-in
counter-offensive
WESTERN FRONT
BRYANSK FRONT
ARMY GROUP CENTRE
SECOND ARMY
STEPPE FRONT (CENTRAL RESERVE FORCE)
CENTRAL FRONT
Kursk
VORONEZH FRONT
Prokhorovka
ARMY GROUP SOUTH
Kharkov
SOUTH-WESTERN FRONT
miles 0
50
100
km 0
50
100

The Battle of Kursk was the waning German Army's third major attempt to break the Russians – after Moscow and Stalingrad. The assault began on the night of 4–5 July 1943 but the Russians were well prepared, and by 10 July the northern pincer (Army Group Centre) had advanced little more than six to eight miles. In the south the fighting was no less fierce but German penetration was greater. The Russian armoured reserves of Steppe Front were sent for and on 12 July the most massive tank battle in history took place near Prokhorovka, involving some 1,500 tanks and self-propelled guns. Here the German armour was beaten back by a huge Russian counterthrust, which finally destroyed Hitler's grip on the Eastern Front.

As the war went on there were big improvements in ammunition. Early anti-armoured rounds had consisted of simple solid, armour-piercing shot (AP), made of alloy steel. While this was satisfactory enough against early forms of armour plate, the introduction of face-hardened armour tended to make AP shot shatter on impact. To overcome this a soft cap was fitted to the basic AP projectile and the round was termed Armour Piercing Capped (APC). The cap, however, had a ballistically poor shape and as increasingly thicker armour required ammunition of even higher velocity to defeat it, a shaped Ballistic Cap (BC) was fitted; this final version of the full-bore shot was known, therefore, as APCBC, and gave significantly better penetration at ranges greater than 500 yards.

The introduction of APCBC was swiftly matched by the use of even thicker armour plate of improved quality, and a more radical approach was required to counter it. The aim was to increase penetration by increasing the velocity of the shot, without at the same time increasing the size of the gun; this became, in essence, a problem of exerting greater pressure on a small projectile within the limits of a gun barrel which had also to fire conventional High Explosive shell. The very successful British solution to the problem, first seen in 1944, has been the Armour Piercing Discarding Sabot (APDS) projectile. In this design the armour-piercing tungsten core is of very much

**below** The V-2 rocket, one of Germany's most dangerous 'secret' weapons. This 46-foot rocket, which entered the war in September 1944, had a range of up to 220 miles and descended on its target at a speed of more than 2,000 mph. Only extensive bombing of V-2 launch sites kept the danger in check before the sites were overrun during the Allied advance across Europe.

**above left** A PIAT projector – an anti-tank weapon used by the Allied infantry – being aimed by a Canadian soldier while another loads it with a 2½-pound bomb: these could pierce four inches of armour plate with the force of a 75-mm gun at ranges of up to seventy yards – qualities which made the PIAT a useful weapon against not only tanks but also against concrete emplacements. The US counterpart to the PIAT was the bazooka, and the Germans devised a short-range *panzerfaust* for essentially the same role. **left** A Czech-produced anti-tank rifle, used by the Germans from 1941.

**left** The amphibious war. In 1939–45 more opposed landings and raids were made than in any previous war, and specialized craft proliferated. In the photograph US marines are seen landing from barges at Guadalcanal in the Solomon Islands, 1942. In the course of this operation over 30,000 US troops were put ashore to oppose the occupying Japanese.

**below** The paratroopers – here preparing for an Allied drop on the Western Front. Airborne units were used on a large scale for the first time in the Second World War, and Commando units gave fresh impetus to the infantry. **right** Armoured warfare in the 1960s. A Soviet tactical missile unit combines on manoeuvres with a tank formation, seen moving forward.

smaller calibre than the barrel itself, and is encased in a lightweight jacket or 'sabot' which increases the calibre of the complete round to the correct full-bore size. Thus a powerful charge, resulting in a very high muzzle velocity, can be applied to the base of a comparatively light projectile without modification to the gun barrel. Once the projectile has left the barrel the sabot falls to the ground, leaving the solid core free to travel on to the target at velocities often in excess of 4,000 feet per second.

In 1939 the Boys Anti-Tank rifle, already obsolescent, was the platoon anti-tank weapon. One is alleged to have shot down a German observation balloon near Dunkirk in 1940, but the records do not appear to credit this weapon with any other successes. It was gradually replaced by the Projector Infantry Anti-Tank (PIAT), which, it was said at the time, was devised to assist those who wished to earn the Victoria Cross. Its short range certainly made its operation somewhat hazardous, but a number of German tanks were stalked or ambushed and destroyed by the PIAT. The PIAT weighed 34½ pounds and its bomb 2½ pounds. Its maximum effective range against tanks was alleged to be 115 yards, but in the view of the present writer it was unlikely to get a 'kill' above 50–70 yards. Its American counterpart was the bazooka, whilst towards the end of the war the Germans invented the *panzerfaust*, a short-range, one-man anti-tank rocket,

122
133
101

of which they made good use in the *bocage* of Normandy and elsewhere. 'Sticky' grenades, and a variety of mines were invented, though the latter, of course, were anti-personnel as well as anti-tank.

### Mortars

Mortars played an important part in the Second World War. In a report dated 30 July 1944 an Operational Research Section reported that the Medical Officers of four different divisions attributed seventy per cent of their units' casualties to mortar fire. By this stage in the war the Germans seem to have set more store by mortars and *nebelwerfer* than conventional artillery. The latter, known to the British soldier as the 'Moaning Minnie', was particularly unpleasant. It had five to ten barrels and was originally designed for making smoke. But in Normandy it was used to fire high explosive, and had a high rate of fire. There were five regiments of them, mostly on the British front. A regiment had sixty or seventy *nebelwerfer*. There were three sizes, as follows:

| *Calibre* | *Projectile* | *Range in yards* |
|---|---|---|
| 150-mm | 75-pound | 7,300 |
| 210-mm | 248-pound | 8,600 |
| 300-mm | 277-pound | 5,000 |

### Hitler's Secret Weapons

Ingenuity in weapons development was by no means confined to the Allies. Indeed after the tide had turned against Hitler he announced, not once but many times, that he had a devastating Secret Weapon. There were in fact two Secret Weapons, the V-1 and the V-2. The V-1 was a flying bomb weighing a ton and delivered by a pilotless aircraft. Its range was about 150 miles, and its speed between 200 and 400 miles an hour. It flew at a steady height and was traceable by radar as well as being visible in flight; it could therefore be shot down by aircraft and also was vulnerable to a near-miss from an anti-aircraft shell. The V-2 was rather more formidable. It was a 46-foot rocket with a range of 200 to 220 miles. Its warhead also weighed a ton. Its trajectory rose to a height of fifty miles. It was so fast that it could not be seen in flight and it came down at more than 2,000 mph. No effective defence against it was ever discovered. The project was not as secret as Hitler thought, however, and was known to British Intelligence by May 1943. Its development was seriously delayed when on 17–18 August of that year an attack by 600 aircraft on the research establishment and factory at Peenemunde did heavy damage, killing many of the key scientists and staff.

The first V-1, or flying bomb, fell on England on 13 June 1944. Indiscriminate attacks on London followed, and though half the V-1s were shot down, either by fighters or anti-aircraft guns, they had an adverse effect on morale. On 8 September came the first V-2. Fortunately for the British the Allied advance swiftly overran the V-2 sites in France and Belgium, although the Germans were able to go on bombarding London, Antwerp, Brussels and Liège from launching sites in Holland until March 1945. Only massive air bombardment kept the V-2 menace within bounds. Altogether the Germans launched 25,649 missiles on the following targets:

### Targets

| | *English* | *Continental* | *Totals* |
|---|---|---|---|
| V-1 | 10,492 | 1,403 | 11,895 |
| V-2 | 11,988 | 1,766 | 13,754 |
| | 22,480 | 3,169 | 25,649 |

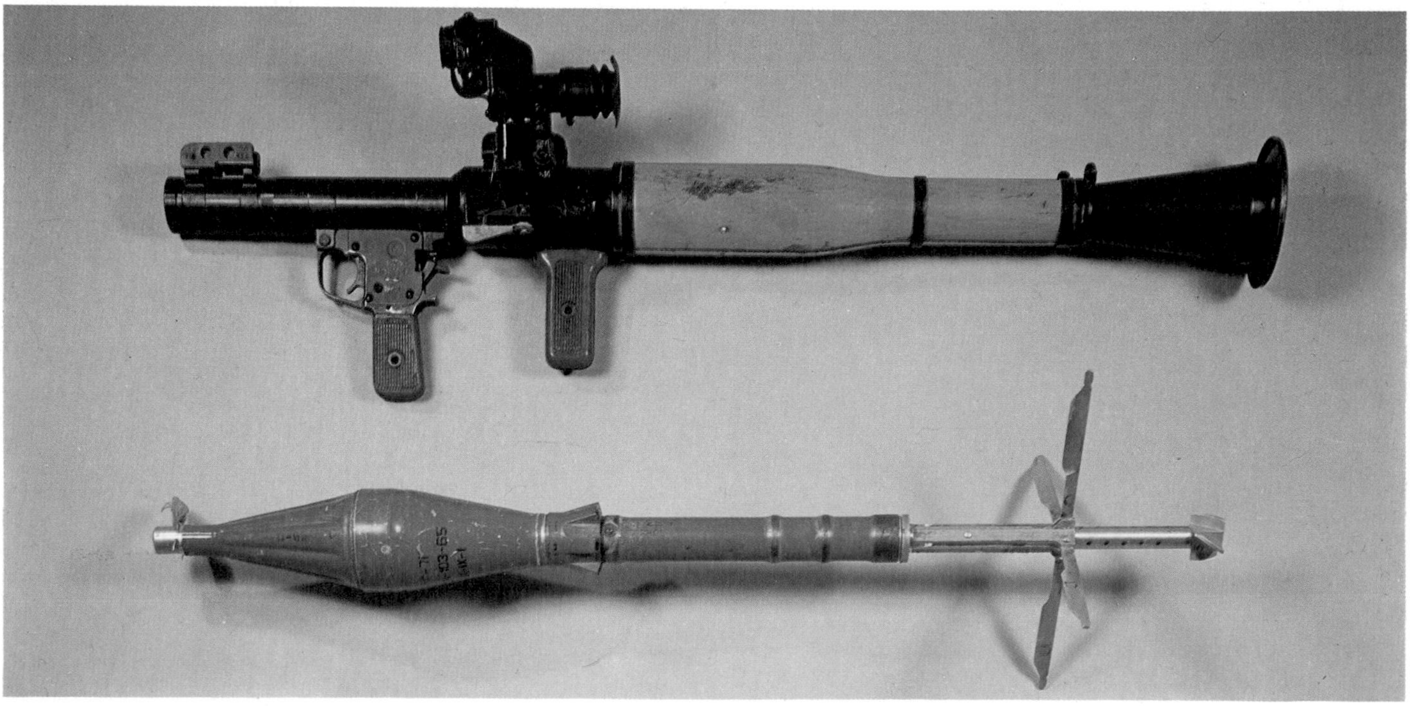

A Soviet anti-tank rocket launcher, the RPG 7, a weapon favoured by many of the conventional armies, guerrilla units and mixed forces that characterize today's battlegrounds from Vietnam to Ulster.

The British Chieftain tank, seen here on manoeuvres, is one of the world's most powerful AFVs. It weighs 51 tons, can travel at up to 26 mph, and its main armament is a 120-mm gun. When it was designed firepower was given priority over mobility: in practice this means that the Chieftain, armed with Armour Piercing Discarding Sabot projectiles – which shed their covers immediately on leaving the barrel – can pierce a 150-mm target from a range of over 3,000 metres. The Chieftain is also equipped to fire HESH (High Explosive Squash Head) projectiles, used mainly against concrete defences and light armoured vehicles. Before the main 120-mm gun is fired, the range of a particular target can first be established by means of a special ranging machine-gun which 'fixes' the distance through short bursts of fire. Other notable features of the Chieftain include its 150-mm frontal armour and the deeply sloped plates on turret and hull. The Chieftain is protected against atomic, bacteriological and chemical weapons by a ventilation system which allows it to remain fully sealed for up to forty-eight hours; it is also equipped for wading through water to a maximum depth of 4.5 metres.

02EB61

A US M551 (Sheridan) tank in Laos. Designed to be air portable, this tank has a number of lightweight aluminium components and can travel at up to 43 mph. However, its performance in Indochina has been erratic. The Sheridan is equipped to fire electronically guided Shillelagh missiles from a 152-mm gun that is also able to fire conventional ammunition.

**Casualties**

| | *England* | *Continent* | *Totals* |
|---|---|---|---|
| Killed | 8,938 | 5,400 | 14,338 |
| Seriously Injured | 24,504 | 22,000 | 46,504 |
| | 33,442 | 27,400 | 60,842 |

The Germans, however, failed in their aim of breaking Allied morale. Nor had they interrupted the flow of supplies to the front. Of the 1,214 V-missiles which landed in the sixty-five square miles of Greater Antwerp, only 302 fell in the port area, and though they sank two large cargo ships and fifty-eight smaller vessels besides damaging the quays, cranes and other installations, they caused no major interruption to the work of the base.

**The Amphibious War**

Besides being a great tank and aircraft war this was the greatest amphibious war of all time. More opposed landings and raids were made than in the rest of the long history of warfare. Numbers of specialized ships and craft proliferated. Numerous devices were invented so that armies could be put ashore over open beaches, in order to avoid the heavy casualties likely in attempting to take a port on D-Day. Two of the most ingenious devices were PLUTO and Mulberry.

PLUTO (Pipe Lines Under The Ocean) supplied petrol from England to France. The most successful pipes were from Dungeness to Boulogne. Eventually eleven pipes were operational and in March and April an average of 3,100 tons a day was being delivered. Petrol, as the French say, is *le sang rouge de la guerre*. With a fully mechanized army the importance of its supply cannot be overestimated. The Mulberry Harbour, built off Arromanches, was an artificial harbour whose piers were protected by breakwaters built of sunken caissons and blockships.

**Airborne Units**

This was the first war in which airborne units were used on a large scale, first by the Germans and then even more ambitiously by the Allies. The parachute and the glider had their disadvantages, however. Once on the ground the airborne troops lost their great mobility, but their power to achieve surprise and to spread confusion played a great part in the 1940 campaign, in Crete, Sicily, Normandy, at Arnhem and in the Rhine Crossing. Airborne troops and the Commandos were a shock to the system of the old-time marching infantryman. But it was useless to expect to carry out complicated amphibious and airborne operations without loading the dice by using specially trained troops. The special conditions of many a previous war had called specialist troops into being: grenadiers, light infantry, rangers, stormtroopers. This war brought forth the airborne divisions and the Commandos. The age of armour was also the age of the parachute and of the assault landing-craft.

**Armoured Formations Today**

In the immediate post-war years, and before the tactical implications of nuclear weapons were fully appreciated, only the Soviet Union continued to view integrated armoured formations comprising all-arms as the principal element in ground warfare. The United States went back to integrating the majority of its tanks into infantry formations while the British, continuing to maintain two armoured divisions, occupied a somewhat indeterminate position in the centre of the controversy. While the British did not fully share the philosophy of the USSR, with its emphasis on mobility coupled with striking power, they did at least introduce a significant technical advance in that direction with their new Centurion, a tank which first reached British service units in 1945 and has proved one of the most versatile AFVs ever built. The Centurion was the first tank to incorporate fully stabilized armament, which meant that for the first time accurate fire on the move was a practical proposition; although the development has been copied in a number of foreign vehicles there is no doubt that the British system has remained the best and the most reliable.

The advent of tactical nuclear weapons, coupled with the realization of the continued Soviet emphasis on armoured forces, gradually brought about a reappraisal of armoured doctrine by the Western nations. Exercises in Germany in the mid-1950s, based on the employment

of tactical nuclear weapons, revealed the need for rapid deployment and concentration of troops on the nuclear battlefield, plus a requirement for first-class communications and protection from nuclear effects. It was painfully obvious that in the British Army at that time only the armoured brigades were capable of meeting that requirement at all and even their infantry battalions were carried in Second World War open half-tracks. However, the need for highly mobile ground forces was appreciated and, with overhead cover, the infantry could at last be properly integrated with tanks into truly versatile armoured formations. Nevertheless, it was not until the late 1960s that all British infantry battalions in Germany were fully equipped with the FV 432 armoured personnel carrier, or that all field artillery regiments finally handed in their towed guns and were equipped with the Abbott 105-mm self-propelled gun.

**Night Fighting**

The limitations on daylight movement and concentration of forces imposed by the threat of nuclear attack caused the Western armies to re-examine the problems of night fighting. The British had examined its possibilities in the 1930s and their research had culminated in the development of the Canal Defence Light (CDL) which was a 30 million candle-power searchlight mounted on a tank and incorporating a flicker device which it was hoped would make it difficult to shoot out. Little operational use was made of the idea because the extreme secrecy which cloaked it made it difficult for crews to gain experience in the necessary techniques. However, one technique which was successfully used was to direct searchlight beams onto low cloud on overcast nights, to provide battlefield illumination from the reflected light. Though successful night advances were fairly frequent during the Second World War, after 1945 no more than lip-service was paid to night operations until the late 1950s, when the first infra-red equipment began to appear.

**Guided Weapons**

During the Second World War a number of infantry anti-tank weapons, all more or less effective, were evolved. The PIAT, the bazooka and the *panzerfaust* have already been mentioned. The continued development of Soviet armoured forces has made even more imperative the need for an anti-armour capability within infantry sub-units. This has led to the development of the anti-tank guided weapon – in original concept an easily portable infantry weapon, although many versions in all armies are now vehicle-mounted and in some cases form an integral part of tank weapon systems. The guided weapon has certainly provided a significant change to the infantryman's armoury, providing as it does an easily concealed weapon with a long-range capability against the heaviest enemy AFVs; it does have the disadvantage of a long time of flight, however, coupled with a low rate of fire and often a poor minimum range. It is unlikely to replace entirely the AFV-mounted tank gun but is complementary to it. For the infantry, however, it does permit a flexibility of response in a combat situation which it has never previously enjoyed on a battlefield dominated by armour.

Although the need for integrated mobile forces of all arms has generally been accepted by all major armies, there are still many different views about the characteristics of the vehicles with which they should be equipped. The British on the one hand have produced the comparatively slow, heavily armoured, powerfully armed Chieftain, equipped with a sophisticated and highly effective fire-control system. With its 120-mm gun this appears to be one of the world's most effective AFVs. The German Leopard on the other hand is a much simpler, more lightly armoured and armed vehicle, capable of great speed. Both these designs reflect the wartime experiences of the two countries in north-west Europe and Russia respectively and also reflect the fact that, as the world's armies move forward into the 1970s, the conflict between protection, firepower and mobility continues. The importance of the armoured fighting vehicle in providing mobile firepower on the battlefield remains undiminished

A FISSION BOMB OF SUPERLATIVELY
DESTRUCTIVE POWER WILL RESULT
FROM BRINGING QUICKLY TOGETHER
A SUFFICIENT MASS OF
ELEMENT U-235.
THIS SEEMS AS SURE AS ANY
UNTRIED PREDICTION
BASED UPON THEORY
AND EXPERIMENT CAN BE.

*REPORT OF THE SECRET COMMITTEE OF THE NATIONAL ACADEMY OF SCIENCE, WASHINGTON DC, 6 NOVEMBER 1941*

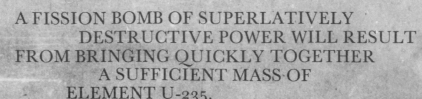

CHAPTER 8

# *The Age of the Nuclear Bomb*

Hiroshima after the bomb, 1945.

On 6 August 1945 the Superfortress Enola Gay (Colonel Paul W. Tibbets) released a bomb which descended five miles by parachute and burst over Hiroshima, the seventh largest city of Japan. The city's population was 343,000 plus a garrison of some 150,000 soldiers. The bomb killed 78,000 people and wounded 37,000 (the majority of them being civilians); 10,000 others were declared missing. Later many more were to suffer from exposure to gamma rays.

If the value of a weapon is measured simply by the number of casualties it causes this missile was by far the most effective the world had ever seen. The 250,000 Frenchmen and Russians who fought at Borodino (7 September 1812) had only managed to kill and wound 68,000 of their number, although the French alone had fired off some 1,400,000 cartridges. On the first day of the Battle of the Somme (1 July 1916), a day notorious in the annals of the British Army for its tragic losses, the casualties were somewhere in the region of 56,000, of whom about one-third were killed. In Normandy (June 1944) the Anglo-American casualties did not reach 60,000 until the landing force had been ashore for twenty days and had achieved far greater results than Napoleon at Borodino or Haig on the Somme. Then, at Hiroshima, without suffering a single wound – except to a few tender consciences already in the know – the Americans laid low 125,000 Japanese. The Pope who long ago had condemned the crossbow, and that French hero the Chevalier Bayard (1473–1524), who used to kill all captured arquebusiers because he disapproved of gunpowder, might have trembled had they seen the results that a Japanese journalist described as follows:

> Suddenly a glaring whitish pinkish light appeared in the sky accompanied by an unnatural tremor which was followed almost immediately by a wave of suffocating heat and a wind which swept away everything in its path.
>
> Within a few seconds the thousands of people in the streets and the gardens in the centre of the town were scorched by a wave of searing heat.
>
> Many were killed instantly, others lay writhing on the ground, screaming in agony from the intolerable pain of their burns. Everything standing upright in the way of the blast – walls, houses, factories, and other buildings – was annihilated and the débris spun round in a whirlwind and was carried up into the air. Trams were picked up and tossed aside as though they had neither weight nor solidity. Trains were flung off the rails as though they were toys. Horses, dogs and cattle suffered the same fate as human beings. Every living thing was petrified in an attitude of indescribable suffering. Even the vegetation did not escape. Trees went up in flames, the rice plants lost their greenness, the grass burned on the ground like dry straw.

In 1944 Field-Marshal Smuts had said, 'We should thank God for Hitler. He has done a great service to the world. He has brought us back to a realization of brute facts. He has got us away from ideals and rhetoric. Facts are the only things that matter. Hitler has shown that Hell is still here on Earth. He has, in fact, taken the lid off Hell, and we have all looked into it. That is his service to the human race.' In 1945 President Truman gave it a couple more glimpses at Hiroshima and, three days later, at Nagasaki.

Although many an American soldier may have felt relief that he was not now to be invited to invade Japan, the human race as a whole did not much like what it saw. It was all too obvious that other powers might develop nuclear weapons. The London *blitz*, the bombing of Rotterdam, Hamburg and Dresden had been bad enough. The prospect of a Third World War was appalling. To quote Smuts again: 'All are aware that the war potential that either side may mobilize is such as to make another war absolute madness, much more so than the madness which led to the two world wars.'

**Warfare Since 1945**

But although, writing in the Autumn of 1972, one can say that there has been no further world war, the 'peace' since 1945 has been much more violent than those between 1815 and 1854, or 1870 and 1914, or 1918 and 1939. Wars in the 1945–72 period seem to have fallen into four categories:

1 Thermonuclear, which has not yet taken place.
2 Conventional.
3 Guerrilla.
4 A combination of 2 and 3.

Although certain other powers have a nuclear capability, the leading nuclear powers are the USA and the USSR, both of which are at pains to give the impression that they are seriously interested in the limitation and reduction of strategic nuclear armament – hence the Strategic Arms Limitations Talks (SALT) of 1971, which do not appear to have made any great progress. Nevertheless since 1963 a 'hot-line' communications link has existed between Moscow and Washington, and on 30 September 1971 two US–Soviet agreements were signed, one to reduce the risk of nuclear war and the other to improve the 'hot line', the primary aim of which is to prevent such a war being sparked off accidentally or without authority.

And so the present great array of enormously expensive inter-continental ballistic missiles (ICBM), submarine-launched missiles (SLBM) and anti-ballistic missiles (ABM), with all the Polaris submarines and strategic aircraft and carriers, may go on grinning at each other year after year until one day somebody discovers that they have worn out. But, supposing they *were* allowed to slip into decay, that might not be such a good thing as it sounds: for it seems that in the last quarter of a century the USA and the USSR, by a process of mutual deterrence, a balance of fear, have achieved a design for living. However, as General André Beaufre has pointed out, 'The stability provided by the nuclear weapon is attainable only between *reasonable* powers. Boxes of matches should not be given to children.'

**Conventional Wars**

The feeling that the nuclear powers will be wary of employing even tactical nuclear weapons has led to a situation where conventional wars, for all their cost in blood and treasure, have remained possible, as in Korea, India and the Sinai Desert. Although the first of these was indecisive in that it left Korea divided, since, as R. E. and T. N. Dupuy's book, *The Encyclopedia of Military History*, puts it, 'the threat of the atom bomb hung heavy over all concerned and throttled exploitation of success', it nevertheless represented a victory for the United Nations. Their battle casualties were about 476,093, as compared to 1,600,000 on the Communist side, sixty per cent of whom were Chinese. For the record, too, about 3,000,000 South Korean civilians died as a result of the war. But, despite the menace of the mushroom clouds, it had been a purely conventional affair.

The two wars between India and Pakistan followed strictly conventional lines – as could be expected when the senior officers on both sides had received their military education in the same tradition – the British – during the Second World War. The second of these wars brought the elimination of East Pakistan and the establishment of Bangladesh; India thereby achieved the strictly limited aim of her policy.

The two most remarkable conventional wars of the period were those between Israel and her Arab neighbours in 1956 and 1967, in which, ironically enough, the Jews showed themselves as the heirs of von Clausewitz, von Moltke and von Manstein. They alone seemed to have learned the secret of that *Schlacht ohne Morgen* (battle with no tomorrow) of which von Schlieffen had dreamed and which had eluded his successors in two World Wars. The methods and armament of the Israelis were those of the El Alamein period brought up to date. Their use of intelligence, mobilization, air and tank power was in fact purely conventional. But, inspired by a fierce patriotism, they did everything superlatively well, with their officers leading from in front. They were not encumbered with soldiers like the disenchanted, ill-doctrinated GIs turned out by ninety days of mass production, who seem to have been wandering for years around the battlefields of Korea and South Vietnam, depending for survival on their massive ironmongery, and feeling all the while that they were a long way from home. From them the world has learned that, despite all the weapons that human ingenuity can produce, morale still counts for something.

Nobody, except perhaps the occasional Egyptian, believes that the Israelis would fail in a third bout of desert warfare. The Egyptians often speak of renewing the war, but they can hardly mean to cross the Suez Canal and invade the Sinai Desert. Nor, given the vulnerability of the cities of the Nile Delta and of the Aswan Dam, does it seem all that likely that they will turn to push-button warfare.

A long-range destroyer: a Polaris A-3 missile breaks the ocean surface after it has been launched from a submerged nuclear-powered Polaris submarine. Missiles launched in this way have a maximum range in excess of 1,500 miles.

S.V.C.G
SVCG
SVCG
SVCG
SVCG

### Guerrilla Wars

Guerrilla warfare has always been the resort of those who, unable to make headway in the field against a better-armed foe, still find the tenacity to struggle on. History abounds with examples: Wilhelm Tell, the legendary Swiss hero of the fourteenth century, Andreas Hofer (1767–1810) in the Tyrol, the Spanish *guerrilleros* of Napoleon's day, the *franc-tireurs* (sharp-shooters) of 1870–1 and the numerous resistance movements of the Second World War. At one time it was thought, because of the experience of the Peninsular War (1808–14), that guerrillas could achieve little without the support of a field army. More modern experience does not altogether support that view. The British in Palestine, Cyprus and in Ulster have been defied by partisans without a field army in the background. So it also was with the French in Algeria.

We are, it seems, back in the days of that accursed General Cluseret, who, from being a respectable French officer (St Cyr, 1843) with a Legion of Honour won suppressing the uprising of 1848, became Minister of War in the Paris Commune and had the bad taste to teach the tricks of street-fighting to his Communard friends. He has much to say that is of interest on such subjects as the timing of attacks (he rightly chose the early hours of the morning); on the importance of shooting the enemy's officers, and on the ruthless destruction of property, even whole towns. But it is his remarks on weapons that are of particular interest here:

> The best basis for making up for a lack of arms is the bomb. This is the speciality of the popular uprising, whether it is directed against its own government or against a foreign enemy. In each case the adversary will be master of the situation, watching the insurgents vigilantly, allowing them no weapons, and forbidding their manufacture. And even if any worker had the facilities for producing arms, he would still not be able to supply all his comrades. Thanks to this, the side of the rich always has overwhelming superiority of force. To be able to shoot, you must first leave cover. In such a struggle as I have explained, a gun is useless, worse still it merely hinders your movements. A locality only allowing man-to-man fighting demands such weapons as the dagger and knife, the axe, the revolver, the grenade and other incendiary and explosive devices, which alone can be used in such a situation.
>
> Bombs have the following advantages: they can be made secretly, and the devastation that they produce is far more significant than that produced by volleys of rifle shots, their explosion creates more panic than injuries, and thrown from an upstairs window they cannot present any danger to the thrower. Such results are obtained when a bomb is thrown through a gap in a wall into a neighbouring room. The explosion sends everything flying in that room and allows the thrower to use the panic to take possession of the place and kill off

Routine checks are carried out to a British Thunderbird II missile launcher panel. This weapon uses a ground radar guidance system which locks onto its target and sends back radar beams to a receiver in the missile, which then homes on the target.

anyone left in there. Mercy must be his very last consideration. The morale effect of bombs is so great that, after a few explosions successfully carried out, the opposition falls to nil, and makes possible a relative lessening of their use.

Of course, it is no longer necessary to leave cover in order to fire a rifle or a submachine-gun. Even so Cluseret's remarks, written before the day of efficient grenades like the Mills bomb, are worth pondering. The fact is that the determined guerrilla, especially in built-up areas and thick country, can get to close quarters with a better-armed enemy; the latter's heavy weapons then lose the benefit of their chief characteristics, be they fire-power, mobility, armour or all three.

The ingenuity of military planners during the next decade or so will be turned not so much to the development of new thermonuclear weapons, new tanks and the means of countering them, as to methods of hunting down and destroying the guerrilla, especially in his new guise of urban guerrilla. The discussion of such methods is beyond our scope. Suffice it to say that armies have occasionally succeeded in suppressing outbreaks of this sort, but always, as it seems to us, by methods that will hardly recommend themselves to civilized politicians: by curfews enforced with draconian severity; by the destruction of the homes of the partisans' supporters and even of whole villages; by taking hostages; by depriving the

**above** A deadly all-rounder. This Northrop N-156 F Freedom Fighter is equipped to carry up to four tons of weapons suitable for a broad range of intercept, strike, ground support and reconnaissance missions. **right** Watching and waiting. An Arab radar installation at a missile base in the desert.

local population of motor transport for days together, and by the lavish bribing of informers.

The fourth of our categories, the combination of guerrilla and conventional war, is the pattern of warfare that we have seen in Vietnam, both during its Gallic and its American periods. It is the pattern foreshadowed by the works of Mao and interpreted, both strategically and tactically, in the campaigns of General Giap, the commander who has been at war for over thirty years.

Much remains left unsaid. If this account has concentrated on weapons and fighting vehicles it is not because good wireless, supply-vehicles and landing-craft count for little or can be taken for granted. There has been no attempt to be all-embracing. The Jeep, the Garand rifle, the MG-34, even the jerrican: all these made their contribution to the mobility or firepower of the armies for which they were devised. The truth is that the weapons and instruments of war are legion, and to attempt to give a paragraph, a sentence or a word to each is no part of a survey of this sort. Nor have the strategy and the tactics of their employment, the ways in which they are used, been discussed as exhaustively as one could wish. The tactics of war vary as widely as those of the senate or the council chamber. Lay down rules as you will, every commander has his own style. For this reason the discussion of tactics has been confined fairly rigor-

ously to the drill and doctrines of the day in the successive periods under consideration.

**The Experience of War**

The Principles of War must be used with discretion for circumstances change and, as General Fuller has pointed out in *The Decisive Battles of the Western World*, the 'full study of war will not seriously assist a subaltern on picket duty . . .' Even so, when I was about half-way through writing this treatise I jotted down my own ideas on how to run a battle (below), based on experiences in the Second World War, during which I commanded everything from a platoon to a brigade, with the Germans, Italians and Japanese 'doing enemy'. If my views are heretical I am very far from apologizing, for a good soldier is afraid of nothing – not even a new idea.

HOW TO FIGHT AN INFANTRY UNIT IN BATTLE

1 Clarify your AIM, whether selected by yourself or another.

2 Study the strength and dispositions of the enemy in every possible detail.

3 Ask yourself the questions: If I were in his position, what would I least expect the enemy to do, and where would I least like to see him?

4 Devise your plan according to 2 and more particularly 3.

FRELIMO freedom fighters trudge through the bush in northern Mozambique.

5 Divide your forces so that they have the maximum tactical flexibility and control. In a battalion this means having five rifle companies (excluding any support company), each with at least three platoons. In a rifle platoon it is probably best to have just two big sections. Brigades should have at least four battalions. Always keep a reserve, since the enemy also may spring surprises. And the moment you have spent your reserve start building up another.
6 When you attack first give the enemy the benefit of all the firepower you can produce from as many different types of guns, mortars, etc., as you can lay your hands on, and keep close to your barrage – even in it. Better to lose a few men from your own fire than a lot from *his*.
7 Avoid frontal attacks in daylight.
8 Train your men to move fast at night, in smoke and dead ground without losing direction.
9 Prevent your men loading themselves like donkeys with loot, comforts, etc., as this destroys mobility.
10 Use strong fighting patrols to make false attacks,

USARV

**right** The guns of Vietnam. A US artilleryman covers one ear against the roar of a big 175-mm gun. **below** A Soviet flamethrower – another of the ground weapons used in Vietnam.

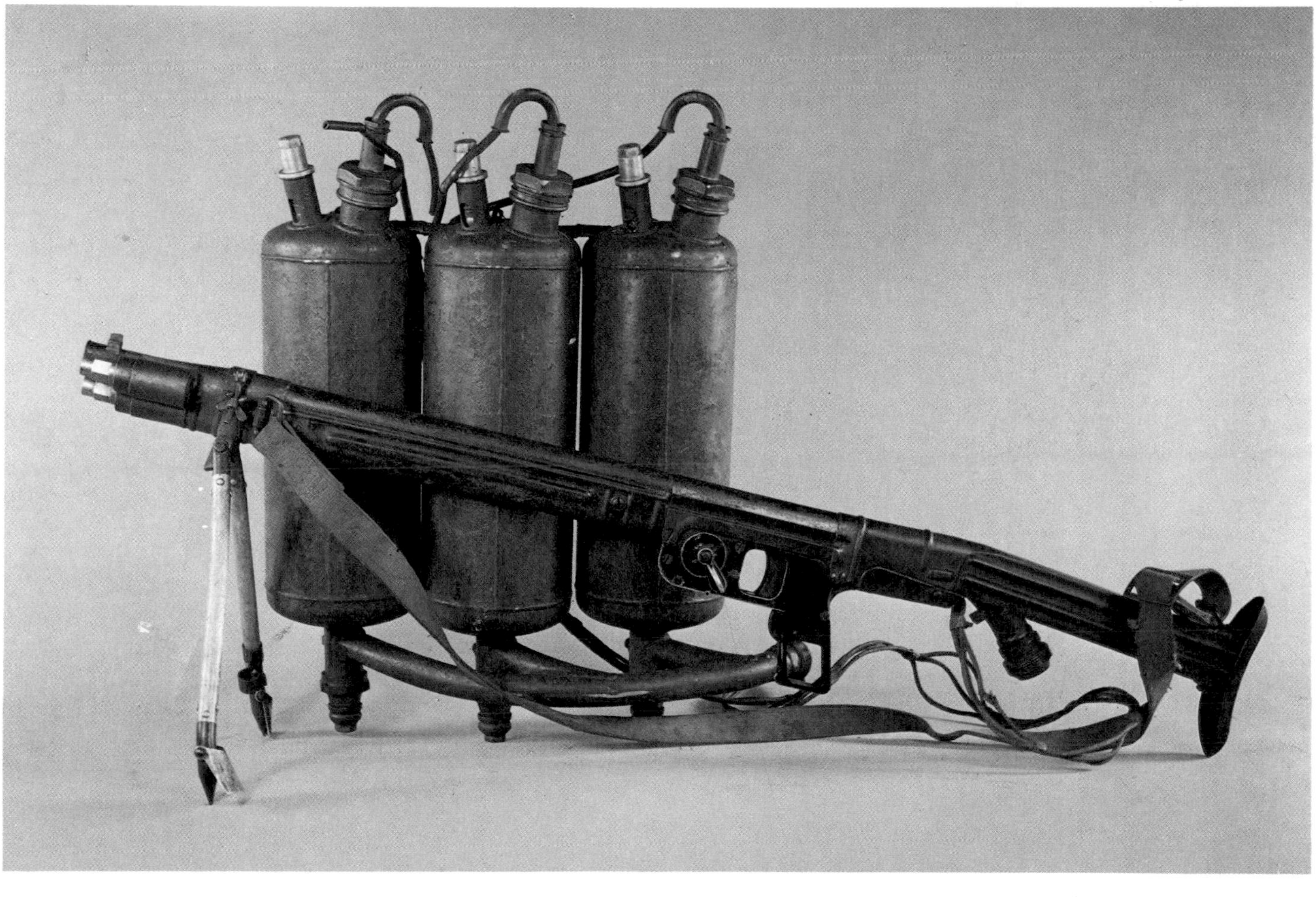

while your real ones go in from other directions.
11 Use strong patrols to prey upon HQ and bottle-necks on the roads in the enemy's rear.
12 In defence conceal the position of your real front. The false front is one of the best devices for cutting down casualties.
13 Never accept anything but the highest standard in training, especially weapon training, signals or logistical support. Most commanders pay lip service to these things. It takes real trouble to see that they actually receive priority.
14 When in the line visit every section every day. This builds up the men's confidence, which is more important to their morale than any other single factor. Only send your second-in-command if it is absolutely impossible for you to go yourself.
15 Beware of launching any tactical movement across ground you have not had a good look at yourself.
16 Study the use of ground.
17 Know your weapons inside out.
18 Sleep with your boots on – and you may survive to die in your bed.

After dealing with howitzers and tanks and atomic bombs it may seem something of an anti-climax to end up talking of platoons and companies and battalions. But after all who wins the war? What use would Wellington have been if his ploughboys had not stood firm? Did the vast air armadas of America halt the North Vietnamese? The truth is that politicians should be somewhat careful of trying to achieve their policies by armed force if they cannot muster a large number of good platoons of trained men imbued with the spirit that Cromwell perceived in his Ironsides: *Men that know what they fight for, and love what they know.*

**top** At Khe Sanh, Vietnam, a Huey Cobra helicopter stands by loaded with rockets, grenades and machine-guns. **above** Machine-gunners of the US 1st Cavalry.

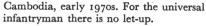

Cambodia, early 1970s. For the universal infantryman there is no let-up.

# INDEX

## ACKNOWLEDGEMENTS

The Editors gratefully acknowledge the courtesy of the following photographers, publishers, institutions, agencies and corporations for the illustrations in this volume.

**Cover**
Musée de la Marine: Bulloz
**Front Flap**
**Page**
6 Ludwig Dieter – Gamma: from the John Hillelson Agency
10 Imperial War Museum
Camera Press
11 Costantini
13 Michael Holford
16 *Melbourne Herald*
18–19 Michael Holford
Michael Holford
20 The Mansell Collection
21 C. M. Dixon
22 Michael Holford
23 Michael Holford
26 Radio Times Hulton Picture Library
The Mansell Collection
Michael Holford
27 The Mansell Collection
28 Radio Times Hulton Picture Library
The Mansell Collection
29 Radio Times Hulton Picture Library
30 Universitetets Oldsaksamling
Universitetets Oldsaksamling
A.T.A., Stockholm
30–31 Michael Holford
The Mansell Collection
Radio Times Hulton Picture Library
The Armories, Tower of London, Crown Copyright
32 The Mansell Collection
33 The Armories, Tower of London, Crown Copyright
The Mansell Collection
The Mansell Collection
The Mansell Collection
34 Radio Times Hulton Picture Library
Radio Times Hulton Picture Library
Courtesy of the Victoria and Albert Museum: Crown Copyright
35 The Wallace Collection: Crown Copyright
C. M. Dixon
The Archbishop of Canterbury and the Trustees of Lambeth Palace Library
36 The Wallace Collection: Crown Copyright
Musée National Suisse, Zurich
The Armories, Tower of London, Crown Copyright
37 The Mansell Collection
The Mansell Collection
The Mansell Collection
38 The Governing Body of Christ Church, Oxford
A.T.A., Stockholm
Pátrimonio National, Madrid: Weidenfeld & Nicolson Archives
39 Radio Times Hulton Picture Library
Waffensammlung des Kunsthistorischen Museum, Vienna: Weidenfeld & Nicolson Archives
40 Kungl. Armée Museum, Stockholm
Courtesy of the Victoria and Albert Museum: Crown Copyright
42 The Mansell Collection
The Mansell Collection
43 The Mansell Collection
45 The Wallace Collection: Crown Copyright
The Armories, Tower of London, Crown Copyright
Musée de Tarbes
46–47 The Mansell Collection
47 National Army Museum
48 National Army Museum
Kungl. Livrustkammaren, Stockholm
50 The Armories, Tower of London, Crown Copyright
52 National Army Museum
The Mansell Collection
National Army Museum
54 Kungl. Armée Museum, Stockholm
55 Radio Times Hulton Picture Library
56 National Army Museum
58 National Army Museum
60 Anne S. K. Brown Military Collection, Brown University, Providence, Rhode Island
National Army Museum
The Armories, Tower of London, Crown Copyright
62–63 Bulloz
64 Photo-Hachette
The Mansell Collection
66 War Museum, Brussels
67 National Army Museum
Radio Times Hulton Picture Library
68 The Mansell Collection
69 Bulloz
70–71 Radio Times Hulton Picture Library
The Mansell Collection
70–71 The Mansell Collection
Radio Times Hulton Picture Library
The Mansell Collection
The Mansell Collection
72 The Museum of Artillery, The Rotunda, Woolwich: Chris Barker
73 Pattern Room Collection, Enfield: Chris Barker
Weidenfeld & Nicolson Archives
74 The Mansell Collection
The Mansell Collection
Pattern Room Collection, Enfield: Chris Barker
75 Pattern Room Collection, Enfield: Chris Barker
Pattern Room Collection, Enfield: Chris Barker
76 Pattern Room Collection, Enfield: Chris Barker
78 The Mansell Collection
79 Pattern Room Collection, Enfield: Chris Barker
Pattern Room Collection, Enfield: Chris Barker
80–81 Library of Congress: BPC Picture Library
The Museum of Artillery, The Rotunda, Woolwich: Weidenfeld & Nicolson Archives
82 The Mansell Collection
82–83 The Mansell Collection
84 Imperial War Museum
88 Camera Press
Camera Press
89 Imperial War Museum
90 Weidenfeld & Nicolson Archives
90 Camera Press
Imperial War Museum
Imperial War Museum
Imperial War Museum
93 Radio Times Hulton Picture Library
Radio Times Hulton Picture Library
Imperial War Museum
94 Imperial War Museum
95 Pattern Room Collection, Enfield: Chris Barker
The Museum of Artillery, The Rotunda, Woolwich: Chris Barker
Bayerische Staatsgemaldesammlungen, Munich
Imperial War Museum
96 Imperial War Museum
Bundesarchiv, Coblenz
Radio Times Hulton Picture Library
Imperial War Museum
97 Imperial War Museum
98 Imperial War Museum
Pattern Room Collection, Enfield: Chris Barker
99 Camera Press
100 Bundesarchiv, Coblenz
Robert Capa: from the John Hillelson Agency
102 *The Times*
103 Pattern Room Collection, Enfield: Chris Barker
Camera Press
104 Pattern Room Collection, Enfield: Chris Barker
Imperial War Museum
105 Camera Press
Imperial War Museum
Imperial War Museum
106–7 Imperial War Museum
Pattern Room Collection, Enfield: Chris Barker
Camera Press
108 Camera Press
Robert Capa – Magnum: from the John Hillelson Agency
109 Camera Press
110 Pattern Room Collection, Enfield: Chris Barker
111 The Ministry of Defence
112–13 Tonnaire – Gamma: from the John Hillelson Agency
114 Camera Press
Camera Press
117 Camera Press
118 C.O.I.
120 Camera Press
121 Cornell Capa – Gamma: from the John Hillelson Agency
122 Camera Press
123 Camera Press
Pattern Room Collection, Enfield: Chris Barker
124 Christian Simon Pietri – Gamma: from the John Hillelson Agency
Gamma: from the John Hillelson Agency
Bailly – Gamma: from the John Hillelson Agency